SOLOMON'S DIVINE ARTS

SOLOMON'S DIVINE ARTS

JOSEPH HALL

INTRODUCTORY ESSAYS BY

E. ANN MATTER

RICHARD A. MULLER

GERALD T. SHEPPARD

MARION TAYLOR

EDITED BY

GERALD T. SHEPPARD

THE PILGRIM PRESS

CLEVELAND, OHIO

Salomons Diuine Arts by Joseph Hall is reproduced by permission of General Theological
Seminary, New York, from a copy in their collection at St. Mark's Library. The original volume
has been enlarged 126 percent for this volume.

The scripture quotations, unless otherwise indicated, are from the New Revised Standard
Version of the Bible, copyright 1989, Division of Christian Education of the National Council
of the Churches of Christ in the United States of America, and are used by permission.

Library of Congress Cataloging-in-Publication Data

Hall, Joseph, 1574–1656.
Solomon's divine arts / introductory essays by E. Ann Matter . . .
[et al.] ; edited by Gerald T. Sheppard.
p.   cm. — (Pilgrim classic commentaries)
Includes bibliographical references and index.
ISBN 0-8298-0918-X (alk. paper) : — ISBN 0-8298-0914-7
(alk. paper) :
1. Bible. O.T. Proverbs—Commentaries—Early works to 1800.
2. Bible. O.T. Ecclesiastes—Commentaries—Early works to 1800.
3. Bible. O.T. Song of Solomon—Commentaries—Early works to
1800. I. Matter, E. Ann. II. Sheppard, Gerald T., 1946–   .
III. Title. IV. Series.
BS1465.H35   1991
223'.07—dc20   91-31085
CIP

This book is printed on acid-free paper.

Printed in the United States of America

10 9 8 7 6 5 4 3 2 1

The Pilgrim Press, Cleveland, Ohio

Contents

FACSIMILE EDITION OF
SALOMONS DIUINE ARTS
Joseph Hall
(1609)

SOLOMON'S DIVINE ARTS

Introduction
Joseph Hall's *Solomon's Divine Arts* Among Seventeenth-Century Commentaries, 1600–1645

GERALD T. SHEPPARD

Joseph Hall (1574–1656), from a poor family but with a privileged Cambridge education, sought throughout his career to stand between the extremes of English Protestantism. His literary style avoided a grand, aristocratic eloquence despite its pitch well above the minimalist condescensions of a Puritan "plaine style." He mastered the use of artistic proverbs and aphorisms that were, despite their subtlety, memorable to common folk. His defense of the episcopate was weak enough to summon the attack of William Laud, though it was also sufficiently strong to elicit steady and stinging derision from John Milton. Eleven months after being appointed an Anglican bishop at Norwich, Hall wept openly as Cromwell's troops demolished the interior of Norwich Cathedral. He spent the last eleven years of his life in a small house about two miles away from that church and the former Bishop's Palace, during which time he signed his books under the name "Joseph Norvic" or "J.H.B.N.," that is, "Joseph Hall, the Bishop of Norwich." He is most famous in the history of biblical interpretation for the magnificent prose and insight of his *Contempla-*

Gerald T. Sheppard is professor of Old Testament literature and exegesis at Emmanuel College of Victoria University in the University of Toronto.

tions on narratives of the Old and New Testament, a massive project
that dominated two decades in the maturity of his life.

As a young scholar, Hall had already distinguished himself as a
promising poet, logician, orator, and dramatist before he became
ordained on December 14, 1600, at twenty-three years of age. Whether
or not his financial needs influenced this decision, there is little doubt
that his thorough training in Ramist logic and biblical exegesis at
Emmanuel College, the "Puritan" center of Cambridge, prepared him
well for a shift in his publications to matters of divinity. A lengthy
and enthusiastic encomium in honor of the succession of King James
I in 1603, entitled "The King's Prophecy, or Weeping Joy," won him
royal approval, leading Hall to a clear decision to be a minister within
the Establishment.

Most of Hall's theological works point in two directions. On the
one hand, he sought to articulate an alternative to the *Spiritual
Exercises*, the "rule" of St. Ignatius and the Jesuits who had earned the
wrath of most Protestants by 1600. In this vein, he published his first
book, *Meditation and Vows* (1605) and, later, *Heaven Upon Earth* (1606),
offering "unruled," aphoristic guides to meditation. After a trip to the
continent, he became convinced of the need for a Protestant "rule" of
meditation and eventually published *The Art of Divine Meditation* in
1606.[1] On the other hand, Hall wanted to reply to the non-Christian
philosophers and to establish the superiority of the Bible. In this
regard, we see the significance of his *Solomon's Divine Arts**. Perhaps
Heaven and Earth comes closest to encompassing both of the goals in
Hall's publications. It was reprinted by John Wesley and shows up, for
example, in Jenner's library in New England. *Solomon's Divine Arts*,
which actually first appeared in print on December 5, 1608, shares
with *Heaven and Earth* Hall's confidence that, "not *Athens* must teach
this lesson, but *Jerusalem*."[2]

Among such a feast of literary works by Hall, the selection of
Solomon's Divine Arts invites justification for its place in this series of
the Pilgrim Classic Commentaries. Both *Heaven and Earth* and *The*

---

*For purposes of research and reference the spelling of the title of this volume
was changed from its original "Salomons Diuine Arts" to conform to contemporary
English.

Art of Divine Meditation have been reprinted recently. The *Contempla-tions* are well known and regularly consulted by scholars. By contrast, *Solomon's Divine Arts* remains grossly underestimated, and its signifi-cance has been barely grasped in the modern history of interpretation. As literature, it is not biblical commentary in the conventional form, which quotes a scripture text and then appends an extensive explica-tion of it. Instead, biblical texts are selectively quoted in *Solomon's Divine Arts* within a logical framework of an extrabiblical sort; or, as is the case with his paraphrase of the Song of Songs, texts are sometimes rendered in a free manner that makes explicit some seman-tic import that may be at most only an implicit possibility. Scholars who are specialists in anthological midrash, translations, Targums, and paraphrases remind us that this literature belongs to an ancient art of interpretation predating what we have conventionally consid-ered to be commentary.[3] The dependence of such literature on the very words of the Bible may seem contradicted by how those same words may be reordered or even altered in paraphrase and re-presen-tation. This circumstance confirms that a tension always exists for the commentator between the Bible as human words and the identification of the Bible, at the same time, with a divine subject matter to which the human words bear witness. Hall's work affords us a prime opportunity to examine the limits and possibilities of that tension so that we can understand why, for Hall, the Bible, as the living Word of God, is a subject exerting pressure upon him rather than merely an object that he could manipulate.

Different options for commentary on the Bible can hardly be better illustrated than in *Solomon's Divine Arts*, with its vigilant avoid-ance of Christian imagery in the books on ethics, economics, and politics, and, by contrast, its overtly christological interpretation of the Song of Songs. Hall's choice of interpretive options is not arbitrary. He thinks he has gone to the heart of the matter, exhibiting here the most obvious significance of these parts of scripture. How Old Testament wisdom should relate to Christian theology is a matter of long debate and continues fully into the modern period—for example, as shown in the controversy over the role wisdom should play within the so-called Biblical Theology Movement from the 1930s to the 1950s.[4] Hall's interpretation invites us to consider once more the relation of Christianity to Judaism in the interpretation of the Old Testament, especially how Solomonic wisdom literature might be accepted as a part of Christian theology with almost nothing added to it by the New Testament.

Another reason for the value of these particular works by Hall lies in their illustration of a long tradition within Christianity that sought to relate biblical wisdom to other modes of human knowledge and behavior distinct from the resources of the revealed law, the prophets, and even the New Testament itself. Hall presumes a compatibility of wisdom with other forms of scriptural discourse, but also accepts it as a self-consistent idiom within scripture. His effort to compare and to refine the identity of biblical wisdom by the use of secular philosophy, logic, and the natural sciences recalls a tradition shared by both premodern Judaism and Christianity.[5] This older strategy has led within modernity to a very different set of debates about "natural theology" and various criticisms of "christomonism."[6] One reason that modern scholars dismissed Hall's approach to wisdom literature is his dependence upon a relationship between the historical identity of King Solomon and the nature of the books associated with his name. Once modern scholars destroyed the foundations for a simple connection between the historical Solomon and the Solomonic books, the very fabric of intertextuality, upon which Hall depends, was rent apart. Only the more recent literary and canonical approaches have offered a fresh perspective from which to reassess the implications of historical criticism, without questioning its negative historical conclusions.[7] Regardless, students of this period will find in Hall's work a vivid demonstration of how one of the most gifted scholars of his time sought to make sense of biblical "wisdom" while warmly embracing the best of non-Christian "wisdom," both classical and contemporary to his own day.

The essays that accompany this reprint begin with Richard A. Muller's "Joseph Hall as Rhetor, Theologian, and Exegete: His Contribution to the History of Interpretation." Muller sets Hall within a broad historical-theological context, with special attention to Hall's major works, his activity as a literary stylist, and his connections with the Protestant Reformation in general. Marion Taylor's "Working with Wisdom Literature: Joseph Hall and William Henry Green" explores both how Hall handles scripture, especially in his advice to women, and why a nineteenth-century historical conservative, William Green, could no longer maintain the same approach as Hall. Next, E. Ann Matter's "Joseph Hall and the Tradition of Christian Interpretation of the Song of Songs" sets Hall's paraphrase within the history of interpretation and carefully investigates various ways that the work reflects his own hermeneutical idiosyncrasies and circumstances of the church in his day. Finally, Gerald T. Sheppard, in his essay "The Role of the Canonical Context in the Interpretation of the Solomonic Wisdom Books," shows how late modern literary and canonical approaches are finding new ways to understand and value Hall's effort.

The scholarly significance of publishing Hall's *Solomon's Divine Arts* alongside the Geneva New Testament, with its annotations and other selected commentaries from the seventeenth century, is far ranging. The Pilgrim Classic Commentaries series provides an unparalleled resource for studies in English Protestant and Puritan social and political history, the Reformation in England and its legacy in New England, the history of biblical interpretation, and assessments of the Westminster Assembly and Confession. It also provides specific sources for the study of the Renaissance heritage of Protestant poetics. A reprint series of this scope has not been undertaken since the well-known Nicholas series in the midnineteenth century.

In Sydney E. Ahlstrom's *A Religious History of the American People*, the late Yale historian argued persuasively that the inheritance from seventeenth-century England in America had not been adequately recognized. Ahlstrom calls for greater attention to ways in which "the Reformation was being carried out of Great Britain" precisely because from this heritage "come the colonial impulses—imperial, commercial, and evangelistic—which would form the chief foundations—political, economic, and religious—of the American tradition."[8] A stridently Protestant America, with little regard for the massive Roman Catholic presence in its midst, grew out of this "Protestant synthesis," giving rise to the Great Puritan Epoch that Ahlstrom thinks came to a close only in the 1960s. English Protestant religious themes of election and predestination of a chosen people composing a "New Israel" took on a powerful political thrust in the milieu of the colonies, themes that were further fueled by the Great Awakening and the American Revolution in the century that followed. What emerged was a uniquely American form of Evangelical Protestantism as spontaneously political as it was religious. Because of this profound connection between England and New England, with a history of persistent influence from the English Protestant Reformation, the Pilgrim Classic Commentaries series concentrates specifically on commentaries that passed from England to New England and played a definitive role in the perception of religion and society both in the history of the United States and in some parts of eastern Canada.

Unlike biblical commentaries in the twentieth century, the antecedents of the commentaries in seventeenth-century England and New England pervasively influenced every level of intellectual, artistic, social, and political life. Books such as Jeremiah, Hosea, and Jonah challenge the assumption of God's continuous covenantal relationship with Israel: English Protestant commentaries on these same books sought to show under what circumstances England (or New England) might be a nation chosen like Israel or similarly rejected by God. Every aspect of social and political life invited a critique from a divine point of view—the role of the king in church affairs, the propriety of owning slaves, the use of East Indians as sources of cheap labor, the pros and cons of tobacco, and so forth. In this "Golden Age of Preaching," the commentaries fully reflected the vibrancy of the lecture hall and pulpit. Those who did not read commentaries heard them quoted, praised, or condemned. "Search the scriptures" (John 5:39) was the rallying cry of the English Protestant Reformation. Because the Bible represented, at least rhetorically, the fulcrum on which the fate of the world rested, biblical commentaries covered a vast range of contemporary issues and often wedded the highest aesthetic gifts to pragmatic concerns of daily life and politics.

When considering commentaries during this period, the editors of the Pilgrim Classic Commentaries are aware that the milieu is still largely that of a Latin church. Older Latin commentaries, including many contemporary Roman Catholic volumes, continued to be treasured by many Protestants alongside the new English contributions. Moreover, the task of selecting which works to include in this collection was complicated by an awareness of the popularity of some continental Reformation commentaries (for example, those on Isaiah,

Jeremiah, and the Gospels), which explains the tendency of English expositors to neglect certain major biblical books. In many cases, a choice was made in favor of the more original contributions rather than the compilations, because they better reflect an indigenous appropriation of continental Reformation themes, cast in uniquely English forms.

Because these commentaries antedate the full impact of the Enlightenment and its modern critical approach to history, they remain among the few extant English works that sustain the biblical text as a literary and coherent whole. At the same time, the seventeenth century was not, by and large, an age of sermons or of interpretations of scripture for any but controversial and polemical purposes. Rather than resolve inner-biblical tensions or contradictions by a speculative appeal to different and autonomous author/editors, the commentators more often found in these instances an opportunity to understand the equally perplexing tensions and contradictions of their own daily and national life. By means of this vision of a canonical text, English Protestant commentators sought to discover within the past tense of Christian scripture a realistic and pragmatically compelling present tense, ripe with implications for their own time. Accordingly, these works warrant a distinct place in the history of English commentary and prove particularly provocative to scholars concerned with a postmodern literary interpretation of the Bible or how it was read as canonized "scripture" within Christian faith.

Theological students will find in these commentaries a primary source for understanding the implications of the famous Westminster Assembly. Many of these same volumes were collected by Old Testament scholar Charles Briggs at Union Theological Seminary in New York City at the end of the nineteenth century. Briggs drew on them for his defense in his historic heresy trial while he was a minister in the Presbyterian Church. Relying on these commentaries and a copy of the *Westminster Annotations*, Briggs argued that the Westminster Confession did not deny the value of modern historical-critical investigations of biblical texts. The close association in the commentaries between exposition of biblical claims and the value placed on the illumination of historical inquiry confirmed for Briggs that the Westminster Divines were at most "precritical" rather than "anticritical" or fundamentalistic in their approach. In the current foment over Bible and history, these volumes mark a pivotal moment in Christian interpretation.

The influence of these commentaries on English literature remains seriously underestimated. For example, when John Milton defends a controversial point in the *Tetrachordon*, he can confidently assert that "I say we conclude no more than what the common expositors themselves give us, both in that which I have recited, and much more hereafter." Most English Protestant commentaries did not bury the biblical text under the debris of arcane historical details or linguistic minutiae. Artistic and literary features were central elements within their style. As part of their commenting on scripture, the expositors often rendered the scriptural text in the form of a poetic paraphrase, transforming the alien traces of Hebrew poetry into the familiar register of rhyme and meter of the great English poets. In this way the aesthetic circle was complete. As the Bible influenced the poets and great prose artists, so the Bible was itself paraphrased to meet the approval of a fastidious cultural idea of literary beauty. Without the aid of the Bible and the guide of these commentaries, English literature in this period is easily distorted.

For literary scholars, these commentaries have drawn increasing attention to the long-neglected influence of Reformed theology on English and American literature and culture. Students of the seventeenth century are often hampered by a lack of primary source materials. This Pilgrim Classic Commentaries series provides precisely the materials necessary to study biblical typology, English Protestant defenses of poetry, the art of biblical translation and paraphrase, the "plain style," the complex manner in which the Bible affords a literary model for Protestant poetry and prose, as well as the intertextual nature of the commentaries themselves. Literary scholars conversant with the great literature and poetry in the seventeenth century will be particularly interested in this series, for it provides essential background material that will bring precision to studies of how Reformed theology directly influenced the poetry and prose of the period.

Grateful acknowledgment is made to David Green, director of St. Mark's Library, General Theological Seminary, for his suggestions and help at various stages in this project. The Northrop Frye Centre, chaired by Eva Kushner, president of Victoria University within the University of Toronto, gave me a generous grant for which I am deeply appreciative. Finally, I feel especially indebted to Barbara Withers, editor at Pilgrim Press, whose support and wise counsel contributed greatly to the quality of this volume. Without her help, expertise, and enthusiasm, this volume would not have been possible.

NOTES

1. For a brief overview of Hall's life and an examination of his contribution to Protestant meditation, see Frank Livingstone Huntley, *Bishop Joseph Hall and Protestant Meditation in Seventeenth-Century England: A Study with the Texts of "The Art of Divine Meditation" (1606) and "Occasional Meditations" (1633)* (Binghamton, N.Y.: Center for Medieval and Early Renaissance Studies, 1981), 1–63.

2. Rudolf Kird, ed., *Joseph Hall, D.D.: Heaven and Earth and Characters of Virtues and Vices* (New Brunswick, N.J.: Rutgers University Press, 1948), 86.

3. For example, see Michael Fishbane, *Biblical Interpretation in Ancient Israel* (Oxford: Clarendon Press, 1985); R. Bloch, "Midrash," in vol. 5 of *Dictionaire de la Bible, Supplément,* ed. Henry Cazelles (Paris: Libraire Letouzey et Ané, 1957), 1263–81; I. L. Seeligmann, "Voraussetzungen der Midrash-Exegese," *VTSuppl* 1 (1963):150 ff.; and Birger Gerhardsson, *Memory and Manuscript: Oral Tradition and Written Transmission in Rabbinic Judaism and Early Christianity,* trans. E. J. Sharp, *ASNU* 22 (Uppsala: Gleerup, 1961).

4. See Henning Graf Reventlow, "Wisdom," in *Problems of Old Testament Theology in the Twentieth Century* (London: SCM Press, 1985), 168–86.

5. Eugene F. Rice, *The Renaissance Idea of Wisdom* (Cambridge: Harvard University Press, 1958); and Gerald T. Sheppard, "Wisdom," in *The International Standard Bible Encyclopedia,* ed. G. W. Bromiley (Grand Rapids: Wm. B. Eerdmans, 1988), 1074–82.

6. For an overview, see Otto Weber, vol. 1 of *Foundations of Dogmatics,* trans. Darrell L. Guder (Grand Rapids: Wm. B. Eerdmans, 1981), 199–227, esp. 204–208; and Karl Barth, vol. 2 of *Church Dogmatics,* trans. G. W. Bromiley (Edinburgh: T. & T. Clark, 1957), 85–128, 172–78.

7. For an overview of standard modern historical criticism on wisdom, see Donn F. Morgan, *Wisdom in the Old Testament Traditions* (Atlanta: John Knox Press, 1981). For more recent literary or canonical approaches, see

David G. Meade, "Authorship, Revelation, and Canon in the Wisdom Traditions," in *Pseudonymity and Canon: An Investigation into the Relationship of Authorship and Authority in Jewish and Christian Tradition* (Grand Rapids: Wm. B. Eerdmans, 1987), 44–72; and Northrop Frye, *The Great Code: The Bible and Literature* (New York: Harcourt Brace Jovanovich, 1982), 121–25. See also the treatment of individual Solomonic books in Brevard Childs, *Introduction to the Old Testament as Scripture* (Philadelphia: Fortress Press, 1979); and Rolf Rendtorff, *The Old Testament: An Introduction* (Philadelphia: Fortress Press, 1986).

8. Sydney E. Ahlstrom, *A Religious History of the American People* (New Haven: Yale University Press, 1972), 83.

Joseph Hall as Rhetor, Theologian, and Exegete: His Contribution to the History of Interpretation

RICHARD A. MULLER

Joseph Hall (1574–1656), better known in the twentieth century for his literary achievements and his contribution to Protestant spirituality than for his abilities as a theologian and interpreter of scripture,[1] belonged to a group of theologians and exegetes of early seventeenth-century England who were caught in the ecclesial and political dilemma caused by a broad commitment to Reformed theology on the one hand and, on the other, a clear rejection of the congregationalist or presbyterian polity associated with English Puritanism.[2] Like James Ussher, Hall stood in the Reformed tradition as an advocate of episcopacy, although his theology was not nearly so "Calvinistic" as Ussher's. In his own time, Hall was renowned as a preacher and exegete and as a writer of considerable rhetorical skill— as evidenced in a secular manner in his two volumes of *Satires* (1597, 1598), and in a theological form in his *Solomon's Divine Arts* (1609),[3] *Contemplations on the Historical Passages of the Holy Story (1612–1615)*,[4] and his *A Plain and Familiar Explication, by Way of Paraphrase, of all the Hard Texts of the Whole Divine Scripture (1634)*[5] If the various exegetical works placed Hall among the notable biblical interpreters of his time, the *Satires* placed him among the major literary figures of his age, if only because he pioneered the form in English. The absence

Richard A. Muller is professor of historical theology, Fuller Theological Seminary.

of reference to his work from several of the standard histories of the interpretation of scripture is a testimony only to the general neglect of the seventeenth-century exegetical and hermeneutical achievement and is no evidence of his stature.[6] In the words of Thomas Fuller, Hall was a writer "not unhappy at controversies, more happy at comments, very good in his characters, better in his sermons, best of all in his meditations."[7]

Hall was born on July 1, 1574 (at "five of the clock in the morning," he notes in his memoirs), at Bristow Park, Ashby-de-la-Zouch, in Leicestershire, where his father, John, served as the local deputy for the Earl of Huntington.[8] His mother, Winifred Bambridge, "a woman of rare sancity," comparable in Hall's mind to Monica, the mother of Augustine, held strongly Puritan sentiments that were encouraged in her by Anthony Gilby, the translator of Beza and himself a notable Puritan thinker, then vicar of Ashby. When the young Hall had finished his training in the grammar school at Ashby, Nathaniel Gilby, son of Anthony and fellow of Emmanuel College, Cambridge, invited him to study at Cambridge, where he matriculated in 1589.[9] Hall was awarded the B.A. in 1592, was elected scholar and fellow of Emmanuel College in 1595, and was awarded the M.A. in 1596. The strongly Reformed and Puritan theological sympathies of Emmanuel College under the leadership of its founding master, Laurence Chaderton, had a profound effect on Hall's thought and on his theological style.[10]

After his graduation from Emmanuel, Hall served for two years as public lecturer in rhetoric and was highly regarded throughout the university for his scholarly achievements. He was "called," Hall comments, "to public disputations often, wilt no ill success: for never durst I appear in any of those exercises of scholarship, till I had from my knees looked up to heaven for a blesing, and renewed my actual dependence upon that Divine Hand."[11] The combination of learning with spirituality characteristic of his later work clearly had its roots in his early training.

In 1601 Hall was offered, through the good graces of Chaderton, a position in the grammar school at Tiverton in Devon, and at the same time, the rectory of Halsted in Suffolk. He recounts a lengthy conversation with Chaderton in which he argued a sense of divine calling to the parish and to ministry. Over some objection from the worried Chaderton, Hall accepted the church position. After a series of difficult encounters with Sir Robert Drury, who was in charge of the parish revenues, Hall and his family accompanied Sir Edmund Bacon on a diplomatic mission to Belgium. There, disguised as a layman, the future bishop engaged in theological debate with Jesuits and other Roman Catholics—who were, he reported in his memoirs, astounded by his command of Christian doctrine and by his skill in Latin, and who were unable to refute his arguments.[12] It was also during his years at Halsted and at Spa in Belgium that he published two volumes of his meditations, his *Meditations and Vows*—two "centuries," or collections, of a hundred aphorisms and short reflections. Frank Livingstone Huntley suggests that Hall's contact with the Jesuits of Belgium may not have been as negative and one-sided as Hall himself indicated; it may have been here, among the followers of Loyola and his *Spiritual Exercises*, that Hall first encountered traditional spirituality and meditative discipline.[13]

The two volumes of meditations brought Hall some literary and theological recognition and, crucial to his later career, the admiration of Henry, Prince of Wales. The prince was so impressed by Hall's prose that he called on Hall to preach a sermon to the court. Hall later reflected that the sermon (which does not appear in his collected works) was "not so well given as taken." Whatever the quality of the sermon, it did result in the patronage of the prince and an appointment as one of the royal chaplains. At about the same time (1608), Hall was given the rectorate of Waltham Cross in Essex by the Earl of Norwich, a position in which he remained until 1627. Hall's relationship to the university continued during the time of his parish service and resulted in his being awarded the B.D. in 1603 and the D.D. in 1612.

After the death of Prince Henry in 1613, Hall remained among the royal chaplains. His skills eventually brought him to the attention of James I, who sent Hall with Lord Doncaster, the Earl of Carlisle, on a mission to France in 1616 and—after appointing Hall dean of Worcester—summoned him to the court in Scotland in 1617 to assist in the development of a more ceremonious liturgy for the Scots church. In 1618 King James appointed Hall, together with several other British theologians known for their Reformed theology, as a delegate to the Synod of Dort in 1618.[14] Hall reports that he was well received and then laments that illness prevented him from remaining at Dort for the entirety of the synod. By his account, his theological perspective, welcomed by many of the delegates, was typical of the irenic approach of the English delegation.[15] Both in the Latin sermon he preached before the synod and in his subsequent treatise, *Via Media, the Way of Peace in the Five busy Articles Commonly Known by the Name of Arminius* (1622), Hall worked for an amicable confessional settlement between the Reformed and the Arminians, albeit from a distinctly Reformed perspective, resting on the theology of Musculus, Zanchius, Polanus, and other Reformed theologians of the age.[16] It is clear, however, both in the sermon and in the debate with English Arminians that inspired his *Via Media*, that Hall's teaching remained fully in the Reformed camp.

This combination of Reformed doctrine with a conciliatory, even ecumenical, interest in international Protestantism remained a feature of Hall's later writings. His treatise *The Peace-Maker: Laying forth the Right Way of Peace in Matters of Religion* (1645) contained an examination of the issue of "fundamental points of religion" and a plea that the "undue alienation of the Lutheran churches from the other Reformed" might be overcome.[17] He continued this effort in his *De pace inter evangelicos procuranda*, a short treatise discussing the Leipzig Colloquy (1631) between the Reformed and the Lutherans, together with a letter sent to the Frankfurt Colloquy.[18]

After the death of James I in 1625, Hall continued to have the favor of the royal court. Indeed, his polemical treatise, *No Peace with Rome* (1611), and his later defense of his views in *The Old Religion* (1627) pleased both the young King Charles I and Archbishop Laud with its views of the church, although Laud remained suspicious of the Calvinistic or Reformed tenor of the greater part of Hall's doctrine. In these treatises, Hall's advocacy of episcopacy and his identification of the true church as visible made clear his differences with the Puritan and Presbyterian theologians of the day—not so much in doctrines of God and redemption as in his doctrine of the church and its polity. Unlike the Puritan and Presbyterian writers, Hall refused to stress the invisibility of the church of the elect, and he insisted that the Roman church was still a part, albeit an errant and aberrant part, of the church catholic. These ecclesial and political aspects of Hall's thought would become central to his later polemic during the era of the Puritan revolution.

In 1627 Hall was elevated to the see of Exeter, but because of the archbishop's distaste for his theology, Hall was watched closely for evidence of Puritan sympathies. In his memoirs, Hall comments that his "ways were curiously observed and scanned"—and, indeed, his willingness to work constructively with the Puritans in his parishes brought him to court on several occasions to answer charges of refusing to inculcate conformity among his clergy. In 1633, when Charles I issued his notorious Declaration of Sport encouraging gaming and hunting on the Sabbath, Hall made no effort to enforce its reading in the diocese of Exeter, and we have no record of any of his clergy having been reprimanded for refusing to read the declaration.

Both in his preaching and in his polemics, as well as in his manner of administering the diocese, Hall showed himself consistently to belong to that minority of English divines, like James Ussher, John Davenant, and Daniel Featley, who became increasingly isolated from both sides of the great religious dispute of the century. On the one side, the Laudian and episcopalian party mistrusted them for their theology; whereas on the other side, the Puritans and Presbyterians mistrusted them for their polity. Hall's difficulties came to a head when he published his *Divine Right of Episcopacy* (1637) and his defense of both episcopacy and liturgy, *An Humble Remonstrance to the High Court of Parliament* (1641). The latter work became the focus of an attack by five Puritan theologians writing under the pen name of "Smectymnuus." Hall's responses, his *Defense of that Remonstrance* and his *Answer to the Vindication of Smectymnuus*, were supported by a treatise by Ussher and attacked by John Milton.

In 1641 Hall was made bishop of Norwich, only to find himself opposed to the antiepiscopal and antiprelatical policies of the Long Parliament. He wrote several treatises in defense of episcopacy and was rewarded with imprisonment for six months in 1642.[19] When he was released from prison, he traveled with his family directly to Norwich, where he attempted to begin his episcopal duties. In the course of 1643, he was expelled from the episcopal residence, deprived of his see, and placed on an allowance by Parliament—a somewhat ironic fate for one schooled in a Puritan college and later accused by Archbishop Laud of having Puritan sympathies! With his family, Hall then rented a cottage near Norwich, where he remained for the next decade. He died on September 8, 1656, at the age of eighty-two. The actual tendency of his theology must be regarded as moderate, somewhat rationalistic, ever practical and oriented toward common sense rather than speculation, genuinely Reformed in its basic tenets, but not averse to finding a ground for agreement with the Arminians, as long as the premise of salvation by grace alone was not compromised. Whereas Haller finds him close in spirit to John Hales and William Chillingworth,[20] it may be more accurate to understand Hall as unwaveringly Reformed in theology, unshakably episcopal in polity, of a generally broad and irenic spirit, and stylistically of a less scholastic bent than the Puritan divines more typically representative of English Reformed theology in his day.[21]

THE RHETOR AND RELIGIOUS LITERARY STYLIST

Late sixteenth- and early seventeenth-century Protestant theologians, teachers, and preachers shared in common a concern for the style and presentation of theology that placed them in the line of development of Renaissance logic and rhetoric as well as Reformation exegesis and exposition of text. Hall's early training at Emmanuel College under Nathaniel Gilby and Laurence Chaderton included the study both of formal rhetoric and of the Ramist logic so closely associated with the plain expository and argumentative style of English Reformed theology.[22] Hall's satires, particularly his *Virgidemiae* (1597–1598), evidence both a mastery of rhetoric and an interest in drawing on the resources of classical style for the defense of Protestantism.[23] His earlier theological works in particular testify to the influence of Ramism, both in their use of a formal pattern of dichotomization in the establishment of the order of argument and in their assumption that the perspicuous order provided by the dichotomies was an aid to the memorization of ideas and, therefore, a support of the meditative exercise.

Hall's writings also testify to his interest in the establishment of a rhetorical style proper to a biblically grounded Christian preaching and teaching. Specifically, they testify to his interest in the development of a "grand style" suitable to the sublime and majestic truths of the faith but also reflective of the rhetorical simplicity of the biblical narrative. This issue of style, moreover, links Hall's work to a common concern of the day—the establishment of a "Christian rhetoric" distinct from the classical, pagan rhetoric of great textbooks like Quintillian, or Renaissance exponents of classical rhetoric like Caussin or Vossius—but nonetheless justifiable in terms of the basic canons of style known to the Renaissance.[24] It was a truism of classical rhetoric that the "plain style" was not properly applicable to religious themes—granting that it was incapable of conveying the majesty of the thought—and that a "grand" or "copious" style, elaborate in its syntax, was necessary in matters of religion.

Neither scripture, however, nor the Protestant models of exegesis evidenced all of the characteristics of the grand style; copious ornamentation and prolixity are characteristic of neither. Nonetheless, the passion, art, and emotionally expressive nature of scripture and its exposition—their ability to move the will and the affections as well as the mind—had affinities with the classical grand style and provided a foundation for a variety of types of grand style in Christian rhetoric.[25] Hall's movement in this direction places him in continuity not only with the general interest in Christian rhetoric characteristic of the era; it also sets him—despite his Ramist inclinations—in some contrast to the Puritan trajectory of English Reformed theology and exegesis, as evidenced in the work of William Perkins. Where Perkins advocated a plain style, devoid of rhetorical device and shows of eloquence, Hall moved clearly in the direction of figurative language and of striking use of metaphor, analogy, and paradox.[27]

First, I offer some comment on Hall's Ramism. Among Hall's early works, the treatise on Christian tranquillity *Heaven and Earth* (1605), *The Art of Divine Meditation* (1606), and *Solomon's Divine Arts* (1609) all evidence the Ramist patterning. *Heaven and Earth* includes a full-page chart of organizational bifurcations that both define tranquillity in all of its parts and aspects, and also offer a road map, so to speak, of the entire argument of the book. *The Art of Divine Meditation* lacks the Ramist charts, but as Huntley has shown, certainly partakes of the pattern of organizational bifurcation typical of Ramism.[27]

The Ramist model—with occasional threefold, in addition to the usual twofold divisions—is particularly evident in Hall's *Solomon's Divine Arts*, where the entire text is conceived of as an essay on "gouernment" that divides into three basic categories of "behaviovr," "common-wealth," and "familie." Each of these categories becomes a separate volume of the work, and each is subsequently subdivided, using Ramist charts, into component parts, identified as the "books" belonging to each volume. Thus ethics is divided into a series of four essays, each of which is concerned with the goals, or "ends," of ethics: book I, felicity; book II, prudence; book III, justice; book IV, temperance and fortitude.

The several books belonging to *Solomon's Divine Arts* are, in turn, also organized according to the pattern of Ramist division. By way of example, the book on justice offers an initial chart in which, first, "justice" is understood as giving "to each his own," and then the categories of the rightful recipients of justice are enumerated, justice "to God," "to God and man," and "to man." This threefold division of justice is then elaborated into further subdivisions of the chart. Justice to God, defined as piety, "comprehends [1] Feare, [2] Honour and respect, [3] Obedience"; to God and man, consists of "[1] Fidelitie, [2] Truth, [3] Loue," with truth being divided into "Truth in words" and "Truth in dealings." Justice "to man only" consists of justice "to others," both in "Mercie" and "Liberalitie"; and in justice "to our selues," understood as "Diligence in our vocations"(39).* Not only does the whole book move carefully and strictly through these initial divisions, but also, in subsequent charts, subdivides the initial divisions still further. Thus love, encountered in the division of justice accorded both to God and to men, is subdivided into the categories of love "[1] To God, rewarded [a] with his loue, [b] with his blessings" and "[2] To men, [a] In passing by offences, [b] In doing good to our enemies" (58). Hall's fundamental intention throughout this exercise is clarity of teaching; and because his arrangement and frequent

*The page numbers in parentheses that follow quotations from Hall's *Solomon's Divine Arts* refer to the 1609 text reprinted in this volume.

rearrangement of the materials of the wisdom literature were for the sake of clarity, he carefully notes and defines the nature of his departure from the biblical form and order. He comments "that euery Concordance peruerts the Text," and his work therefore "only en-deuoured to be the common-place-booke of that great king [Solomon], and to referre his diuine rules to their heads [i.e., topical divisions], for more ease of finding, for better memory, for readier vse"* (A3 verso).

Solomon's Divine Arts, particularly in the paraphrase of the Song of Songs published together with it, also exemplifies, albeit not quite as expertly as in his sermons or in a somewhat later work like the *Contemplations on the Historical Passages of the Holy Story*, Hall's quest for a religiously and theologically suitable form of grand style. The more simple forms of the text are consistently expanded toward a more "copious" style through parallel metaphors, even as the physical imagery of the text is drawn out toward spiritual meanings. Thus, "I am black, O daughters of Jerusalem, but comely"—traditionally understood as an allegory of the church—is elaborated as "Neuer vpbraid mee (O ye forraine congregations) that I seeme in outward appearance discoloured by my infirmities and duskish with tribulations: for, whatsoeuer I seeme to you, I am yet inwardly wel-fauoured in the eyes of him, whom I seeke to please"(4).

THE THEOLOGIAN AND PREACHER[28]

Hall is remembered as having balanced his rather high views of episcopacy and divine right with a simple style of life and a close attention to the duties of a pastor. His religious and theological works, all written during his years as a cleric, taken as a whole evidence strong concern for doctrinal integrity as well as for episcopal polity, for the right presentation of the faith as well as for the spiritual and moral care of souls. Thomas Fuller, who was, some years after Hall's time, also the rector of Waltham Cross, spoke highly of Hall's ministry: "I must pay the tribute of my gratitude to his memory," wrote Fuller, as building upon his foundation; beholding myself as his great-grandchild in that place, three degrees from him in succession—but, oh, how many from him in ability! His little catechism hath done great good in that populous parish; and I could wish that ordinance more generally used over all England.[29]

The work indicated by Fuller is most probably Hall's *Brief Sum of the Principles of Religion* (1607), a basic catechism distinctly Reformed in its theology, as indicated by its strongly stated views on human sinfulness and election in the questions concerning human nature:

Q What must we know of ourselves?
A What we were, what we are, and what we shall be.
Q What were we?
A We were made at first perfect and happy, according to God's image, in knowledge, holiness and righteousness.
Q What are we?
A Ever since the fall of our first parents, we are all naturally the sons of wrath, subject to misery and death: but those, whom God chooseth out to himself, are in part renewed through grace, and have the image of God in part repaired in them.[30]

Even so, Hall's *Via Media, the Way of Peace in the Five busy Articles Commonly Known by the Name of Arminius* is so invested in the theology of the moderate majority of the Synod of Dort and in the works of major voices of the Reformed churches of the sixteenth century, like Musculus, Zanchius, and Polanus, that its "middle way" is not argued between the Reformed and the Arminian parties, but rather takes a confessional, infralapsarian approach to election, between the strict supralapsarianism of contemporaries like Perkins, Twisse, Gomarus, and Maccovius, and the synergistic view of the Arminians.[31] Similarly, in his *De pace inter evangelicos*, his presentation of doctrine, though irenic and hopeful of future concord between the Reformed and the Lutherans, is distinctly Reformed on such issues as grace and election.[32]

This Reformed cast of Hall's thought is also evident in his polemics against Rome, most notably, *The Peace of Rome* (1609), *A Serious Dissuasive from Poperie* (1609),[33] *No Peace with Rome* (1611),[34] and

The Old Religion (1627).[35] In virtually all of these writings, Hall identifies his church as "Reformed," albeit in a moderate and genuinely catholic and unitive manner. Thus he could write:

> Let us all sweetly incline our hearts to peace and unity. Let there be amongst us, as said Jerome to St. Augustine, pure brotherhood. Neither let us suffer ourselves, upon every slight quirk of opinion, to be distracted and torn asunder. Let us forget that there were ever any such, in respect of the devotion of a sect, as Luther, Melanchthon, Calvin, Zuinglius, Arminius, or if any other mortal name; for what have we to do with man? Let us breathe nothing, let us affect nothing, but Jesus Christ.[36]

At the same time, he could offer a strictly Calvinistic or Reformed reading of the message of salvation given in scripture. In commenting on the so-called golden chain of Romans 8:29–30, Hall could insist that "there is a strong and indissoluble chain of mercy and grace in God towards his elect, the links whereof can never be broken or severed; for those whom he did predestinate, them also in his due time he effectually calleth; and those, whom he thus calleth, he also justifieth; and those, whom he justifieth from their sins, he doth also fully, at last, glorify."[37]

Although only a comparatively small number of Hall's sermons have survived, the hortatory cast of his *Contemplations* and the homiletical thrust of most of the comments in his *Plain and Familiar Explication, by Way of Paraphrase, of all the Hard Texts of the Whole Divine Scripture*, offer evidence of the breadth of his approach to the text of scripture and of his consistent effort to move from theology and exegesis to application of theological learning in the daily life of the church. The forty-two surviving sermons are models of biblical learning, rhetorical skill, and religious eloquence—tending more toward the Anglican style of the day than toward the Puritan, despite the Calvinistic character of Hall's theology. His homiletical style has been favorably compared to that of Lancelot Andrewes and Jeremy Taylor.[38]

An illuminating contrast can be made between Hall's homiletical approach to the text as it appears in the published versions of his meditations and sermons, and the style of the Puritan preacher Thomas Manton, ordained by Hall in 1640, when Hall was bishop of Exeter. Although comparatively few of Hall's sermons survive in their original manuscript forms, it is highly probable that the larger number of his meditations were originally given in the form of sermons. We know from Hall's own account of his life that he preached three sermons each week and that he wrote each sermon out in full manuscript form—over a period of some forty years. Not only is it the case that forty-two surviving sermons of the bishop hardly illustrate this effort; it is also the case that the many published meditations bear the characteristics of sermons. They move from exposition of text to application, and they evidence use of rhetoric that might well indicate oral delivery.[39]

Despite Hall's strong advocacy of Reformed theology, his meditative and homiletical style, as evidenced in works like the *Contemplations*, in his sermons, and even in the Ramist *Solomon's Divine Arts*—lacks the tendency toward scholastic organization and doctrinal or even dogmatic exposition characteristic of sermons by his Puritan contemporaries. Whereas it is characteristic of the Puritan sermon—as in virtually every one of Manton's—to line out at the very beginning the structure of the sermon as a whole, the various doctrinal points to be covered, and the "use" of the doctrine, and then to develop the body of the sermon in strict accordance with this pattern, noting explicitly (at least in the finalized written form) all of the sections and subsections, Hall's meditations seldom present such an explicit structure and follow an approach more discursive than logical or argumentative.

Even in a highly theological sermon, delivered before a learned audience, such as the sermon on Ecclesiastes 7:16 delivered before the Synod of Dort,[40] or sermons on doctrinal themes, such as the two sermons on "The Impress of God,"[41] or the sermon on "The Enemies of the Cross of Christ,"[42] where Hall operates within the confines of a fairly formal outline, his style is highly rhetorical, filled with metaphors and similes to attract the attention and grasp the memory of hearers. The outline is intended more to press the meaning and the rhetorical power of the text on his hearers than to argue a doctrinal point. Thus the last noted sermon, on the text of Philippians 3:18–19

("For many walk of whom I have told you often, and now tell you even weeping, that they are the enemies of the Cross of Christ Whose end is destruction"), begins with a section on "the fidelity of the Apostle" in which Hall draws his hearers attention to three issues—the apostle's "warning," its "frequence," and its "passion"—all based on the rhetorical structure of the first two clauses of the verse: "his warning, *I have told you*; the frequence, *I have told you often*; the passion, *I now tell you weeping*."[43] The sermon then passes on to a second section on "the wickedness of these false teachers" that is divided into four parts in which the false teachers are "described by their number, motion, quality, [and] issue," respectively: "their Number, *many*; their Motion, *walk*; their Quality, *enemies to the cross of Christ*; their Issue, *destruction*."[44] The organization is carefully drawn, but it serves the rhetorical and textual rather than a scholastic and doctrinal purpose.

In his *Contemplations*, moreover, Hall evidences a greater interest in the way historical figures throughout scripture function as examples for faith and life than in the doctrinal or dogmatic implications of the text. By way of example, in the meditation on Jacob and Esau, Hall clearly recognizes the working out of the divine purpose that the elder should serve the younger, but his emphasis falls not on the problem of the eternal decrees, but instead on the working out of the divine purpose in and through the lives of individuals—principally Jacob and Rebecca—and the lesson that this history holds for believers in the present:

> That God which had ordained the lordship to the younger, will also contrive for him the blessing: what he will have effected, shall not want means. . . . Now God inclines the love of the mother to the younger, against the custom of nature, because the father loves the elder, against the promise. The affections of the parents are divided: that the promise might be fulfilled, Rebecca's craft shall answer Isaac's partiality; Isaac would unjustly turn Esau into Jacob; Rebecca doth as cunningly turn Jacob into Esau: her desire was good; her means were unlawful. God doth oftentimes effect his just will by our weaknesses; yet neither thereby justifying our infirmities, nor blemishing his own actions.[45]

The whole passage stresses the human and the mediate working of God, even as it draws the personal, moral conclusion and refrains from making the doctrinal point concerning election. In addition, stylistically, it moves by short, rhetorically juxtaposed phrases, pressing toward paradox and manifesting in their verbal opposition both the patterns of the human dilemma and the hidden, seemingly contradictory, divine working. There is, in addition, no recourse to theological terminology or, indeed, to scholastic distinction to explain the point.

Manton, by way of contrast, evidences a massive grasp and use of Protestant scholastic theology and its technical language. Thus, in his exposition of the text "With God all things are possible" (Mark 10:27), Manton distinguishes between God's "absolute" and God's "actual" or ordained power, between God's "extraordinary" or miraculous and God's "ordinary" power. He then offers his hearers a distinction between *"impossibilia naturae"* and *"impossibilia natura,"* things impossible to nature and things impossible by nature: God can do what nature cannot, but God cannot do what is by nature impossible—that is, negative or contradictory acts do not belong to the divine omnipotence.[46] As far as Manton was concerned, such distinctions belonged not only in a theological system but also in the sermon, inasmuch as they "have their use in many controversies that are about religion" and that threaten the faith of Christians.[47]

The contrast between Manton's more dogmatic and Hall's more rhetorical and discursive method is nowhere more clear than in their sermons on Zechariah 14:20–21 ("In that day there shall be upon the bells of the horses, Holiness unto the Lord; and the pots in the Lord's house shall be like the bowls before the altar. Yea, every pot in Jerusalem and in Judah shall be holiness unto the Lord of hosts"). They agree substantially concerning the meaning and import of the text; it concerns the divine "inscription" or "impress"—in Manton's words, the "eminent and notable sanctification both of things and persons" that the prophets expect to occur in the fulfillment of God's promises.[48] In style and approach to text and exposition, however, the two writers are significantly different.

Manton offers a tripartite division of the material, consisting of a brief examination of the text in terms of "(1) The inscription or impress; (2) The things on which it is graven; (3) The time when it is done," followed by a discussion of the doctrine presented in the text, and concluded with an examination of the "use" of the doctrine in the lives of believers. The connection between the text in Zechariah and its application to the lives of believers is identified by Manton in the prophet's citation of Exodus 28:36, "Holiness unto the Lord," inasmuch as these words were, according to the text of Exodus, to be inscribed on the "frontlet" of the priests of Israel to indicate that they had been set apart to God. Now, according to Zechariah, all things—from the bells of horses to household utensils—are to be consecrated.[49]

The time of this consecration, indicated by the phrase "in that day," Manton argues, is not "any particular time, but the whole state of things under the gospel," inasmuch as "the time of the gospel" is a day "full of light and grace" unlike any other time in history.[50] The text, therefore, offers a prophecy of the age of the gospel and of the duties of believers during that age. In Manton's model, the remainder of the sermon is, formally, quite simple: he offers a doctrinal and practical exposition of the proposition that "God in and by the gospel will effect an eminent and notable sanctification both of things and persons."[51] What follows is a strict division of the discussion that first offers an explication of the "doctrine" and then a presentation of its "use."

Hall's approach is quite different. Literary style, classical allusion, and overt Latinity are far more important to him than to Manton, and the sermon as a whole is not framed out of a concern for the strict definition of doctrine and its use. In short, the search for an appropriate theological grand style is evident in Hall's work, whereas Manton's remains within the realm of the plain style advocated by his Puritan predecessors. Indeed, Hall's exposition is more closely tied than Manton's to the style and circumstances of the text itself, understood as a vehicle for oratory rather than, in a restrictive sense, as the foundation for doctrine.

From a discussion of the "Emblem or Word," "impress," that is similar in content to Manton's introductory comments, Hall passes on to an analysis of the "Subject and Circumstances" of the text. Here, like Manton, he finds that "it is under the Gospel that this posy of

Holiness shall be so common; *in illâ die*; and *this is that day*. . . . It is
the fashion of the true Church, to grow up still, from worse to better;
as is said of the head of the Church, *Crescebat et corroboratur*." [52]
Punctuation of the text with Latin phrases is typical, and the key
phrase from the text itself, *in illâ die*, becomes a motif repeated
throughout the sermon.

When he comes to his concluding exhortation, Hall raises the
pitch of his rhetoric and presses his point—as well as illustrates his
erudition—with a host of examples and, above all, with close attention
to the emblems or symbols offered in the text:

> O our misery and shame! All things else are holy; Men, Christians
> are unholy. . . . How oft would God have written this title upon our
> foreheads! and, ere he can have written one full word, we blot out
> all. One swears it away, another drinks it away, a third scoffs it away
> . . . and I would to God it were uncharitable to say, that there is as
> much holiness in the bridles of the horses, as in some of the riders.
> . . . We have many titular saints, few real; many, which are written
> in red letters in the calendar of the world, "Holy to the Lord,"
> whom God never canonizes in heaven, and shall once entertain with
> a *Nescio, I know you not*. These men have holiness written upon them;
> and are like, as Lucian compares his Grecians, to a fair, gilt, bossed
> book: look within, there is the Tragedy of Thyestes, or perhaps
> Arrius' [sic] Thalia; the name of the muse, the matter of heresy; or
> Conrad Vorstius's late monster, that hath *De Deo* in the front, and
> atheism and blasphemy in the text. [53]

Hall concludes with a brief exhortation to personal holiness. Careful
rhetorical crafting of argument is evident in the movement from the
emblem "Holy to the Lord" to a direct use of the biblical reference to
the bridles of horses in contrast to contemporary Christian riders
unworthy of the emblem. Hall laments the presence of the title "Holy"
on so many who fall short. The metaphor of writing the emblem on
the forehead then shifts, by way of classical allusion, to the image of a
beautiful book; but like the false saint, the book is inwardly a great
tragedy. Another classical allusion leads to an example from the early
church: the heretic Arius, who named his book after the muse of
comedy and bucolic poetry—"the name of the muse, the matter of

heresy." The point is made contemporary with the example of Vorstius.

Manton, who teaches much the same substance as Hall, offers no classical allusions; uses Latin only to offer technical theological terms; and, of most significance, when he comes to his discussion of the practical "use" of the sermon, makes no broad or grand rhetorical point, but rather in the plainest prose addresses his hearers directly:

> Undertake nothing but what will bear this inscription upon it, "Holiness to the Lord." This question should be put to ourselves, Can I dedicate this to God? In worship, Am I now acting for God or for myself? In your callings, Is this for God? Is it consistent with my great end, or impertinent to it? If it be inconsistent, it is plain treachery to my covenant vow; if impertinent, it is a diversion not voluntarily to be allowed. . . . Be sure to exercise your general calling in your particular; your general calling is to be a christian, your particular calling is that way of life to which God hath designed you by your abilities and education for the common good. . . . God should be worshipped by every faithful person in his own house in as God-like a manner as he was worshipped by the Jews in the temple. . . . Therefore when we familiarly converse, we should show most of holiness, ordering all our affairs and actions as may best demonstrate the sincerity of our hearts.[54]

Thus Manton's conclusion, like the body of his sermon, contains no flowery language, no grand metaphors, and makes no attempt to write timeless prose. Because of this, far more than Hall, Manton is able to strike directly at the heart of his hearers in their present context.

This contrast between the methods of Manton and Hall does not, of course, indicate that strict dichotomy can be made between Anglican and Puritan on the basis merely of the style of homilies and meditations. A highly exegetical Anglican preacher like Lancelot Andrewes had frequent recourse in his sermons to the text of scripture in the original languages and, more often than not, presented at the outset of his meditation a tight outline, leading from text, to doctrine, to application, of the issues to be addressed in the sermon.[55] Nonetheless, the grand style belongs more clearly to the Anglican, as does the classical allusion and the high rhetoric that gives pleasure to the ear;

whereas the direct address to the heart of the hearer and the stress on
praxis belong to the Puritan. Hall, despite his theological views, was
Anglican not only in polity but also in literary style.

THE EXEGETE AND INTERPRETER

The biblical works of Bishop Hall occupy an important place in
the Protestant and, specifically, English Protestant exegetical and
interpretive tradition.[56] Hall does not rank as one of the major
linguists, text-critics, or technical exegetes of the seventeenth century.
He cannot be compared to the likes of Buxtorff, Lightfoot, or Walton
for linguistic or text-critical prowess, nor should he be compared with
exegetes like Ainsworth or Poole for detailed grasp of the linguistic
and theological workings of the text in whole and in part. Nonetheless, he remains an important example of the way in which seventeenth-century exegetes and theologians bridged the gap between the
technical establishment and examination of the text of scripture and
the popular or churchly explanation and application of the text. Or,
as we might say in the language of modern hermeneutics, Hall was
adept at making the transition between the establishment of *meaning*
and presentation of *significance*. Primary examples of this effort are his
Solomon's Divine Arts, and his *Plain and Familiar Explication . . . of all
the Hard Texts of the Whole Divine Scripture*, each of which approaches
the problem of contemporary significance in a different way.

In the first of these works, *Solomon's Divine Arts*, Hall offered a
guide, resting on biblical wisdom, to the so-called *scientiae practicae*,
or "practical ways of knowing," of the day. His gathering together of
the three forms of "gouernment"—"ethickes," "politickes," and "oeconomicks"—pertaining to the ordering of personal, civil, and family
behavior echoes the concern of other Reformed theologians of the
day, like Keckermann and Perkins, to incorporate the entire category
of human life and work into a large-scale Christian encyclopedia of
knowledge. Perkins not only wrote a treatise on *Oeconomie, or House-
hold-Government*,[57] he also offered a diagram of the various "sacred
sciences" into which "the bodie of holy scripture is distinguished." [58]
The diagram offers a simple Ramist bifurcation between the "princi-

pall" science in scripture, theology, which is the "science of living well and blessedly for ever," and other sciences that stand as "attendants or handmaides" to theology. Indeed, for Perkins, these other sciences all offer instruction in "living well and blessedly" in this world. As preparation for the next, Perkins enumerates seven ancillary sciences: "I. *Ethiques*, a doctrine of living honestly and civilly"; "II. *Oeconomickes*, a doctrine of governing a family"; "III. *Politikes*, a doctrine of the right administration of a Common-weale"; "IV. *Ecclesiasticall discipline*, a doctrine of well-ordering the Church"; "V. *The Iewes Common-weale*, in as much as it differeth from Church government"; "VI. *Prophesie*, the doctrine of preaching well"; "VII. *Academie*, the doctrine of governing Schooles well: especially those of the Prophets." [59] Keckermann similarly saw the need for the Christian theologian—in his case, acting as the rector of a Gymnasium—to raise the issue of the larger body of knowledge in its relation to theology. The second volume of Keckermann's collected works offers his lectures on ethics, economics, politics, rhetoric, Christian rhetoric (as a distinct discipline), and theology. [60] The intention of many Reformed theologians at the end of the sixteenth and the beginning of the seventeenth century was to meet the challenge of the institutionalization of the Reformation by creating a cohesive body of Christian doctrine that could address not only religious issues but that could also apply the Protestant *sola Scriptura* to all aspects of human life. [61] Hall's work, therefore, belongs to a conscious effort on the part of Protestants to organize biblical wisdom and present it as an alternative, at least in part, to the purely secular traditions of ethics, politics, and the other humane disciplines. As Hall notes in his meditation on inward tranquillity, *Heaven Upon Earth* (1627), "Not *Athens* must teach this lesson, but *Jerusalem*." [62]

Hall's *Solomon's Divine Arts* not only accepts the disciplinary model of ethics, economics, and politics; it also reflects the strong concern for method, understood as the right way through a body of knowledge, that was characteristic of the age in general and of Reformed theology in particular. Even so, his identification of ethics as "*a Doctrine of* wisedom and knowledge *to liue wel*, and of the madness and foolishness *of vice:* . . . *The end wherof is* to see *and attaine* that *chiefe* goodnes of the children of men" is quite in accord with the

Ramist and Perkinsian definition of theology as the "science of living well and blessedly for ever." [63] In addition, if we understand wisdom and knowledge to mean *sapientia* and *scientia*, Hall has pointed his readers toward the two kinds of knowing traditionally associated with theology—knowledge of first principles as it is directed toward goals or ends (*sapientia*) and knowledge of first principles together with the conclusions that can be drawn from them (*scientia*). Indeed, the entirety of Hall's exposition indicates how the conclusions of *scientia*, drawn from the principles offered in the text, direct the life of believers in the present, and how that rightly directed life, assisted by the *sapientia*, also drawn from the text, can be led toward "the end" of seeing and attaining the "chiefe goodnes of the children of men." The resulting work is a well-ordered handbook of biblical wisdom—not strictly a work of exegesis, but certainly an essay in biblical theology constructed with sensitivity to the genre of wisdom literature.

Hall's *Plain and Familiar Explication . . . of all the Hard Texts of the Whole Divine Scripture* is a handbook of English-language biblical interpretation that begins with Genesis 1:1 and proceeds to examine a host of passages—in fact, nearly the entirety of the Bible—and to offer brief explanations as far as Revelation 22:20. The work itself sprang out of Hall's concern for the use of scripture by the laity in the face of Roman Catholic objections:

> The inconveniences, that are pretended to have followed upon the open and free permission of Scriptures in vulgar languages, have sensibly arisen from the misunderstanding of them. Remove that peril; and the frequence and universality of them can be no other, than a blessing. This service I have here endeavoured to perform; having commonly, in the passages of this work, trod in the steps, as I have judged, of the best interpretations.[64]

The work, then, is an attempt to support the Protestant *sola Scriptura* and right of free access to the text by all believers through the creation of a bridge between the more technical tradition of the Protestant biblical commentators and the needs of the literate laity. There are but few signs in the paraphrase of technical exegesis, but the lines of interpretation reaching into the Protestant exegetical tradition and linking Hall's Reformed theological sympathies to his episcopal polity and to his spiritual interests are quite clear.

As in *Solomon's Divine Arts*, the wisdom of the text is made accessible in a form suited to Hall's historical and cultural context and capable of resolving difficulties in doctrine caused by untutored readings of the text. In addition, Hall's meditative concern for the life of the inward person, so evident in his spiritual works, evidences itself throughout the paraphrase. Thus, on Psalm 69:2: "I sink in deep mire, where there is no standing," Hall offers a paraphrase that interprets the metaphors of the text while at the same time acknowledging the moral predicament of the psalmist, and brings it to bear on the life of the church in his own time: "O God, I am ready to be utterly swallowed up with the evils, which are come upon me: I find not any ground of comfort to rest my soul upon." [65] Hall's interest in traditional, indeed, in Roman Catholic spirituality and its direct application to the needs of contemporary Protestantism is evident in his comment on John 3:29: "He that hath the bride is the bridegroom . . .," where he comments:

> It is he, who is the true and only Bridegroom, and Husband of his spouse, the Church: this honour is proper to him therefore to enjoy her, whom he hath chosen and betrothed to himself in truth and righteousness: as for me, and all other faithful servants, we are the friends and attendants of this Blessed Bridegroom; and therefore, as our duty is, we wait upon him, and hold it to be our greatest joy and glory, that we hear his voice, and that we see the happy success of this Spiritual Marriage. [66]

A strongly Reformed accent, echoing Calvin's views on human self-knowledge and sin and echoing also the Canons of Dort on the problem of human inability, is heard in Hall's comment on John 1:5: "And the light shineth in the darkness; and the darkness comprehendeth it not":

> It is true indeed, that the faculties of man's knowledge and understanding are now so overspread with darkness of ignorance and misconceit, that he cannot rightly apprehend and conceive the things

of God; yet the means of this divine knowledge are offered and held forth unto him, howsoever the indisposition of man's depraved nature is such, that he doth not entertain them, and make use of them accordingly.[67]

Hall's exposition not only draws the text out of its metaphor into a clear contemporary paraphrase; it also offers a theological interpretation geared to the problems of his seventeenth-century English hearers and readers, who were pressed to decide between a Reformed and an Arminian approach to the problem of salvation.

Similar in method, although quite different in content, is the comment on Matthew 16:18–19, where, in truly Protestant fashion, the identification of Peter as the "rock" or stone points not to the bishop of Rome, but to Christ, "the chief Corner Stone" on whom the "foundation of [the] Prophets and Apostles" rests; whereas in a thoroughly episcopal manner, Hall can also point to the authority of binding and loosing given to this "prime Apostle, and to the rest of [his] fellows."[68] Hall's way of directing the text toward his seventeenth-century audience is not obtrusive, but the paraphrase does consciously and consistently move from inherent grammatical meaning to contemporary significance.

CONCLUDING REFLECTION

The meditations, paraphrases, sermons, and theological treatises of Joseph Hall, taken as a whole, stand as a major contribution to the Protestant tradition of spirituality and biblical interpretation. Hall's approach to the text of scripture, whether in the rhetorically rich style of the sermons and contemplations or in the somewhat more plain and direct style of the paraphrases and of *Solomon's Divine Arts*, stands in continuity with the developing Protestant hermeneutics of the late sixteenth and early seventeenth centuries. His interpretations evidence at once a concern for the literal meaning of the text and for the situation of the text in the context of the larger meaning of scripture.

This latter consideration is particularly apparent in the case of *Solomon's Divine Arts*, where the paraphrase and interpretation stays exceedingly close to the meaning of the text but nevertheless understands the text as directly applicable to Hall's own audience. Hall's only recourse to allegory occurs in the paraphrase of the Song of Songs, where the traditional understanding of the text—grounded in rabbinic and patristic exegesis, as an allegory of the love of God for his people—quite understandably occupies Hall's attention and serves his meditative, spiritual purpose. The examination of texts from Proverbs and Ecclesiastes, however, is highly literal and seeks consistently to establish the meaning of the text within the context of Solomonic wisdom—understood by Hall as a unified perspective on human life and institutions.

Granting the Reformed understanding of the unity and distinction of the testaments, in their common themes of the covenantal history of salvation and the movement from prophecy to fulfillment, Hall was able to understand scripture as a unified whole offered as revelation for the doctrinal and spiritual direction of the church. Nonetheless, his reading of the text evidences also the restraint characteristic of the more literal of the Reformed exegetes from the time of Calvin onward. He manifests no desire to invest the Old Testament with christological content merely for the sake of churchly application. He searches out the meaning of the text as such: Jacob and Esau need not be allegorized or understood as types, and the Pauline language of election need not be pressed against the text of Genesis. What the text reveals about God's relationship with human beings becomes Hall's central interest in interpretation, and the wisdom of the text is allowed to speak directly to Hall's seventeenth-century audience.

NOTES

1. On Hall's spirituality, see Frank Livingstone Huntley, *Bishop Joseph Hall and Protestant Meditation in Seventeenth-Century England: A Study with Texts of "The Art of Divine Meditation" (1606) and "Occasional Meditations" (1633)* (Binghamton, N.Y.: Center for Medieval and Early Renaissance Studies, 1981); and John Booty, "Joseph Hall, the *Arte of Divine Meditation*, and Anglican Spirituality," in vol. 2 of *The Spirituality of Western Christendom*, ed. E. Elder (Kalamazoo, Mich.: Cistercian Publications, 1984), 200–228.

2. On the life and works of Joseph Hall, see Frank Livingstone Huntley, *Bishop Joseph Hall, 1574–1656: A Biographical and Critical Study* (Cambridge, Eng.: D. S. Brewer, 1979); and Leonard D. Tourney, *Joseph Hall* (Boston: Twayne, 1979). There is also a substantial biographical essay available with an introductory memoir and notices of Hall's other works by the Right Reverend Charles Wordsworth, in Joseph Hall, *Contemplations on the Historical Passages of the Old and New Testaments* . . . (London: SPCK, 1871). All discussions of Hall's life must, moreover, begin with his personal memoir "Observations of Some Specialties of God's Providence in the Life of Joseph Hall, Bishop of Norwich, Written in His Own Hand," in *The Works of Joseph Hall, D.D.*, 12 vols. (Oxford: D. A. Talboys, 1837–39).

3. Joseph Hall, *Solomon's Divine Arts* (London, 1609); also in *Works* 8: 427–84. In this essay, all of Hall's writings, with the exception of *Solomon's Divine Arts*, will be cited from the collected *Works*. The citations of *Solomon's Divine Arts* follow the 1609 text reprinted in this volume.

4. Hall, in *Works*, vols. 1–2.

5. Ibid., 3–4.

6. Cf., e.g., Frederick W. Farrar, *History of Interpretation* (New York: Dutton, 1886; repr., Grand Rapids: Baker Book House, 1961); with *The Cambridge History of the Bible*, 3 vols. (Cambridge: Cambridge University Press, 1963–70).

7. Thomas Fuller, *Worthies of England*, ed. Nuttall, 3 vols. (London, 1840), 2: 130.

8. Hall, "Observations," in *Works* 1: xi.

9. Cf. ibid., xii, xiv; with Canon G. G. Perry, *Dictionary of National Biography*, ed. Leslie Stephen and Sidney Lee (New York: Macmillan, 1885–1912) s.v., "Hall, Joseph," vol. 8: 959.

10. Cf. Marshall Knappen, *Tudor Puritanism: A Chapter in the History of Idealism* (Chicago: University of Chicago Press, 1939; repr., 1965), 470–71, 475.

11. Hall, "Observations," in *Works* 1: xvii.

12. Ibid., xxi-xxii.

13. Huntley, *Bishop Hall and Protestant Meditation*, 18.

14. The other delegates were Dr. George Carleton, bishop of Llandaff; Dr. John Davenant, then master of Queen's College, Cambridge, and later bishop of Salisbury; Dr. Samuel Ward, master of Sidney Sussex College, Cambridge; Walter Balcanquall, fellow of Pembroke Hall, Cambridge (as representative for the Church of Scotland); and John Hales of Eton, the chaplain to the royal ambassador to the Hague, Sir Dudley Carleton. Hall left the synod before its end and was replaced by Dr. Thomas Goade.

15. Hall, "Observations," in *Works* 1: xxxi-xxxii.

16. *Works* 10: 471–98.

17. Ibid., 7: 49–51, 54–57.

18. Ibid., 11: 492–511.

19. On Hall's *An Humble Remonstrance to the High Court of Parliament, by a Dutifull Sonne of the Church* (1641) and the ensuing debate with the pamphleteers jointly known as Smectymnuus, see William Haller, *Liberty and Reformation in the Puritan Revolution* (New York: Columbia University Press, 1955; repr., 1963), 32–40.

20. William Haller, *The Rise of Puritanism: or, The Way to the New Jerusalem as Set Forth in Pulpit and Press from Thomas Cartwright to John Lilburne and John Milton, 1570–1643* (New York: Columbia University Press, 1938; repr., New York: Harper & Row, 1957), 327–28.

21. See Sara Jean Clausen, "Calvinism in the Anglican Hierarchy, 1603–1643: Four Episcopal Examples" (Ph.D. Diss. Vanderbilt University, 1989).

22. On the development of rhetoric in the English Renaissance, see Debora K. Shuger, *Sacred Rhetoric: The Christian Grand Style in the English Renaissance* (Princeton: Princeton University Press, 1988). For discussion of Ramist logic and its impact on English theology, see Keith L. Sprunger, "Ames, Ramus, and the Method of Puritan Theology," *Harvard Theological Review* 59 (1966): 133–51; and Donald K. McKim, *Ramism in William Perkins' Theology* (New York: Peter Lang, 1987).

23. On Hall's religious satire, see J. W. Blench, *Preaching in England in the Late Fifteenth and Sixteenth Centuries: A Study of English Sermons, 1450–c. 1600* (Oxford: Basil Blackwell, 1964), 337–38, 340–42, 345.

24. On this issue, see Shuger, *Sacred Rhetoric.*

25. Cf. ibid., 69–76, 84–100.

26. Cf. William Perkins, "The Art of Prophesying," in *The Workes of that Famous Minister of Christ in the University of Cambridge, Mr. William Perkins*, 3 vols. (Cambridge, 1609–18), 2: 643–73.

27. Huntley, *Bishop Joseph Hall and Protestant Meditation*, 20–21.

28. For a discussion of preaching in England, see Blench, *Preaching in England*; and Irvonwy Morgan, *The Godly Preachers of the Elizabethan Church* (London: Epworth Press, 1965). Also see Erwin R. Gane, "The Exegetical Methods of Some Sixteenth-Century Anglican Preachers: Latimer, Jewel, Hooker, and Andrewes," *Andrews University Seminary Studies* 17 (1979): 23–38, 169–88; and Gane, "The Exegetical Methods of Some Sixteenth-Century Puritan Preachers: Hooper, Cartwright, and Perkins," *Andrews University Seminary Studies* 19 (1981): 21–36, 99–114.

29. Fuller, *Worthies of England*, ed. Nuttall, 2: 129–30.

30. Hall, "Brief Sum of the Principles of Religion, Fit to be Known of Such as Would Address Themselves to the God's Table," in *Works* 7: 423–26.

31. Hall, in *Works* 10: 471–98.

32. Ibid., 11: 499.

33. The two works were published together: Hall, "The Peace of Rome: Proclaimed to all the World, by her famous Cardinall Bellarmine, and the no lesse famous casuist of Navarre . . . whereto is prefixed A Serious Dissuasive from Poperie" (London, 1609), in *Works* 9: 1–156.

34. Hall, "No Peace with Rome: Wherein is Proved, that as Terms now Stand there can be no Reconciliation of the Reformed Religion with the Romish," in *Works* 11: 277–381.

35. Hall, "The Old Religion: A Treatise, in which is laid down the True State of the Difference between the Reformed and the Romish Church; and the Blame for the Schism is Cast upon the True authors," in *Works* 9: 305–95.

36. Hall, "A Serious Dissuasive," in *Works* 9: 45.

37. Hall, "A Plain and Familiar Explication . . . of all the Hard Texts," in *Works* 4: 318.

38. Perry, *Dictionary of National Biography* s.v. "Hall, Joseph," 8: 963.

39. Huntley, *Bishop Joseph Hall and Protestant Meditation*, 8–9.

40. Hall, in *Works* 11: 465–87.

41. Ibid., 5: 47–66.

42. Ibid., 172–87.

43. Ibid., 172.

44. Ibid., 179.

45. Hall, *Contemplations*, 3:i. (*Works* 1:42).

46. Thomas Manton, in *Works* 17: 86–87.

47. Ibid., 87.

48. Ibid., 441–42; cf. Hall, in *Works* 5: 47–48, 51–52.

49. Manton, in *Works* 17: 441.

50. Ibid.

51. Ibid., 442.

52. Hall, in *Works* 5: 51–52: *"In illâ die,"* "in that day"; *"Crescebat et corroboratur,"* "he grew in stature and was strengthened."

53. Hall, in *Works* 5: 54–55.

54. Manton, in *Works* 17: 449–51.

55. See Gane, "The Exegetical Methods of Some Sixteenth-Century Anglican Preachers: Latimer, Jewel, Hooker, and Andrewes," 179–81.

56. On the methods and patterns of Protestant exegesis in sixteenth- and seventeenth-century England, see Richard A. Muller, "William Perkins and

the Protestant Exegetical Tradition: Interpretation, Style, and Method in the Commentary on Hebrews 11," in William Perkins, *A Commentary on Hebrews 11*, facs. ed., ed. John H. Augustine, Pilgrim Classic Commentaries Series, ser. ed. Gerald T. Sheppard, (New York: Pilgrim Press, 1989). Also see Gane, "The Exegetical Methods of Some Sixteenth-Century Anglican Preachers: Latimer, Jewel, Hooker, and Andrewes" and "The Exegetical Methods of Some Sixteenth-Century Puritan Preachers: Hooper, Cartwright, and Perkins."

57. Perkins, *The Workes of . . . Mr. William Perkins*, 3: 668–700. For a description of the various editions of the three-volume *Workes,* see Muller, "William Perkins and the Protestant Exegetical Tradition," in Perkins, *A Commentary on Hebrews 11*, ed. Augustine.

58. Perkins, "A Golden Chaine: or, The Description of Theologie," in *Workes* 1:1.

59. Ibid.

60. See Bartholomaus Keckermann, *Operum omnium quae extant*, 2 vols. (Geneva, 1614).

61. On Keckermann, see Richard A. Muller, "Vera Philosophia cum sacra Theologia nusquam pugnat: Keckermann on Philosophy, Theology and the Problem of Double Truth," *The Sixteenth Century Journal* 25, no. 3 (Fall 1984): 341–65.

62. Hall, "Heaven Upon Earth: or, Of True Peace and Tranquillity," in *Works* 6: 4.

63. Cf. Hall, *Solomon's Divine Arts*, 1–2, with Petrus Ramus, *Commentariorum de religione christiana* (Frankfurt, 1576), 1:i and with Perkins, "A Golden Chaine," in *Workes* 1: 11, col. 1.

64. Hall, "Plain and Familiar Explication . . . of all the Hard Texts," in *Works* 3: ix.

65. Ibid., 203.

66. Ibid., 4: 227.

67. Ibid., 221; cf. John Calvin, *Institutes of the Christian Religion*, ed. John T. McNeill, trans. Ford Lewis Battles (Philadelphia: The Westminster Press, 1960), I.iv.1–4; v.1–5; "Canons of the Synod of Dort," in Philip Schaff, *The Creeds of Christendom: With a History and Critical Notes*, 3 vols. (New York, 1919; repr., Grand Rapids: Baker Book House, 1977), 565, 588.

68. Hall, "Plain and Familiar Explication . . . of all the Hard Texts," in *Works* 4: 154.

Working with Wisdom Literature: Joseph Hall and William Henry Green

MARION TAYLOR

J oseph Hall (1574–1656) was a renowned wit and poet, a prolific writer of elegant prose and of practical and devotional literature. William Henry Green (1825–1900) was celebrated as "the Nestor of the conservative Old Testament School" at Princeton Theological Seminary in the second half of the nineteenth century. In this essay, I will compare Joseph Hall's treatise *Solomon's Divine Arts*, which deals with the biblical books associated with Solomon, with William Henry Green's extant works on the wisdom books of the Old Testament. I will do this with a view to understanding not only the similarities in how they understood and used the scriptures but also their differences, which were rooted for the most part in changes brought to biblical studies through the forces of the Enlightenment. Such a comparison will show that Hall's approach to interpretation, which was typical of the older way of working with the Bible, could not be sustained in exactly the same way even by conservatives in the nineteenth century. The hermeneutical issues raised in the study will also challenge interpreters in the postmodern period to reconsider some of the fundamental issues involved in interpreting Solomon's wisdom for the church today.

SOLOMON'S DIVINE ARTS

In the dedicatory inscription to *Solomon's Divine Arts*, Joseph Hall speaks quite candidly about his endeavor to present to Robert, Earl of

Marion Ann Taylor is assistant professor of Old Testament, Wycliffe College in the University of Toronto.

Essex, *"those precepts, which the Spirit of God gaue"* to Solomon, *"the royallest Philosopher and wisest king"*(A2).* His focus is clearly on the proverbial wisdom of Solomon, which he also describes as *"his diuine rules"* and *"diuine Morals"* (A3 verso). Hall then arranges these precepts, rules, or morals by subject into what he calls *"the common-place-booke of that great king"* (A3 verso). Hall is quite defensive about his method. Although he admits that Solomon *"could not erre"* and that contrariwise he himself could not *"but haue erred; either in art, or application, or sense, or disorder, or defect,"* he asks those who might raise an objection and imply that he has tried *"to correct Salomons order, or to controule Ezekias seruants"* to understand his purpose to be one that is practical and edifying for the readers, *"for more ease of finding, for better memory, for readier vse"* (A3 verso).

Certainly, by selecting and then arranging the proverbs under various headings, Hall brought a new shape and even new meanings to many of the biblical proverbs. Moreover, his own understanding of the biblical texts is implicit in his work. For example, in his presentation of Solomon's economics or the government of the family, Hall prescribes that the model wife be "1. Faithfull to her husband; Not wanton. 2. Obedient, 3. Discreet, 4. Prouident and hous-wife-like" (155). He supports his prescriptive outline with a catena of proverbial sayings (or half sayings) on women, joined together by his own interpretive comments. He begins his disquisition on the faithful wife by extolling the priceless value of "a Vertuous Wife . . . the Crowne of her husband" by joining together the first half of Proverbs 12:4 and Proverbs 31:10 (155). He then defines the qualities of a virtuous wife and places great emphasis on her fidelity in contrast to the loose woman who is frequently featured in the book of Proverbs:

> *Shee is true to her husband's bedde*; such as the heart of her husband may trust to, *as knowing that she is tied to him* by the couenant of God; *not wanton and unchaste; such one* as I *once* saw from the window of my house. (155)

---

*The page numbers in parentheses that follow quotations from Hall's *Solomon's Divine Arts* refer to the 1609 text reprinted in this volume. The italics mark Joseph Hall's own words.

In Hall's description of the model wife, it is noteworthy that it is Hall and not Solomon who defines the wife as being *"true to her husband's bedde . . . not wanton and unchaste"* (155). To be sure, this depiction of a wife is assumed in the book of Proverbs and would be supported by the larger canonical context of the Old Testament. But the texts that Hall presents as support for this prescription are not clearly about a wife's fidelity to the marriage bed. Notably, as the parallel half verse in Proverbs 31:11 intimates, the context of the stichos "such as the heart of her husband may trust to" is not sexual (155); it is far more open-ended. Moreover, Hall completes this half verse with his own words and a reference to the covenant of God, a phrase taken from the middle of the discussion of the loose woman in Proverbs 2:17, *"as knowing that she is tied to him* by the couenant of God," a reference that may or may not refer to a contract of marriage in its original context (155). Without a doubt, there is much of Hall in this document. Although the theme of fidelity is found in the book of Proverbs, Hall has given it a new shape by placing it within his discussion of the economics of family, particularly the wife. He has brought a definite culturally conditioned preunderstanding of what constitutes a virtuous wife to his discussion of the subject, and he has selected and construed the biblical material to support his view.[1]

Similarly, Hall's claim that Solomon's economics prescribes that a wife *"is duetifull and obedient"* is supported with a very general precept taken from Proverbs 15:1, the larger context of which suggests that the advice given is to a son (159). Hall continues his discussion by imposing a marriage context upon part of a verse from Ecclesiastes 4:9: "Two bee better then one," and joins it together with Proverbs 21:19 (not 27:19 as the text suggests) as support for his contention that Solomon advocates that a wife is dutiful and obedient (160). In fact, none of the verses that Hall cites to support his outline are directly related to the subject of a wife's obedience.

Again, in his treatment of Solomon's economics of the master and servant and his ideal courtier, Hall freely alters the import of the biblical proverbs to suit his own agenda. To support his contention that the servant must be diligent, for example, he cites Proverbs 27:23, a text that is addressed not to servants, but rather to those who own livestock: "Be diligent to knowe the estate of thy flock (*or rather*, the face of thy cattel), and take heed to the heardes" (174). Then, to find textual support for his contention that according to Solomon's commonwealth, a courtier is to be discreet, religious, humble, charitable, diligent, and faithful, Hall freely narrows the focus of some very general proverbs. Thus, although the term *courtier* is not found in the biblical texts, Hall intends the reader to understand that the ideal courtier is being depicted in the following rather generic proverbs:

> Hee that seeketh good things getteth fauour; . . . the righteous is more excellent then his neighbour: *and besides these,* humble; The reward wherof is glory: *for,* before glory goeth humilitie . . . *whom if he see moued,* he pacifieth by staying of anger, *and* by a soft answer breaketh a man of bone; *not aggrauating the faults of others.* (130)

Clearly, Hall has construed the biblical proverbs to support his own conception of how life should be ordered and regulated at the personal, family, and societal levels. Moreover, in doing so he has brought new meaning to many of the biblical texts. Hall's claim that *"the matter is all his* [Solomon's]; *nothing is mine, but the methode"* is really not true (A2–A3 verso). What is his own in *Solomon's Divine Arts* is not to be disparaged, however. It constitutes not only an important resource for the history of biblical interpretation but also for studies in English Protestant and Puritan social and political history.[2]

HERMENEUTICAL ISSUES

The question that faces a modern reader is, How can Hall adapt the proverbs so liberally for his own purposes? How can he change the original referent of a particular proverb and piece together half verses from Ecclesiastes with parts of verses from Proverbs and even the Song of Songs, and then claim that *"the matter is all his* [Solomon's]" (A2)? To be sure, a number of interrelated factors stand behind Hall's use of the biblical materials. His lack of sensitivity to the particular historical and literary contexts of the material he is working with allows him to move quite freely in the material that he attributes to the hand of one author. Indeed, Hall's assumption of the Solomonic authorship of the books of Proverbs, Ecclesiastes, and the Song of Songs enables him to treat these biblical books as one book, a common resource from which to draw his analysis or synopsis of the only extant wisdom sayings of *"the royallest Philosopher and wisest king"* (A2).

Moreover, Hall works with an understanding of the "scope" of Solomon's writings that permits him to reorder, to rewrite, and to reinterpret Solomon's proverbs in ways he feels are consonant with the larger canonical context of the particular proverbs he is using and in light of his own understanding of the purpose and present function of Solomon's writings within the Christian community.[3] The fluidity with which he treats the texts shows that his high view of inspiration does not stop him from a relatively bold and at times precariously free use of the text. Certainly in his prefatory comments, Hall speaks of the divine nature of the biblical texts. He even speaks of the inerrancy of Solomon's writings: *"the royallest Philosopher and wisest king, giuing you those precepts, which the Spirit of God gaue him. The matter is all his. . . . In that, he could not erre"* (A2–A3 verso). But Hall also recognizes the human aspect of the wisdom writings and speaks of the words as being Solomon's and the arrangement attributed to Solomon and the servants of Hezekiah.[4] However, the freedom with which Hall uses, reshapes, and reinterprets the material demonstrates that his fidelity to the text is not fastidious. Still he concedes that interpreters of the inspired text can in their admittedly frail ways only attempt to interpret and apply the scriptures: *"I cannot but haue erred, either in art, or application, or sense, or disorder, or defect"* (A3 verso).

Further, like his contemporaries,[5] Hall believed that the scriptures functioned in a prescriptive way for "the gouernment of behauiour, common-wealth, and familie" (title page).[6] Clues to Hall's understanding of the prescriptive nature of the biblical wisdom literature are found within *Solomon's Divine Arts*. His discussion of wherein felicity lies exemplifies this:

> *Wherein then doth it consist?* Let vs heare the end of all; Feare God, and keep his Commandements; for this is the whole of Man, *the* whole *dutie, the* whole *scope, the* whole *happinesse*; for Life is in the

waie of righteousnesse, and in that path there is no death; *and attending thereon, all* Blessings are vpon the head of the righteous. (12–13)

Hall clearly regards the proverbial wisdom as a divine source of principles or rules for living, for the governing of personal behavior, the commonwealth, and the family. Thus he comments in his paraphrase of Proverbs 1:2:

"To know wisdom and instruction."]–The use whereof is to give true, moral, and spiritual wisdom and instruction to those that do carefully read or hear them.[7]

Similarly, Hall relates the knowledge of wisdom and morality in his paraphrase of Ecclesiastes 1:17:

"I gave my heart to know wisdom, and to know madness and folly."]–I addicted myself moreover to the disquisition and study of morality; and therein I did not only labour to know what pertained to wisdom, but also on the contrary, to understand what belongs to folly and madness, that I might perfectly comprehend all the fashions and courses of men; and I found this to be no better than vexation of spirit.[8]

The keeping of the law, or the following of the prescriptive principles found in scripture, was part of what Hall understood to be the God-given means of finding wholeness in life and of approving oneself before God. To put it another way, Hall regards the contents of the Solomonic books as *"the rule whereof is Gods Lawe"* (21–22). This sentiment is fleshed out in Hall's discussion of virtue, where he writes:

Vertue consistes in the mean; vice in extreams. Let thy wayes bee ordered aright; Turne not to the right hand, nor to the left, but remoue thy foote from euill; *The rule whereof is Gods Lawe:* for the commandement is a lantern, and instruction a light; and euery word of God is pure. My son, hearken to my words; incline thine eare to my sayings: Let them not depart from thine eies; but keepe them in the midst of thine heart. For, they are life vnto those that finde

them, and health vnto all their flesh. Keepe my commandements and
thou shalt liue, and mine Instruction as the apple of thine eye: Binde
them vpon thy fingers, & write them vppon the Table of thine heart.
(21–22).

This catena of verses that focuses on the importance of God's words
as law, as commandment, as light, and as instruction for life reflects
Hall's own understanding of the nature of the contents of Solomon's
biblical writings; that is, they are inspired writings that continue to
function as "law," as prescriptive for the life of the follower of God,
as words that bring life and light.

Nevertheless, Hall's willingness to rework Solomon's proverbs
into a systematic presentation that he calls *Solomon's Divine Arts of
Ethics, Politics, and Economics* shows that Hall's view of this material as
law is very general. Hall envisions Solomon's proverbs or, perhaps
more appropriately, his own recasting of Solomonic proverbial wisdom literature as law in a very broad sense. Hall believes that the
Solomonic literature can function prescriptively in that wisdom brings
life. Thus he writes of the didactic and spiritual function of the law of
God in his paraphrase of Proverbs 13:14:

> "The law of the wise is a fountain of life, to depart from the snares
> of death."]–The law of God, which is the matter and scope whereto
> all instruction of wise teachers tendeth, is that fountain from which
> spiritual and eternal life floweth, and the only means to deliver the
> soul from the snares of everlasting death.[9]

Functionally then, Hall views Solomon's precepts as broad guidelines
or principles for Christian living, material that lends itself to practical
applications such as those he himself attempted in mapping out the
government of behavior, commonwealth, and family.

It follows that Hall's stated desire to order the proverbs in a way
that will make *"for more ease of finding, for better memory, for readier
use"* has to be understood within his broader understanding of the
purpose of Solomon's wisdom literature as prescriptive, as words that
"both direct his [the reader's] *life, and iudge it"* (A3 verso-A3 recto).
Here it is important to note that because Hall believed that Solomon's

wisdom was preserved for *"our good"* as well as *"glory to himselfe,"* he purposefully sought to make practical moral and religious applications of this material to a Christian audience (A3 recto).

WILLIAM HENRY GREEN AND SOLOMON'S WISDOM BOOKS

William Henry Green (1825–1900) taught at Princeton Theological Seminary for over fifty years and propagated what was known as "the reverent and conservative school of higher criticism" far beyond the walls of the theologically conservative Princeton Seminary. As the controversy about the scriptures intensified during the last quarter of the nineteenth century, Green stationed himself on the front lines of the battle and emerged as "the Nestor of the conservative Old Testament School," an "Athanasius against the world," "one of the last of the active professors of Old Testament literature in American universities who held the views concerning that authorship and inspiration of the Bible which were generally adopted by evangelical leaders a generation ago."[10] Because Green stood in the conservative Protestant reformation tradition and taught and published material related to the biblical books associated with Solomon, and yet lived at a time when the traditional conception of the verbal inspiration and authority of scripture was being attacked and traditional ascriptions of authorship and dating questioned, his work provides an interesting point of comparison with that of Joseph Hall.

Unlike the practical focus of Hall's unique treatise *Solomon's Divine Arts*, Green's extant work on Solomon's wisdom books is primarily academic in its focus, taking the form of a journal article on the book of Ecclesiastes and lecture notes.[11] This academic slant is useful because it fleshes out the critical issues at stake for interpreters in the second half of the nineteenth century. An extant syllabus of Green's lectures in his course on Special Introduction in 1866, for example, shows that critical issues related to the questions about the authorship, integrity, and structure of Solomon's wisdom books had already taken central stage in terms of Green's approach to teaching Proverbs and Ecclesiastes.[12] In his teaching, Green systematically exposed his students to the critical challenges to the traditional understanding of these books and then tried to equip his students with the apparatus for dealing with such challenges. At the same time, he focused his attention on issues related to the structure and design of each book and its relationship to other parts of the canonical scriptures.[13] Although Green's sensitivity to the literary aspects of the biblical texts is striking in and of itself, his commitment to treat a book as a whole and to discern its plan and scope soon became one of the most important weapons in Green's arsenal in the battle that he waged against those forms of higher criticism that Green regarded as being antibiblical in nature and grounded upon presuppositions that he felt were inimical to the Christian faith.[14]

GREEN ON PROVERBS

Green's lectures on the book of Proverbs demonstrate that he, like Hall, believed that the biblical proverbs were both inspired and free from error and yet also of human origin.[15] Yet because of his awareness of the growing body of comparative literature, Green felt particularly constrained to address the issue of the nature of the biblical proverbs. In his lecture notes, he spoke of the abundance of proverbs in the East, of the wide use of proverbs for teaching "in every nation on the globe," and of their very human origin either as "wise utterances of sages," like Solomon, or as expressions of "the general common sense of the people," like those found in Proverbs 27:17 or 24:13.[16]

Moreover, like Hall, Green was interested in the question of the general character and hence the usefulness of the proverbs for teaching in the Christian community. This question raised the issue of the relationship between the book of Proverbs and law. Although Hall's position on this matter is implicit in *Solomon's Divine Arts*, Green struggled to articulate his view of the relationship between the book of Proverbs and the law of God. Green averred that the book of Proverbs "stands in a most intimate relation to law, which is represented in the light of Wisdom." "The law," Green declared, "as a guide of life, is here shown to be practically useful as well as good."[17] Thus, although Green worked with a very broad understanding of torah as "all God's law however communicated," he also wanted to embrace the notion of torah that goes beyond instruction to include "divine authoritative law." Hence Green argued that although law in Proverbs was distinct from Mosaic law, it was nevertheless connected to it through the idea of wisdom in Proverbs 3:19:

> Proverbs does not deal with sacred observances of Levitical ordinances; nor as is the case with the prophets, with what specifically applies to Israel. It concerns itself with ordinary matters and everyday life. It refers to men as men in their daily duties. Hence we do not expect to find in it citations from the Mosaic law. There is, however, a connection with that law (3:19).[18]

Although Green certainly acknowleged the very pragmatic nature of the instruction given in Proverbs, he, like Hall, stressed the importance of its religious character and aim. Thus Green taught that "Proverbs set forth the ordinary working of God's law in which piety is the ground and condition of a happy and peaceful life."[19] However, Green also felt that the book of Proverbs had to be read together with the other wisdom books in the Old Testament. But unlike Hall, who read the Solomonic books together rather indiscriminately, Green argued that the book of Proverbs had to be read with a sensitivity to its aim together with the wisdom books of Ecclesiastes and Job, which he felt provided a corrective to Proverb's simple and potentially misleading equation of prosperity and piety.[20] Thus one of Green's students wrote:

> Job, Proverbs, Ecclesiastes, the results of careful reflection upon God's ways, they may in a sense be said to represent the philosophy of the OT. The common characteristic of these books is shown by the frequent use of [the] word Wisdom. To fear and obey God, the only true wisdom is the teaching of this book. It is to exceptional aspects of God's good that Job and Ecclesiastes are devoted. . . . To this [Proverb's thesis that piety brings prosperity] there are two exceptions: 1. Piety without prosperity—Job sets forth this in the extremist case. 2. Prosperity without piety—Ecclesiastes and [sic] shows that it is all vanity and vexation.[21]

By grouping the Old Testament wisdom books together, Green was thus able to shift the focus of the book of Proverbs away from practical application and a view of the book as a resource for Christian ethics, morals, and government toward a more philosophical view of the book.

Further developments in biblical studies since the time of Hall that affected Green's approach to the book of Proverbs included a new understanding of the nature of Hebrew poetry and of the structure and style of biblical proverbs; a more refined understanding of Hebrew grammar, comparative philology, and the history of the Hebrew language; and a new critical approach to the biblical texts that fostered debates about the authorship, dating, and structure of the book.[22] These developments brought new insights into how the book of Proverbs should be read and raised new issues that Green had to face as an interpreter. Thus, although points of similarity can be drawn as to how Hall and Green understood and used the book of Proverbs (i.e., its inspiration, its inerrancy, its Solomonic authorship, its usefulness for teaching in the church), it is clear that Green's basic approach was different. Notably, Green was sensitive to issues related to the genre, literary form, and function of a biblical text within its larger canonical context. Hence he was committed to interpreting each proverb in its complete form, using the immediate context to shed light on meaning where available and its larger canonical context, especially other wisdom books, as a further control on interpretation. It is not surprising that Green's hermeneutical principles not only led him to interpret the book of Proverbs very differently than did Hall, but also to disparage the atomistic type of interpretation practiced by Hall. Moreover, because of Green's knowledge of the history, culture, and comparative literature of the ancient Near East, he was more conscious of the differences between the world of the Old Testament and the world in which he lived, and also more sensitive to the hermeneutical issues that these differences raised for the interpreter who wants to make the message relevant to the needs of the present community of faith. Finally, Green's more academic approach to the book of Proverbs brought him face to face with the complex critical issues at stake in the nineteenth century, issues related to questions about the integrity, authorship, date, and inspiration of the book of

Proverbs that he felt obliged to address and that certainly changed the traditional approach to the study of the book of Proverbs.

GREEN ON ECCLESIASTES

Green's approach to the book of Ecclesiates is remarkably different from Hall's. To be sure, Green, like Hall, felt that the proverbs within the book contained practical wisdom that continued to function didactically for the Christian community. However, Green believed that because "the general truths inculcated by the proverbs of course admit either of being taken in their widest extent, or of receiving an indefinite number of particular applications," the only way of determining "the precise intent" of the writer was by discovering the place the individual proverb holds within the larger plan of the book. Unlike Hall, then, whose treatment of the various proverbs—and even parts of proverbs—in Ecclesiastes as detached sentences would certainly have come under Green's censure, Green emphasized the importance of discovering the author's intended meaning as a guide and control on interpretation.[23] This emphasis reflects one of Green's fundamental hermeneutical principles:

> In order to [gain] the proper understanding of any treatise, it is necessary to gain clear and correct ideas of its scope and plan. There is no book of the Old Testament to which this remark applies with greater force than Ecclesiastes, and none in which the neglect of it has been and must be attended with more serious injury to its exposition. Its proverbial dress creates a special need of taking comprehensive views of the writer's main design, and not being diverted from this by cleaving too anxiously to the tenor of each individual expression. The ill success of too many attempted expositions has shown, that if the clues thus furnished to all its intricacies and windings be not discovered or be lost sight of, the book becomes a labyrinth, within whose mazes the improvident adventurer is hopelessly entangled; and each verse becomes to him a new passage leading to fresh perplexity, however honestly and assiduously he may labour upon its interpretation.[24]

Furthermore, Green would have criticized Hall's use of the book of Ecclesiastes as a source for principles of living. Thus he wrote:

> Attention has sometimes been directed to too great an extent to the seemingly miscellaneous character of the proverbs . . . and the conclusion has hence been drawn that the design of the book is to give rules for the conduct of life, and to teach wisdom in general. This goes to the extreme of extending the theme too widely. . . . Its aim becomes too vague and indefinite. . . . The writer does not spread his thoughts over the whole range of human action or the proprieties of life; but he has one definite subject before him.[25]

Contrariwise, Green argued that the book of Ecclesiastes had a main design or scope that centered around the seeming inequalities of divine providence.[26] He cited as support for this thesis first of all "the testimony of the author himself" at the end of the book (Ecclesiastes 12:13, 14, verses on which Hall also placed great weight), where he sets forth "the final result of the experience, observations, and reasonings recorded in his book." Second, Green pointed to both the recurring negative statements about the vanity found in "those accumulations and sources of gratification which men so eagerly covet, and after which they so unceasingly toil" and also the more positive statements about the enjoyment, pleasure, and happiness that are "a greater good than all these vain acquisitions which are attended with so little satisfaction."[27] Because of Green's belief that the book of Ecclesiastes had a definite aim and purpose and his concomitant commitment to interpreting individual proverbs within the book in light of the overarching plan of the book, his fundamental approach to interpreting the individual proverbs within the book was different from Hall's. Indeed, Green would have been quite critical of Hall's noncontextual use of the proverbs from Ecclesiastes in *Solomon's Divine Arts*; for whereas Green's view of intentionality led him to give great weight to the context of individual proverbs within Ecclesiastes, Hall treated the proverbs as a collection.

Furthermore, Green's approach to Ecclesiastes, like his approach to Proverbs, was affected by new data, new questions, and new challenges to traditional views of the authority, dating, and authorship of the book. Notably, Green's knowledge of Hebrew and other Semitic languages allowed him to engage in the critical debates about the dating and authorship of the book of Ecclesiastes based on the language of the book. The rather cryptic notes on Green's lectures on Ecclesiastes from 1866 show that Green was aware of the problem of the Aramaic character of the language, but that he had not yet seriously wrestled the problem through. Thus the notes read: "The peculiarity of the Hebrew explained in part by nature of subject and mode of treatment. Aramaeisms not always criterion of age. Solomon's foreign connections. Proverbs of this book close resemblance to Book of Proverbs." [28] However, the later notes of Green's lectures from the decade of the eighties in which the battle over critical methodology was taken much more seriously by American interpreters reveal that the more mature Green struggled at a much deeper level with the objections to the Solomonic authorship of Ecclesiastes based on the language and style of the book.[29] For after defending the various "trivial" objections to Solomonic authorship, Green addressed the serious problem that "the fact seems to be, that the Hebrew of this book is so Aramean that it must belong to a period later than Solomon; and the style is unlike that of any other of the writings of Solomon." [30] Although he tries to mount a possible defense of Solomonic authorship based on language and style, Green clearly feels himself torn between his commitment to a traditional understanding of authorship and date—a commitment influenced by his personal conservatism, his Old School Presbyterianism, his philosophical commitment to Scottish commonsense philosophy, and his extreme distaste for German speculative thought—and an intellectual decision based on his extensive knowledge of the history of the Hebrew language.[31] His dilemma was not unlike that faced by Gotthold Lessing (1729–81), who likened his intense struggle to relate the eternal truths of abstract philosophy and religion to the variable and seemingly accidental historical process to "the ugly broad ditch which I cannot get across." [32] Green was torn between his deep sense of loyalty to tradition and his personal intellectual attraction to the scholarly consensus that Solomon did not write Ecclesiastes. Yet there is no evidence that Green conceded to his intellectual drives. Perhaps he felt that if he conceded on this issue of authorship, he would open the way to even greater concessions, like those that were more at the center of the battle that was waging at the time over the authorship of the Pentateuch. Clearly, the traditional consensus regarding the Solomonic authorship had been broken by the late nineteenth century. No longer could the interpretation of Proverbs, Ecclesiastes, and even Song of Songs be uncritically wed to assumptions about their Solomonic authorship.

CONCLUSIONS

A comparison between Hall's way of working with wisdom in the early seventeenth century with that of William Henry Green in the second half of the nineteenth century has shown not only family resemblances due to similarities in presuppositions about the nature, authority, and function of the biblical texts within the Christian community of faith, but also major differences that can be traced to some of the larger philosophical and ideological changes that were rooted in the Enlightenment. Of great consequence was the issue of the authorship of the biblical texts. For as Green seemed to realize, once the idea of the Solomonic authorship of Ecclesiastes and Proverbs was dispensed with, all sorts of new issues related to the interpretation of the books were raised. In particular, the use of the biblical persona, Solomon, as a key to unlock the wisdom books was lost. To be sure, Green's more modern sensitivity to the literal sense of a text within its historical and canonical context and his knowledge of Semitic languages had pushed him away from the very free and fruitful associations that Hall had made between the various texts that he attributed to the pen of King Solomon. Yet unlike many of his successors, Green seemed unable to sever the idea of authorship and the biblical "authors" as persons associated with biblical texts. His sensitivity to the issues related to the unity of various biblical books based on his awareness of the scope and canonical shape of a book fueled his commitment to the idea of a single author, the identity of whom tradition and common sense assumed was the purported biblical author. Still, although modern critical studies in the twentieth century have drawn firm the lines of distinction between authorship

and the biblical personae associated with particular texts, some interpreters in the postmodern period have realized the theological importance of such traditional associations, and new lines of continuity
between the ways that premodern and late modern interpreters work
with wisdom have opened up.[33] It is with renewed interest, then, that
modern interpreters read a work like *Solomon's Divine Arts,* which uses
the identification of author and biblical persona as an important
hermeneutical clue.

A further issue that Hall and Green raise for postmodern interpreters relates to the question of how biblical wisdom should function
within the Christian community. To be sure, Hall's lack of sensitivity
to the historical particularity of the text warns of the dangers of
moving too quickly from the world of Solomon to the world of today.
Nevertheless, both Hall and Green wrestled with the important issue
of the relation of law and wisdom, and they both felt that wisdom's
expression of the good and obedient life was one that continued to
operate in some sort of prescriptive sense for the community of faith.
Moreover, Green's insight that the books of Ecclesiastes, and Job
served to correct Proverb's potentially misleading equation of piety
and prosperity and to direct interpreters toward a more general and
less legalistic application of the "ordinary" principles of life found in
Proverbs remains important. Green's unexplored suggestion that
Proverbs, Ecclesiastes, and Job represent the philosophy of the Old
Testament is also thought provoking in that it confers to the biblical
wisdom books a very different type of function than that fleshed out
by Hall. Furthermore, as Green's analysis of the scope and plan of
Ecclesiastes showed, a commitment to interpreting individual verses
within their immediate and larger canonical context brought a greater
sense of control to the task of interpreting biblical wisdom in the
church.

Finally, a study of how interpreters in the past have worked with
wisdom reminds us again of the subjectivity involved in the interpretation of the scriptures. The new information available to interpreters
in the nineteenth century about Hebrew poetry and the structure and
style of biblical proverbs, Hebrew grammar, comparative philology,
the history of the Hebrew language and comparative literature, together with the new critical approach to the biblical texts that engen-

dered discussions about the inspiration, authorship, dating, and structure of the biblical books necessarily brought changes to the way they
worked with the wisdom literature in the Old Testament. Developments in the twentieth century would bring yet further changes.
However, a comparison of the ways Hall and Green worked with
biblical wisdom suggests that in spite of the differences in audience
and in spite of the new data and new methods of interpretation that
were available to Green, such basic presuppositions as the inspiration
of the scriptures and their usefulness for the Christian community
ensure that family resemblances can be seen in the way Christian
interpreters handle the scriptures even over time.

NOTES

1. Similarly, Hall's comments on Proverbs 31:25 point to his rather
traditional views on women: " 'Strength and honour are her clothing.'] –
She so demeans herself as that all her actions and carriages are full of honour,
and bewray a masculine strength and fortitude" (Joseph Hall, "A Paraphrase
upon the Hard Texts of the Whole Divine Scripture," in vol. 3 of *The Works
of the Right Reverend Joseph Hall, D. D.*, ed. Philip Wynter [Oxford: Oxford
University Press, 1863], 266).

2. See Gerald T. Sheppard, "William Perkins' Exposition Among Seventeenth-Century Commentaries, 1600–1645," in William Perkins, *A Commentary on Galatians*, facs. ed., Pilgrim Classic Commentaries Series, ed. Gerald
T. Sheppard (New York: Pilgrim Press, 1989), x.

3. See Gerald T. Sheppard, "Between Reformation and Modern Commentary: The Perception of the Scope of Biblical Books," in William Perkins,
A Commentary on Galatians, facs. ed., Pilgrim Classic Commentaries Series,
ed. Gerald T. Sheppard (New York: Pilgrim Press, 1989), xlviii-lxxvi.

4. By identifying King Lemuel as King Solomon, Hall associates Proverbs 31 with Solomon and his mother: "The words of king Lemuel, the
prophecy that his mother taught him."]—The words which king Solomon,
whom his mother in a style of love termed Lemuel, received from his mother
in his younger years, and that divine counsel which she gave him (Hall, "A
Paraphrase upon the Hard Texts of the Whole Divine Scripture," 265).

5. Sheppard, "Perkins' Exposition Among Seventeenth-Century Commentaries," x-xi.

6. Compare Hall's view of the function of the scriptures in his paraphrase of Ecclesiastes 12:11: " 'The words of the wise are as goads, and as nails fastened by the masters of assemblies, *which* are given from one shepherd.'] – The words of the wise and holy prophets of God are of singular benefit, for they are as goads to prick us forward to all good duties: yea, they go yet deeper; they are as nails driven up to the head by gracious teachers, so as they cannot easily be pulled out: which words, however they be delivered to us by several messengers, yet they come all originally from one hand, even from the great Pastor of his Church, the Word of his Father" (Hall, "A Paraphrase upon the Hard Texts of the Whole Divine Scripture," 289). (Hall's italics.)

7. Ibid., 237.

8. Ibid., 268.

9. Ibid., 244.

10. Titles like these were bestowed upon Green at the celebration of the fiftieth anniversary of his appointment as a teaching assistant at Princeton Theological Seminary in 1846. See *Celebration of the Fiftieth Anniversary of the Appointment of Professor William Henry Green as an Instructor in Princeton Theological Seminary, May 5, 1896* (New York: Charles Scribner's Sons, 1896). E. L. Curtis, Professor of Hebrew Language and Literature at Yale University Divinity School, paid the following tribute to Green: "In America, if not in the world, he is *facile princeps* in expounding and defending the sacred Scriptures of the old covenant upon the lines of the traditional views of the Christian Church, and however much some of us may feel, in certain particulars, compelled to differ with him in opinion, it is a delight to honor one who in solid learning, judicial fairness, and Christian courtesy has been surpassed by none in these days of controversy over the nature of the Bible" (Letter of Regret from E. L. Curtis, *Celebration*, 134).

11. William Henry Green, "The Scope and Plan of the Book of Ecclesiastes," *Biblical Repertory and Princeton Review* 29 (1857): 419–40; *Syllabus of Dr. Green's Lectures: Special Literature of Old Testament* (Princeton, N.J.: Blanchard's Print, 1866); G. F. Greene and D. W. Woods, eds., *Old Testament Literature: Lectures on the Poetical Books of the Old Testament, Psalms, Song of Solomon, Proverbs and Ecclesiastes* (Trenton, N.J.: Edwin Fitzgeorge, 1884). The notes were printed on only one side of the page so that Green's students could take additional notes during the class lectures. The extant copy of this work in the archives of Princeton Theological Seminary contains the handwritten notes of Paul Martin, a student in the middle class in 1884 at Princeton Theological Seminary.

12. *Syllabus*, 28–29.

13. Greene and Woods, eds., *Old Testament Literature*, 38–62.

14. Green's apologetic based on the notion of an organic and Christo-centric unity of the Bible was fundamental to his defense of the unity of the book of Genesis and of the Pentateuch. See especially William Henry Green, *The Unity of the Book of Genesis* (New York: Charles Scribner's Sons, 1896), and *The Higher Criticism of the Pentateuch* (New York: Charles Scribner's Sons, 1896).

15. Greene and Woods, eds., *Old Testament Literature*, 39.

16. Ibid.

17. Ibid., 38.

18. Ibid., 38–39.

19. Ibid., Paul Martin's class notes opposite p. 38.

20. Cf. Peter Craigie's similar evaluation of the function of Job and Ecclesiastes in relation to the book of Proverbs. See Peter Craigie, "Biblical Wisdom in the Modern World I. Proverbs," *Crux* 15, no. 4 (1979): 7–9; "Biblical Wisdom in the Modern World II: Ecclesiastes," *Crux* 16, no. 1 (1980): 7–10; "Biblical Wisdom in the Modern World III: Job," *Crux* 16, no. 2 (1980): 8–10.

21. Ibid.

22. Green's knowledge of the Hebrew language and of the style of Hebrew proverbs helped him explain why it was so difficult to see the interconnectedness of the various proverbs in Ecclesiastes: "Another difficulty . . . arises from the absence of particles in every case to indicate the connection or the relation of dependence which the various sentences or paragraphs sustain to each other. This is partly due to the venerable simplicity of the Hebrew language. . . . It is partly due to the proverbial style . . . which characteristically delights to state truths in the general and the absolute, leaving their limitations and specific relations to be gathered from the connection in which they are adduced" (Green, "The Scope and Plan of the Book of Ecclesiastes," 806–807).

23. In this vein, Green wrote: "An erroneous view of this theme or of the method of its discussion, will necessarily involve attaching meanings to passages very different from those which they were intended to bear. . . . The inattentive and superficial reader might infer . . . that this book is composed of loose and detached sentences, without orderly consecution or intimate coherence" (ibid.).

24. Ibid., 806.

25. Ibid., 810.

26. Green suggested that the solution to the problem discussed in the book was twofold: "1. A proper estimate of men's fortunes and of their

characters will show these inequalities to be much fewer than they will appear to be. 2. There is a righteous government to rectify whatever inequalities may temporarily exist" (ibid.).

27. Ibid., 811–12.

28. *Syllabus*, 29.

29. In Green's opening lecture of the fall term in 1881 at Princeton Theological Seminary, he expressed his concern for the future of orthodoxy as it faced what he described as "the eve of an agitation upon the vital and fundamental question of the inspiration and infallibility of the Bible, such as it had never known before. . . . The battle rages around the citadel. No drones or cowards are wanted now. . . . There is a demand now, as never before for high Biblical scholarship, for well-trained exegetes and critics,— for men well versed in the critical and speculative attacks made upon the Word of God, and who are well prepared to defend it" (William Henry Green, *Moses and the Prophets* [New York: Robert Carter and Brothers, 1883], 9, 31).

30. Greene and Woods, eds., *Old Testament Literature*, 55.

31. Greene's lecture notes attest to his dilemma: "We agree with Delitzsch that if the book is Solomon's we must give up everything like a history of the Hebrew language. And this is the uniform opinion of scholars at the present time." Paul Martin notes that "Dr. Green does not see how to answer objections from style against this being by Solomon." (Greene and Woods, eds., *Old Testament Literature*, 55–56; see also Paul Martin's comments on the page facing p. 55.)

32. Gotthold E. Lessing, *Lessing's Theological Writings*, ed. Henry Chadwick (Stanford: Stanford University Press, 1957), 31.

33. Here the insights of Brevard S. Childs and Gerald T. Sheppard regarding the canonical shaping of biblical texts and the canonical function of such hermeneutical clues as the superscriptions in the books of Proverbs and Ecclesiastes have been foundational. See especially Brevard S. Childs, *Introduction to the Old Testament as Scripture* (Philadelphia: Fortress Press, 1979), 78–80, 551–52, 583–84; and Gerald T. Sheppard, *Wisdom as a Hermeneutical Construct: A Study in the Sapientializing of Old Testament Traditions.* Beihefte zur *Zeitschrift für die alttestamentliche Wissenschaft* (Berlin: Walter de Gruyter, 1980).

Joseph Hall and the Tradition of Christian Interpretation of the Song of Songs

E. ANN MATTER

Unique among the books of the Bible, the Song of Songs owes its place in both the Jewish and the Christian canon to an understanding of the text that modern readers would perceive as allegorical. That is, in the many centuries of interpretation of this book by communities of faith, there has been a prevailing assumption that what the poems "seem" to be talking about (human sexual desire, frustration and fulfillment) is by no means what they "really mean." The interpretations championed by both Jews and Christians are complex, but rather similar.

Jewish exegesis has traditionally understood the Song of Songs as either the story of the love between God and Israel confirmed at the giving of the Torah on Mount Sinai, or as the song of love commemorating the installation of the Ark of the Covenant in the Temple of Jerusalem.[1] These interpretations were so well established by the beginning of the Common Era that Rabbi Akiba is said to have defended the holiness of the text (against those who wished to use it as a secular love song) with the famous statement: "The whole world is not worth the day on which the Song of Songs was given to Israel, for all the Scriptures are holy, but the Song of Songs is the Holy of Holies."[2]

E. Ann Matter is professor of religious studies, University of Pennsylvania.

For Christians, the Song of Songs has been traditionally understood as the song of love between God and the church or between God and the individual soul. These adaptations of the traditional Jewish allegories were first conceptualized by Origen of Alexandria (185–ca. 254), a Christian Platonist who spent many years in Palestine and probably studied with Jewish sages in the circle of Rabbi Yohanan.[3] Origen was the author of two works on the Song of Songs, a commentary and a series of homilies, both of which survive only in fragments and only in Latin translations of the Greek originals.[4] The surviving Latin texts were widely influential and are the literary model for what I have argued is a genre of medieval Latin Christian literature.[5] Between the translation of Origen's exegesis of the Song of Songs and the end of the flowering of monastic culture (that is, between the fourth and the thirteenth centuries), there are more than sixty Latin commentaries on this book of the Bible. All of these are allegorical, explicating the text either as the love song between Christ and the church, Christ and the soul, or, in a few cases, God and the Virgin Mary. Even Nicholas of Lyra, the late medieval champion of the "literal" sense of the Bible, argued that the Song of Songs must be understood according to these allegories.[6]

Early Protestant movements accepted this allegory and used it to emphasize the sanctity of the True Church and the immediate connection to God of the individual believer. This generalization is true from the very beginning of what could be called Protestantism in England. The Middle English Wycliffe Bible, for example, explicitly describes "the booc that is clepid Songus of Songis" as "of the bridalis of Crist and of the Chirche."[7] Even English Bible versions based on the Hebrew (rather than the Latin) text of the Song of Songs followed this tradition, as, for example, the Geneva Bible, a translation of English Protestant exiles during the reign of Queen Mary and a text very close to Joseph Hall's Bible text. The first edition of the Geneva Bible (1560) introduces "An Excellent Song Which was Solomons" with this argument:

In this Song, Solomn by moste swete and comfortable allegories and parables describeth the perfite love of Iesus Christ, the true Salomn and King of peace, and the faithful soule his Church, which he hathe sanctified and appointed to be his spouse, holy, chast and without reprehension. So that here is declared the singular love of the bridegrome toward the bride, and his great and excellent benefites wherewith he doeth enriche her of his pure bountie and grace without anie of her deservings. Also the earnest affection of the Church which is inflamed with the love of Christ desiring to be more and more ioyned to him in love, and not to be forsaken for anie spot or blemish that is in her.[8]

The Geneva Bible is printed with marginal glosses that spell out the "most swete and comfortable allegories and parables" hidden in the text.

The marginal glosses of the Geneva Bible can be understood as one of the earliest deliberately allegorical commentaries on the Song of Songs from Protestant England, but in no way is this an idiosyncratic interpretation. A number of English sermons and texts from the sixteenth century continue the ancient allegories of the Song of Songs. For example, the sermons preached by Bartimeus Andreas on the fifth chapter of the Song of Songs and published in London in 1583 explain that this text shows "the pure, free, perfect, eternall and constant love of Christ Jesus towards his Church, and every faithfull soule," while dismissing "the Romish Church" and all its trappings as "painted Harlottes that drive Christe farre from them, though they seeme to carry him in their bosomes."[9] Other contemporary English authors followed this pattern, such as Richard Schilders, whose 1587 poetic English translation and commentary (which promises "as little libertie in departing from the words as any plaine translation in prose can use") offers an interpretation that incorporates the Holy Ghost and Christ and the church.[10] Nor did this tradition end with the generation of Joseph Hall. English and American Protestant writing throughout the seventeenth and eighteenth centuries was rich in allegorical commentary on the Song of Songs, as is evident by the extant treatises of J. Dove, Henry Ainsworth, John Cotton, Richard Sibbes, and William Guild.[11]

Coming in the midst of such a venerable tradition of allegorical interpretation of the Song of Songs, it is little wonder that Joseph Hall's "open and plaine Paraphrase, vpon the Song of Songs" should be a continuous exposition highlighting the love between Christ and the church. This is one of Hall's earliest texts, written the year after his appointment as tutor to Prince Henry.[12] The paraphrase, dedicated to Edward Lord Denny, Baron of Waltham, was printed at the end of a treatise entitled *Salomons Diuine Arts of 1. Ethickes, 2. Politickes, 3. Oeconomics*. This is a compendium of practical advice; the first book of the Politics is, in fact, a "mirror of princes." *Solomon's Divine Arts* is a highly schematic work conceived in an Aristotelian model and made up entirely of quotations from Proverbs, Ecclesiastes, and the Song of Songs.[13] It was dedicated to Robert, Earl of Essex. All of this contextual evidence suggests that Hall wrote these Solomonic commentaries in the context of a newly flourishing career, as thanks for patronage.

Although Hall was thirty-four years old when he was appointed Prince Henry's tutor, this was his first major position. It was the beginning of an ecclesiastical career that led to his consecration as bishop of Exeter in 1627, and of Norwich in 1641, but which had a rapid demise. At the time of this appointment at Norwich, Hall was immersed in the defense of the episcopacy and liturgical practice against John Milton and a group of five Puritans known (by the acrostic of their names) as the Smectymnuuans. There is some irony in Hall's opposition to this Puritan group, because he had been trained at Emmanuel College, Cambridge, the "nursery of Puritan thought," and probably had few theological differences with the Smectymnuuans other than those of the role of bishops and the form of the liturgy, which were in some senses political issues.[14] Because of his position in this so-called Bishop's War, Hall was deposed from his bishopric at Norwich in 1643. The remaining years of his life until his death in 1656 were devoted to devotional writings, including extensive exegesis of the New Testament.

The works presented in this volume were, then, written at a time when Joseph Hall was coming into prominence as an ecclesiastical figure, and when his concern for church and state was gaining influence. He seems to have written the *Open and plaine Paraphrase vpon the Song of Songs, Which is Salomons* as an appendix to *Solomon's Divine Arts* rather than to have ignored the allegorical meaning of the Song of Songs. As he says to Lord Denny:

When I would haue withdrawen my hand from diuine Salomon: the heauenly elegance of this his best Song drewe me vnto it; and would not suffer me to take off mine eies, or pen. (N2)*

This is a text of mystical rapture, Hall explains, one of the hard passages of scripture. He claims no originality for his interpretation of the allegory, but he does promise clarity:

Two things make the Scriptures hard: Prophecies, Allegories; . . . this whole Pastoral-marriage-song (for such it is) is no other then one Allegory sweetly continued: where the deepest things of God are spoken in riddles, how can there be but obscurity and diuers construction? All iudgements will not (I know) subscribe to my senses yet I haue beene fearefull and spiritually nice in my choice, not often dissenting from all interpreters; alwaies, from the vnlikeliest. (N2 verso–N3 recto)

Hall's paraphrase of the Song of Songs is set up as a dialogue, mostly between the church (who speaks first) and Christ, but including a few other interlocutors, such as the "Forraine Congregations," who ask the Church "whether is thy welbeloued gon?" at 5:17 (58), and "The Iewish Church," who speaks twice, plaintively, at 8:1 (76) and 8:6 (80). In this, the paraphrase follows an ancient tradition of dramatizing the Song of Songs by means of rubrics indicating speakers, a tradition going back at least as far as the second century, well developed in the Latin Middle Ages, and also visible in the Wycliffe Bible and the Geneva Bible.[15]

Hall's dialogue does not exactly follow these English Bible divisions of the text into dialogue. A good example of how he goes his own way in assigning voices can be seen in his treatment of a repeating refrain ("I charge you O daughters of Ierusalem, by the roes and by the Hinds of the field, that ye stirre not up, nor waken my Loue, vntill he please"), which appears in Song of Songs 2:7, 3:5, and 8:4. The Wycliffe Bible places these words consistently in the mouth of Christ, the Geneva Bible, which constructs its dialogue along chapter

---

*The page numbers in parentheses that follow quotations from Hall's *Open and plaine Paraphrase vpon the Song of songs* refer to the 1609 text reprinted in this volume. The italics mark Joseph Hall's own words.

lines, always has them spoken by the church. Hall follows neither lead and in fact takes liberties with the idea of this repeating text as a constant rhetorical marker of the allegory hidden in the Song of Songs. In chapter 2, Hall leaves these verses in the middle of a long discourse (Song of Songs 2:3–3:5) by the church (18); at 3:5, the refrain begins the discourse of Christ (29); and at 8:4, the admonition not to stir up the beloved ends a speech by "The Iewish Church" (76).

The "Iewish Church" becomes a rather important speaker at the end of Hall's paraphrase, taking over most of the first-person referential statements (8:6, "Set mee as a seale"; 8:10, "I am a wall"). The answering voice in these passages is Christ's, and the answering message is the expectation of the coming of the true church. In Song of Songs 8:5, Christ asks "Who is this that commeth out of the wildernesse, leaning vpon her welbeloued?" and answers:

Is it not my Church? it is she, whom I haue loued, & acknowledged of olde: for, euen vnder the tree of offence, the forbidden fruit which thou tastedst to thy destruction, I raysed thee vp againe from death; Euen there, thy first mother conceiued thee; while by faith shee layd hold on that blessed promise of the Gospel, whereby she, and her beleeuing seed were restored. (79–80)

This tension between the "Iewish Church" and the church after the fullfillment of the coming of Christ emphasizes one moment of redemption. But Hall's paraphrase ends with a reminder that the church is not perfect, nor is redemption complete, until the second coming of Christ. The church gets the last word, if only to emphasize that she is not the last word. At Song of Songs 8:14 ("Oh my welbeloued, flee away, and be like vnto the Roe, or to the yong Hart vpon the mountaines of spices"), the church concludes the dialogue with anticipation of the parousia:

I Will most gladly doe what thou commaundest, O my Sauiour but, that I may performe it accordingly; be thou (which art, according to thy bodily presence, in the hyest heauens) euer present with me by thy spirit, & hasten thy glorious comming, to my full redemption. (86–87)

Joseph Hall's paraphrase on the Song of Songs is thus a very complicated text. It takes its basic insights from an ancient tradition of Christian allegorical exposition, particularly that of reading the text as a commentary on the life of the church. But, like most examples of the genre of Song of Songs exposition, Hall's paraphrase reflects the portrait of the church in which he lived and wrote.[16] This short paraphrase would, I think, repay close study as a commentary on the English Protestant church at the beginning of the seventeenth century; it was written by an ecclesiastic who was to become an important and controversial figure in that institution and community.

NOTES

1. Arthur Green, "The Song of Songs in Early Jewish Mysticism," *Orim* 2, no. 2 (Spring 1987), reprinted in *Modern Critical Interpretation: The Song of Songs*, ed. Harold Bloom (New York: Chelsea House Publishers, 1988), 141–53.

2. Rabbi Akiba's statement is quoted in the *Mishnah, Yadayim* 3.5; other comments on the sanctity of the Song of Songs attributed to Akiba are found in *Tosefta, Sanhedrin* 12.10, and the *Babylonian Talmud, Sanhedrin* 101a.

3. Reuven Kimelman, "Rabbi Yohanan and Origen on the Song of Songs: A Third-Century Jewish-Christian Disputation," *Harvard Theological Review* 73 (1980): 567–95; E. E. Urbach, "The Homiletical Interpretations of the Sages and the Exposition of Origen on Canticles," *Scripta Hierosolynitana* 22 (1971): 248–75; N. Lange, *Origen and the Jews* (Cambridge: Cambridge University Press, 1976). For a general study of Origen, see Joseph Wilson Trigg, *Origen: The Bible and Philosophy in the Third-Century Church* (Atlanta: John Knox Press, 1983).

4. Both are edited by Baehrens, *Origenes Werke* 8, GCS 33 (1925): xiv–xx and 26–60 for the homilies; xx–xxviii and 61–241 for the commentary. These texts have been reedited by O. Rousseau, *Sources chrétiennes* 37bis (1966). There is also an English translation by R. P. Lawson, *Origen: On the Song of Songs: Commentary and Homilies*, Ancient Christian Writers Series 26 (New York: Newman Press, 1957).

5. E. Ann Matter, *The Voice of My Beloved: The Song of Songs in Western Medieval Christianity* (Philadelphia: University of Pennsylvania Press, 1990).

6. "Postillae venerabilis Patris, Fratris Nicholai de Lyra super Canticum Canticorum," in *Biblia Sacra cum glossa interlineari, ordinaria et Nicholai Lyrani Postilla . . ."* (Venice, 1588), 3:355r–368v.

7. Josiah Forshall and Frederic Madden, eds., *The Holy Bible Containing The Old and New Testaments With the Apocryphal Books, in the Earliest English Versions made from the Latin Vulgate by John Wycliffe and his Followers* (Oxford: Oxford University Press, 1850), 3:73.

8. *The Geneva Bible: A Facsimile of the 1560 Edition*, with an introduction by Lloyd E. Berry (Madison: University of Wisconsin Press, 1969). See also Peter Levi, *The English Bible, 1534–1859* (Grand Rapids: Wm B. Eerdmans, 1974), 87–109, for a brief description and other excerpts from the Geneva Bible.

9. *Certaine Verie Worthie, godly and profitable sermons, upon the fifth chapiter of the Songs of Solomon preached by Bartimeus Andreas* (London: Printed by Robert Waldegrave for Thomas Man, 1583), 5, 100.

10. Richard Schilders, *The Song of Songs . . . Translated out of the Hebreu into English meeter, with as little libertie in departing from the words as any plaine translation in prose can use . . .* (Middelburgh, 1587).

11. J. Dove, *The Conversion of Solomon. A Direction to Holiness of Life, Handled by way of commentary upon the whole Booke of Canticles* (1613); Henry Ainsworth, *Solomon's Song of Songs in English Metre with Annotations and references to other Scriptures for the easier understanding of it* (1623); John Cotton, *A Brief Exposition of the Whole Book of Canticles, pointing at the gloriousnesse of the restored Estate of the Church of the Jewes and the happy accesse of the Gentiles in the approaching daies of the Reformation* (London, 1642–48); Richard Sibbes, *Bowels Opened: or, A discovery of the near and dear love, union, and communion betwixt Christ and the church, and consequently betwixt Him and every believing soul. Delivered in divers sermons on the fourth, fifth, and sixth chapters of the Canticles*, 3d ed. (London: Printed by R. Cotes for J. Clark, 1648); William Guild, *Loves entercors between the Lamb and His bride, Christ and His Church: or, A clear explication and application of the Song of Solomon* (London, 1648). See also Marvin H. Pope, *Song of Songs. A New Translation and Commentary*, The Anchor Bible 7C (New York: Doubleday & Co., 1977), 245ff.; and Prudence L. Steiner, "A Garden of Spices in New England: John Cotton's and Edward Taylor's Use of the Song of Songs," in *Allegory, Myth, and Symbol*, ed. Morton W. Bloomfield, Harvard English Studies 9 (Cambridge: Harvard University Press, 1981), 227–43.

12. For Hall's life, see "Bishop Hall's Account of Self," in *The Works of Joseph Hall, D.D.*, 12 vols. (Oxford: D. A. Talboys, 1837), 1: xiv; and T. F. Kinloch, *The Life and Works of Joseph Hall* (London: Staples Press, 1951).

13. Song of Songs 3:9 and 3:10 are quoted in Ethics, Book 1, Felicity (p. 7); Song of Songs 6:7 in Politics, Book 1, King (p. 110). These citations do not follow the allegorical meanings given to these passages in the *Paraphrase*.

14. For information about Emmanuel College and its impact on Hall, see Kinloch, *The Life and Works of Joseph Hall*, 16; and Douglas Bush, *English Literature in the Earlier Seventeenth Century* (Oxford: Clarendon Press, 1945), 341–42. For the "Bishop's War," see William Haller, *The Rise of Puritanism* (New York: Columbia University Press, 1938), 325.

15. See the facsimile edition of the Codex Sinaiticus by Constantinus Tischendorf, *Codex sinaiticus petropolitanus* (St. Petersburg, 1862), vol. 3; D. de Bruyne, "Les anciennes versions latines du Cantique des Cantiques," *Revue benedictine* 38 (1926): 118–22; and the Wycliffe Bible and the Geneva Bible, notes 7 and 8 above.

16. See Matter, *The Voice of My Beloved*, chap. 4, "The Song of Songs as the Changing Portrait of the Church."

The Role of the Canonical Context in the Interpretation of the Solomonic Books

GERALD T. SHEPPARD

A s indicated in the introduction to this volume, Joseph Hall was preoccupied with the goals of ascertaining a Protestant alternative to Roman Catholic rules of meditation, on the one hand, and of establishing biblical wisdom as superior to classical or recent humanistic philosophy, on the other.[1] Certainly, the exact nature of wisdom and its proper relation to theology became a significant matter of debate throughout this period.[2] Hall's re-presentation of Proverbs and Ecclesiastes under the topics of ethics, politics, and economics is a prime example of an effort to take up a traditional approach and to enrich it with the latest advances in logic and argumentation.

In a recent study of Thomas Aquinas, Lawrence Boadt sought to show how the Bible itself informed Aquinas's perspective on wisdom even more than did his extrabiblical knowledge of philosophy.[4] That essay is full of insight, but it is weakest in its tendency to detect ways in which Aquinas seems to anticipate later modern historical critical ideas about wisdom in ancient Israel. What needs further consideration is how Aquinas relied upon his own literary vision of the canonical context of the biblical wisdom literature. My aim in this essay will be to examine this work of Hall with that specific question in mind. Finally, I will comment on some implications for late modern

Gerald T. Sheppard is professor of Old Testament literature and exegesis at Emmanuel College of Victoria University in the University of Toronto.

hermeneutical theory and practice in the contemporary interpretation of scripture.

What seems immediately obvious from the most simple literary perspective is that the Solomonic books lack key themes found elsewhere throughout scripture. Within the intertext of scripture, the Solomonic books are remarkable for their silence on matters central to Israel's faith, including the Exodus, the giving of the law, the role of the prophets, the proper form of prayer and sacrifice, and the history of God's covenant with Israel. Solomonic wisdom books have few narrative genres, valuing instead short sayings that can be easily borrowed by other cultures and religions, and, therefore, seem open to conversation and competition with the world on a level utterly foreign to the rest of scripture.

The positive depiction of the visit by the Queen of Sheba (1 Kings 10) to "examine the truth of foreign relations" illustrates this dimension peculiar to Solomonic wisdom within the Bible.[5] The "test" of Solomon by the Queen of Sheba is reported with pride, in absolute contrast to any openness to a foreign evaluation of Israel's prophets. Although the biblical prophets repeatedly condemn any reliance on foreign prophets and show little or no interest in the opinion of the nations about the validity of Israel's prophets, the same texts are replete with a desire for other nations to recognize that Israel is full of "wise" people and is an exceptionally "wise" nation among the others.[6] Hall is acutely aware of this aspect of the canonical context of the Solomonic books in scripture and depends on this evidence in order to re-present Solomonic wisdom in its full strength. He hopes its superiority to other sources will be self-evident to the present age, which had been reawakened to the ancient wisdom of the philosophers and might be seduced away from the Bible by its own contemporary knowledge and sophistry.

Hall finds continuity in the Bible between the activity of the historical Solomon depicted in 1 Kings 3—11 and Solomon as depicted in the books of Proverbs, Ecclesiastes, and Song of Songs without feeling a need to defend such a position historically. He allows for some complexity in the formation of biblical books but treats this aspect as negligible and unobtrusive. Only in the modern period did the connection between the biblical prehistory and the presentation of history within biblical books become a consistent and serious rather than negligible "difference" that could threaten the integrity of the biblical "books" themselves. Although acknowledging this new, distinctly modern sense of historical "differences," a canonical approach allows us to view the biblical books from the perspective of the later intertext of scripture so that we can recognize, even in a late modern vision of the biblical text, how Hall perceived and exploited warrants within the scriptural context itself. By this perspective, we can also offer some modest criticism of his effort on his own terms. Any criticism must, of course, follow upon a profound appreciation and is always in danger of arrogance and anachronistic self-righteousness. A canonical approach provides us with a fresh way to avoid some of the limitations of earlier modern assessments of such efforts in the history of interpretation.

INTERTEXTUAL PREUNDERSTANDINGS INTEGRAL TO HALL'S BOOK

In his dedication to *Solomon's Divine Arts*, Hall offers some brief, subtle, and highly significant generalizations about King Solomon and how the biblical books derive from him and relate to Hall's own re-presentation. He calls Solomon *"the royallest Philosopher and wisest king"* (A2).* Although the Bible supports the latter claim explicitly (e.g., 1 Kgs. 3:12; 4:29–24; Eccl. 1:16; 2 Chr. 9:22; Matt. 12:42; Luke 11:31), the former attribution of "royallest philosopher" betrays Hall's own biblically oriented criticism of secular philosophy. For Hall, Solomon's wisdom surpasses the achievements of Aristotle and other classical philosophers not only in content but in the superiority of its form. For this reason, Hall's own earlier philosophical writings frequently employ an aphoristic strategy reminiscent of the Solomonic books of Proverbs and Ecclesiastes.

*The page numbers in parenthesis that follow quotations from Hall's *Solomon's Divine Arts* refer to the 1609 text reprinted in this volume. The italics mark Joseph Hall's own words.

What appears quite postbiblical is Hall's reliance upon Ramist logic to reorganize his *"common-place-booke"* (A3 verso). Hall argues for the legitimacy of his approach by a subtle appeal to features within the canonical context of Proverbs itself. He insists that the biblical proverbs themselves offer inerrant information (*"he* [Solomon] *could not erre")* but admits that his own *"methode"* of organizing the same should *"submit to censure"* (A3 verso). He presupposes that we know about the unusual editorial notation found at Proverbs 25:1: "These are also parables of Salomon, which the men of Hezekiah King of Iudah copied out" (Geneva Bible). Unlike a modern redaction critic, Hall does not interpret these words as evidence that Hezekiah's servants functioned as editors. They serve merely as scribes who "copied" a proverbial collection already arranged, according to Hall, in *"Salomons order"* (A3 verso). The Geneva Bible similarly supplies the following marginal gloss upon the words "copied out": "That is, gathered out of divers bokes of Salomon." [7] This note implies a premodern theory of tradition history, one that imagines various Solomonic books from which derives the one, later biblical book of Proverbs. Why Hezekiah's servants would tamper with the earlier "divers bokes" at all and how their formation of the present singular book of Proverbs would not alter the older "order" of the earlier collections remain questions unexplored.

Hall carefully states that his goal is neither to correct Solomon nor to manipulate, *"to controule"* (A3 verso), the scribes of Hezekiah. He feels he can justify his reordering of the proverbs on strictly limited, pragmatic grounds by analogy to a concordance. The result is helpful because it will allow the reader more easily to find, to remember, and to apply biblical proverbs. This rationale does not intentionally depreciate the canonical context that serves other semantic purposes and needs no correction in its own right. Hall reorders the biblical presentation of Proverbs solely to accentuate the positive relationship between the text of the Solomonic books and various primary and immediate subtopics within the larger subject matter of biblical "wisdom."

Two conspicuous features of Hall's work are his dependence upon the logic system of Peter Ramus and his use of commonplace methods in overarching justification for his re-presentation of wisdom in this form. First, Hall, as did William Perkins, studied under the first master of Emmanuel College, Laurence Chaderton, from 1584 until 1622.[8] Though Chaderton published nothing, his lectures on "the Ars logica of Peter Ramus" are reported to have "roused a great interest in that study through the University."[9] He also earned a wide reputation as a preacher who railed against the threat to the "orders" in society, which were exactly as they were meant to be.[10] Hall undoubtedly found inspiration both in logic and social disposition from Chaderton. For the purpose of this essay, it will suffice to say that Peter Ramus (1515–1572), a Protestant who taught mostly in France and never in England, became a favorite among many scholars at Cambridge University who stood against the more positive Aristotelian approaches that held sway at Oxford. Ramus proposed a nonsyllogistic system of logical oppositions that started with the most general and moved to the particulars. Detailed reviews of Ramus's logic are readily available. We need observe here only that this theory of logic accounts for Hall's regular effort to treat each major topic by appealing to sets of oppositions of increasing particularity.

The commonplace method employed by Hall is indicated by his effort to assign dogmatic topics (e.g., felicity, prudence, justice) to biblical texts on the assumption that such a correlation exists, in fact, between the literal sense of these texts and the analogy of faith. The method itself goes back to the Loci communes of Melanchthon, who made a topical organization of Paul's doctrinal teaching in Romans.[11] By the early sixteenth century, commonplace method had become popular as a rhetorical device among the northern humanists. Robert Kolb notes that "Rudolph Agricola and Desiderius Erasmus had refined the method out of material supplied in part by Aristotle and in part by Cicero."[12] It spread into other university disciplines and was, subsequently, borrowed by many English Protestants in the sixteenth and seventeenth centuries. The role of commonplace method as a rhetorical aid that might accompany a commentary explains Hall's effort to compare it to a concordance rather than to a conventional form of biblical commentary. However, I would argue that Hall's representation of the biblical text, with Ramist oppositions (cf. his use of transitions between scriptural citations, such as "contrarily," e.g., 224, 227, 228, 248, 250, 251) exceeds identification of a few obvious topics typical of the commonplace method. Hall's use of biblical citations often implies a strong interpretation of these same texts in a manner far closer to the nature of commentary and not what we would expect to find merely by use of a topical concordance.

For his definition of wisdom, Hall assumes that we know well the narratives about Solomon and especially the praise of Solomon in 1 Kings 4:29–34, where the range of such knowledge and skill is circumscribed. There we are told: "He composed three thousand proverbs, and his songs numbered a thousand and five. He would speak of trees, from the cedar that is in the Lebanon to the hyssop that grows in the wall; he would speak of animals, and birds, and reptiles, and fish" (vv. 32–33, NRSV). Comparing this description with the actual contents of Proverbs and Ecclesiastes, Hall considers why God *"thought good to bereaue mankinde of Salomons profounde commentaries of Nature"* (A3 verso). It is a simple fact that there are no such texts among the Solomonic books in scripture, though we should perhaps not underestimate the excessive display of esoteric knowledge about nature in poetic descriptions within the Song of Songs (e.g., 1:14–17; 4:12–15; 5:10–16). Hall reasons that such detailed knowledge of nature would only *"feed mans curiositie"* (A3), whereas the extant books offer us *"his diuine Morals"* (A3 verso) and serve the greater purpose of directing and judging our lives. Hall identifies the expression of these "morals" in terms of "diuine rules" and "precepts," employing extrabiblical jargon to distinguish the content of this biblical "wisdom" from case law, oracles of prophecy, hymns, or other types of literature found elsewhere in the Bible. This rhetorical strategy depends directly on commonplace method.

Finally, Hall plays upon the narrative about Solomon's receiving wisdom as God's gift (1 Kings 3) when he declares these *"precepts"* were things *"which the Spirit of God gaue him"* (A2). Hall is surely aware of similar claims within the book of Proverbs itself (e.g., Prov 2:6; 8:22). Unlike modern interpreters of wisdom, Hall does not define wisdom by any appeal to human experience or to the effort to wrestle gnomic expressions of order out of the chaos of ordinary human perception and circumstance.[13] Of course, the Solomonic books themselves also lack words for "experience" and "order." Debate over the epistemology and original life settings of Proverbs is properly a modern concern that Hall does not raise. His phrase *"which the Spirit of God gaue him"* occurs nowhere in the Solomonic books and is a traditional Jewish and Christian formula indicative of the canonical status, the revelatory capacity, or the "inspiration" of Solomon's words as scripture.[14] Hall, thereby, ascribes to the Solomonic books the same scriptural capacity for mediating revelation as he does for the other books of the Bible. We are reminded that the premodern attribution of scriptural status does not require that the biblical author be identified as a "prophet." I think that the paucity of commentary production on these books in some periods results only from the proper perception of their limited subject matter compared with other books rather than from any questions about their revelatory status.[15] Finally, it is important to observe that Hall holds together an acceptance of the full humanity of these words, assigned to Solomon, and a confidence in the inerrant capacity of his words to mediate the word of God in spite of Solomon's fallibility as a human being. Hall readily acknowledges the human failings of Solomon, though he, also, speculates on the basis of Ecclesiastes 7:25–26 (esp. v. 26b: "who so pleaseth God shall be delivered, from her, but the sinner shall be taken") that Solomon probably repented "in the Autumne of age."[16]

Hall does not read these ancient proverbs *as scripture* for insight into the nature of wisdom in the time of Solomon, but for the wisdom of God, which is the same in every time and place. This radical, from a modern perspective, "misreading" of the "original" ancient sayings is warranted for Hall by the larger canonical context of scripture itself in which Solomon (Hall's "wisest king") receives the greatest gift of God's wisdom that will ever be given to a human, parallel to Moses as the only human to hear the Torah while speaking with God "face to face" (cf. Deut 34:10; 1 Kgs 3:12; Eccl 1:16). The many historical problems raised by this position did not demand a response from Hall in the way that it would in the centuries that followed. In late modernity, these issues have emerged once more in theology and are now accompanied by a postmodern suspicion regarding the limits of earlier modern "solutions," whether liberal or conservative. Whatever the outcome of that debate, Hall reminds us that he has literary support from the canonical context for his effort, which on its own terms is neither an uncritical nor biblicistic interpretation of the Solomonic books.

Finally, we should consider why Hall divides his *"common-place-booke"* on wisdom into the categories of ethics, economics, and politics. Perhaps his choice of ethics is the most self-evident, for the serious consideration of ethics as a major concern of the classical philosophers made it a natural topic of Solomonic and biblical wisdom. What might surprise us is that ethics can be treated topically, with the same reserve as found in the biblical wisdom books; that is to say, with no reference to the Exodus, election of Israel, or the teaching of the Old Testament prophets, much less any direct recollection of the gospel. Although ethics is a general discipline, the other two topics—politics and economics—take a different orientation, for they are predicated upon two of the three social systems commonly acknowledged in the seventeenth century as belonging to the "order" of society that God had made. John Cotton, for instance, speaks of God's "appoyntment of mankind to live in Societies, first, of Family, Secondly Church, Thirdly, Common-wealth."[17] The first and third of these groups are exactly the ones Hall considers as the proper domains of economics and politics, respectively.

The only omitted one, the church, is self-consciously excluded from Solomonic wisdom both because it is an institution belonging to a period after Solomon and because the nature of biblical wisdom is that it brackets out of its vocabulary idiosyncratic expressions of faith peculiar to Israel and, by implication, should do the same in the Christian period in regard to the distinctive confessions and institutions of the church. There is, accordingly, a long wisdom tradition within Christianity before Hall's own effort that brackets out talk of Christ, cross, and resurrection for the same reason. The three sections in Hall's treatment prove to be unevenly chosen. Ethics is a transcendent humanistic topic, whereas politics and economics derive their definitions from commonwealth and family, two of the three social systems providentially maintained by God in both Jewish and Christian society. Just as Solomon omits reference to a distinctly Jewish understanding of the Temple or synagogue, so Hall omits the church as either a topic of biblical wisdom or even the social center of ethics within the larger idiom of biblical wisdom.

HALL'S PERCEPTION OF WISDOM AS ETHICS

Despite his affirmation of Solomon's lack of error in these biblical books, Hall demonstrates, at the outset, that he is not a biblicist by his reliance on Ramist logic, by his highly selective use of biblical citations, and by his dependence upon extrabiblical categories to refine the subject matter of biblical wisdom itself. The substantive role of this last feature is proven by Hall's choice of the first element in his entire presentation—a definition of "ethickes," a term not found within the biblical traditions themselves.

We might be surprised that Hall does not find his best resource for a definition of ethics in the most obvious canonical description of wisdom in the prologue to Proverbs (1:1–7). Instead, he depends on Ecclesiastes and cites a pertinent verse in the opening chapter spoken in the first person by "the Preacher" (Luther's contagious translation of the uncertain Hebrew, perhaps a sage official with the title "One who calls an assembly"). Hall has already told us in the dedication that the wisdom of the Preacher embraces many different subjects, including natural sciences, completely outside the domain of ethics. So, ethics is, in terms of a commonplace book, one of the chief topics of biblical wisdom. Hall claims here only that ethics forms an integral part of Solomonic wisdom that includes a much larger agenda. Ecclesiastes alone and not the prologue to Proverbs demonstrates such a concern for ethics in a manner compatible with Hall's Ramist predilection to define a profound topic by means of the richness of logical oppositions within it. The Geneva Bible translation of Ecclesiastes 1:17, which Hall notes in the margin, reads in its entirety: "I gave my mind to knowe wisdom & knowledge, madness & foolishnesse: I knewe also ỹ this is a vexaciõ of the spirit." In his actual use of this verse, Hall omits the last half of it, which might have been heard as a challenge to his positive presentation of such wisdom as a source of ethics.

Hall marks his nonbiblical expressions by putting them in italics so that we readily see what part of a verse he uses in his definition of ethics. His citation calls attention to the polarities exactly as he finds them here in Ecclesiastes 1:17, namely, "wisedom and knowledge"; and "madness and foolishnesse" (1). However, he clearly conceives of ethics as a discipline committed to practical guidance rather than as a theory of ideas about moral actions. Later, under his treatment of felicity, he quotes both 1:16 and 1:18, the immediate context of 1:17, to show explicitly that wisdom and knowledge, by themselves, do not constitute a sign of ethical understanding (9–12). Both 1:16 and 1:18 ("wisdom is much griefe") might endanger Hall's purpose of offering a positive definition of ethics and for that reason he qualifies 1:17 by citing Ecclesiastes 7:27 (Geneva Bible; in NRSV, 7:25) in the margin. The reader might ask why he bothers with 1:17 at all, if 7:27 would verbally serve his purpose better. I think the answer lies in his assumption that the purpose of a book is usually visible in its opening or closing verses rather than hidden arbitrarily somewhere else in that book. An opening verse is more likely to reflect the scope of the canonical context, and Hall is determined to follow and maintain this strategy even if the verses immediately associated with it could cause him a problem. So, in the margin, he cites as secondary support Ecclesiastes 7:27, which he does not quote, to justify his own specific interpretation. He concludes that "wisdom and knowledge" are pursued in ethics, again in his own words, *"to liue wel,"* whereas insight into "madness and foolishnesse" allows one to know the limitations and negative consequences, again in his own words, *"of vice"* (1). Hall had to search through several chapters of Ecclesiastes to find the particular verse that speaks exactly of this need "to know the wickednes of folie, and the foolishnes of madnes" (Eccl 7:27). It is the first instance in the book that assigns an ethically constructive function to one's knowledge of folly and madness, in contrast to 1:17a (cf. 2:3, 12). In this use of the biblical book, he follows a conventional practice of letting a more precise expression within the larger context clarify a more ambiguous saying found at an expected or conspicuous place.

Moreover, Hall's predisposition toward Ramist logic helps explain his preference for many of his quotes from Ecclesiastes. Often, Ecclesiastes more than Proverbs offers the better resource for Hall's negative oppositions in the definition of a topic. From Hall's perspective, such a use of Ecclesiastes alongside Proverbs provides ready answers to the implicit questions within the Ramist logical strategy Hall adopts from his Cambridge mentor, Chaderton. The reorganization of biblical texts conforms to this logic and is, for Hall, a convenience rather than a source of any really new information.

Only after this initial definition of ethics most suited to his commonplace method does Hall offer a complementary definition based on the more obvious prologue of Proverbs. From the standpoint of scripture itself, he could not ignore this part of the canonical context. Hall exhibits his literary-poetic aptitude observing exactly where the Hebrew poetry culminates in the first three verses, citing only the final line of Proverbs 1:3, "iustice and iudgement and equitie" (2). To this general definition of wisdom, Hall adds a qualification by means of a phrase he cites from Ecclesiastes 3:12, "and to doe good in our life" (2). This last aspect, once more, refracts the larger agenda of wisdom specifically in the direction of ethics, as distinguished from its many other concerns. Finally, Hall secures a precise definition by quoting, also, Ecclestiastes 2:3, with its further confirmation of the goal of ethics in a search for "goodnes" in human activity and conversation (2). Undoubtedly, Hall's assumptions about the nature of ethics in this period reflect contemporary views, including the Aristotelian concern with conceptions of "the good."[18] By his selective employment of biblical wisdom texts, Hall manages to fill the term *ethics* with biblical language, while respecting, at the same time, a Renaissance understanding of something called "ethickes," distinct from other humanistic concerns. The consequence is, at least in his mind, not a distortion of the Bible but a demonstration of the capacity of scripture to respond to more precise questions and categories enjoyed by later generations of faithful believers who continue to look to scripture as an authoritative guide to revelation.

"FELICITIE" AS A PRIMARY AIM OF ETHICS

By identifying the aim of ethics as "felicitie," Hall accepts an extrabiblical ideal of ethics advocated by Aristotle and many others.[19] Thus a eudaemonic goal for ethics can find support in the Solomonic books far more readily than in the law and the prophets. Only after treating felicity as an essential aim of ethics does Hall illustrate the means to attain it in the form of the "virtues" of prudence, justice, temperance, and fortitude. Again, in his selection of these categories he needs no explicit biblical warrant, but accepts contemporary notions about what topics integral to the analogy of faith pertain properly to ethics. By giving prominence to felicity, Hall interprets in his own way a utilitarian, eudaemonic dimension to biblical wisdom that modern historical criticism has often attributed to ancient wisdom. It is precisely this dimension that has allowed some modern scholars to suggest that the biblical wisdom is entirely "humanistic" or that it sprang up as an alternative to other "prophetic" religious options in ancient Israel.

Hall and other interpreters in the premodern period saw no such conflict between the biblical traditions and explored, instead, lines of continuity and discontinuity between the content of the Solomonic books and that of other biblical books. In Hall's citation of Proverbs 1:3, "justice" is the only term that recurs as a "virtue." By focusing first on "felicitie" and "goodnes," Hall succeeds in distinguishing wisdom's special concern with justice as a virtue in ethics, separate from his treatment of justice as a general concern under other topics as well. Clearly, the justice of God is the same wherever it is found, so Hall manages to retain and emphasize only that the wisdom idiom of justice has its own style and modes of expression distinct from a concern with justice elsewhere in the Bible. In the latter case, a much wider set of issues related to God's justice attains address through an entirely different set of genres, for example, by means of laws, narratives, oracles, and prayers of lamentation. At most, Hall has shown that biblical wisdom complements the rest of scripture by taking up a common concern in scripture—justice—and by articulating it through wisdom's own specialized idioms such as ethics. Naturally, this presentation leaves unexplored a whole set of questions about the relationship of sapiential ethics to law, to prophetic pronouncements, to priestly instruction and religious ritual, and to the Christian gospel itself. What may seem quite remarkable is Hall's full retention of Solomonic wisdom from the Old Testament as a self-sufficient source of ethics, without any overtly Christian corrective.

Dividing the main theme of felicity into certain illuminating oppositions, Hall begins with three subsections regarding what it is not. Here, Ecclesiastes provides his primary resource of biblical citations. Conversely, when he turns to address the positive properties of this same topic (12–15), he employs mostly Proverbs along with only a few quotations from Ecclesiastes. This section illustrates very well how Ecclesiastes often provides Hall with his best examples of the "wickednes of folie, and the foolishnes of madnes" (Eccl 7:27), whereas Proverbs remains the primary resource for a positive appropriation of "wisedom and knowledge." The dynamic of oppositions in Ramist logic serves him well by allowing an ample use of Ecclesiastes as a contrastive complement to Proverbs, showing how only the hearing of the two books together renders the full richness of divine wisdom.

When Hall turns to a positive estimate of felicity, he moves to a key place within the canonical context, namely, the epilogue to Ecclesiastes. In my judgment, the prominent use of this unique summary from the end of Ecclesiastes in his treatment of felicity shows how heavily Hall depends on parts, especially beginnings and endings, of biblical books most likely indicative of its scope. Only in the late modern period have contemporary critics rediscovered the editorial effect and semantic implications of such late additions to the beginnings and endings of biblical books. Just as modern critics now see in Ecclesiastes 12:13 an editorial summation of wisdom that seeks to secure a bridge between the Solomonic books and the Mosaic Torah, so Hall finds here a crucial warrant for how to read the wisdom books.[20] He quotes the verse—"Let vs heare the end of all; Feare God, and keep his Commandements; for this is the whole of Man, *the* whole *dutie*"—then adds epexegetically, *"the* whole *scope, the* whole *happinesse"* (12–13).

Ecclestiastes 12:13 is significant as an intertextual clue because it is rare in the Solomonic wisdom books to hear of "his Commandements," when the commandments signify the revealed laws of God rather than the "teaching" (torah) of a sage. By linking the leitmotiv of wisdom "fear the Lord" (cf. Prov 1:7) with observance of the law, an overt connection is presupposed between Solomonic wisdom and revealed Mosaic law. Jews and Christians have long observed this equation between wisdom and law, using one idiom to interpret the other. Jewish interpreters could read the wisdom books as commentary on legal observance or draw out wisdom sayings from the legal and narrative portions of the Torah.[21] This complementarity was ensured by the confidence that the Word of God had integrity despite the different idiomatic manifestations of it within scripture. Hall seeks to confirm the relation between wisdom and law by concluding this brief subsection with a citation from Proverbs 29:18, which in the Geneva Bible reads "hee that keepeth the lawe." Because the word *torah* in Hebrew can be translated either as "law" or "instruction," the fact that it lacks a definite article in Proverbs 29:18 explains why modern translations properly prefer to avoid here a reference to law. So, the Jewish Publication Society version (1985) offers "he who heeds instruction." In general, Hall asserts this complementarity between wisdom and law and assumes that wisdom's own unique contribution will only enhance rather than conflict with similar concerns for justice found elsewhere in the law and prophets.

Hall's additional words *"the* whole *scope, the* whole *happinesse"* expand the implications of Ecclestiastes 12:13 in a highly sophisticated manner. In this use of "scope," we see the influence of Matthias Flacius Illyricus and the recovery of the Eastern Church's exegetical tradition by continental theologians on English Protestants.[22] The beginning and endings of books were precisely the places where one might expect to find insight into the "scope" of a book. The term *scope* at this time had a richer significance than simply an author's purpose, for one could also speak of a "scope" of land; therefore, the text can be considered as a territory for which the scope served as a compass and guide to its essential value and purpose. The author's intent was thought to coincide. We have already observed that Ecclesiastes 12:13 allows such a scope to wisdom that is complementary with other parts of scripture. The final phrase *"the* whole *happinesse"* returns full force to the topic of ethics and allows Hall to clarify that felicity can be found according to terms familiar throughout scripture, namely, "In approuing ourselues to GOD" (12).

"ETHICS": ITS "VERTUES" OF PRUDENCE, JUSTICE, TEMPERANCE, AND FORTITUDE

Hall's priority given to felicity as a distinctive and definitive feature of ethics is qualified by his subordination of the other topics in this category as representing "All Vertues" (23) that belong to the constellation of felicity itself. His introductory statement on "Prudence" is entirely extrabiblical: *"Vertue consistes in the mean; vice in extreams"* (21). His emphasis in this short section is on *"the rule,"* which he identifies, once more, as *"Gods Lawe"* (21–22). Hall defines "Gods Lawe" by a catena of citations about "my commandements and . . . Instruction" (22), which, within the book of Proverbs itself, obviously refers to the teaching of the sage and, despite many figural correspondences, does not explicitly refer to the law as revealed by God to Moses. However, the problem is built into the formation of the book itself, because the comments on ritual performance cited by Hall, "binde them vpon thy fingers" (Prov 7:3), do echo a similar procedure in Deuteronomy meant to honor the revealed law. Consequently, Hall uses the word *law* in a general manner that potentially includes the Mosaic law, though the Mosaic law is explicitly expressed only outside of the restrained language of the Solomonic books themselves.[23] In this way, Hall has allowed for a subtle distinction between the "Gods lawe," which supports "the rule" that governs our recognition of "vertues," and the clusters of revealed law given to Moses in Genesis through Deuteronomy. Hall makes no effort to bridge this distinction between differing manifestations of God's law by a theory of natural law, nor does he find the law adequately revealed in other religions. He maintains, consonant with the epilogue to Ecclesiastes, the ancient identification of wisdom and law in a sophisticated, unharmonized, intertextual manner.

As seen in the Geneva Bible, "prudence" is a biblical term (e.g., Eccl 2:14, Prov 8:12, 14:8) primarily concerned, for Hall, with one's understanding of "his way" (24–28), foreknowledge (28–29), and discretion (30–32). As a counterpoint, Hall explores what stands in opposition to virtue, that is to say, *"the extreams"* (32–37). Here he draws chiefly on the half verses that occur so frequently in Proverbs about the actions of the fool or the wicked in contrast to the deeds of the wise and the righteous.

"Justice" receives more attention than any other subcategory in Hall's re-presentation of the Solomonic books (39–81). As a category in Solomon's "ethickes," Hall organizes it by first distinguishing the various social domains in which it functions: in relation to God, "to

God & man," and "to man only" (39). By an unusual marginal note (39), he admits that some of his associations of virtue with one of these categories could pertain equally well to others (see counsellour, 121). In its essence, justice is defined extrabiblically and precisely by Hall as *"in giuing each his owne"* (40). This description best circumscribes for him the range of biblical admonitions regarding the implementation of piety into righteous and just actions toward God and humanity. The opposite is participation in "euill" (40). Subvirtues pertinent to the virtue of justice include: fear, honor, respect, obedience, fidelity, truth, love, mercy, liberality, and diligence in our vocations. By this means, Hall can introduce into the wisdom literature classical categories of virtues that are addressed and amplified by biblical citations. Furthermore, they are distinguished by the idiom of wisdom as a guide to ethics distinct from but complementary to the other biblical idioms of revealed law, prophecy, and gospel. Obviously, these virtues are treated elsewhere in scripture, but Hall allows here for a distinctive mode of instruction that can be appreciated on its own terms and valued even by a foreign monarch, as in the prior case of the Queen of Sheba in the time of Solomon (1 Kings 10).

Both temperance and fortitude are extrabiblical terms that help Hall interpret biblical texts concerned with virtues such as sobriety, modesty, humility, continence, refraining from anger, and, in the second, confidence and patience. The vast majority of his citations come from the book of Proverbs and confirm, once more, his certainty that the wisdom books have a self-sufficiency of their own and provide an ample and biblical guide to virtues within a postbiblical discipline of Christian ethics. Some of Hall's depictions elsewhere in his works of persons exhibiting vices seem so unequivocal and one-sided that a supporter of Hall is quoted by McCabe to have said, "Because he had overcome vices in himself, he took liberty to whip them in others."[24]

THE SECOND MAJOR SECTION:
ON "POLITICS," OR "COMMONWEALTH"

Under this topic, Hall treats the affairs of king, counselor, courtier, and subject without attempting any biblical justification for the social system itself. For the king, Hall makes plain his preference for dynastic succession and his belief that the privileges of a king, as well as the plight of the poor, express divine "decrees" (108). The king's status should, consequently, be "natural" and "morall" (108). In the latter case, Hall primarily observes the negatives a moral king should guard against; the king should not be lascivious, riotous, hollow and dissembling, childish, imprudent, or oppressive. Hall comments in only two and a half pages at the end on the positive virtues of a just and merciful ruler (116–18).

Hall, next, gives special attention to counselors who play an essential supporting role to the king. We may, of course, see here some of Hall's own self-interest. On the benefit of many competent counselors, Hall cites Proverbs 11:14 and 24:6. The highest form of service in this role is *"Counsel for the soule,"* offering a "vision" that in Hall's own words, "requires both holinesse and wisedome" (119). Clearly, this very work by Hall is a prime example of such inspiring counsel. As in the other sections, Hall exploits the capacity of the biblical text to express virtues and vices. So, here an ideal counselor exercises wisdom (discussion of causes, foreknowledge), piety, and justice (with freedom from partiality, bribes, and oppression) (121). Hall puts emphasis on one's ability to judge wisely and impartially.

Hall briefly considers the political role of "courtiers" (129–31) and, more extensively, that of "subjects" (132–42). Although courtiers should be discreet, religious, humble, charitable, diligent, and faithful, each subject of the king is bound by a double sense of duty both to "His prince" and to "Fellow subjects" (132). The two principal virtues that a subject should exercise in relation to the prince are "reuerence" (or respect) and "obedience" (132). In his own words, Hall adds to his citations from scripture specific references to the "lawes" enacted by the king that all subjects should obey (133). Beside exploring various virtues of friendship, diligence in work, and openness in commerce, Hall presumes that society is highly segmented so that one might readily know who are one's superiors, inferiors, and equals. These distinctions are not drawn to outline conditions to be changed, but they simply describe accepted social systems of relatively fixed social strata. The chief goal of wisdom is for each person to honor his or her divinely ordered role through virtuous conduct. This acquiescence and support of the status quo is easily reinforced by sayings found within the Solomonic books, in contrast to the blistering social criticism of the prophets. In this period, the Puritans in general, whether pro-Establishment, as Hall, or disestablishmentarian, rejected direct challenges to the secular order. Still, Hall has appealed minimally at most to sayings found in both Proverbs and Ecclesiastes that describe the tragic plight of the poor or the ease with which wealth and privilege allow the wicked to usurp the rights of the poor. He does not find in the irony of these wisdom sayings a reason to question the justice of the present social order.

THE THIRD MAJOR SECTION: ON "OECONOMICKS," OR "FAMILY"

In our consideration of this section, I want to examine more closely two different forces at work within the singular event of Hall's interpretation: Hall's vision of the canonical context of "the text," which exerted pressure upon him, and the cultural conventions of family life that Hall attempted to influence by his compelling reading of that text. This dual focus of our investigation presumes that a hermeneutical understanding of Hall's interpretation can be enriched to the degree we know more about the dialectical relationship existing between his pragmatic vision of a text (and, hence, the pressure it exerts upon him as a reader) and the living situation addressed (and, by that, the political pressures challenged or vindicated by the act of interpretation itself). Without the one, we may become preoccupied with projections and prejudice of the reader's response to a text; without the other, we are left with merely abstract historical comments on a reader's vision of "the text" without any measure of how the text could confirm, disturb, console, and irritate those who read it.

This model of criticism applies especially to the type of biblical interpretation found here, namely, to efforts like that of Hall to read and to view the Bible as though it is a revelatory mirror of reality—that is to say, to view it as a "scripture" of a religion with the capacity to render the reality of its readers through its inspired and realistic depiction of the world. The "mainstream of Calvinist episcopalianism," to which Hall belonged, never tired of calling the Bible a "mirror," a favorite metaphor of Calvin and many earlier Christian interpreters.[25] One may even argue that this general view of the Bible as scripture is one integral to the traditional understanding of "the literal sense" of scripture within the history of Christianity.[26] Such a claim need not deny either the value or the validity of the nearly infinite variety of other, completely different ways one might read the Bible. It should, however, generate criteria so that one may evaluate how profitably other readings contribute to an interpretation of the Bible as scripture. For an assessment of Hall in this section, we will consider, first, how we may describe his pragmatic vision of the biblical text and, second, comment on the audience he wants to address in each subsection of his economics.

Hall's Vision of the Biblical Text and Its Canonical Context

In his identification of economics specifically as the "government" of the family or household, Hall seizes upon a distinctive feature already marked within the biblical Solomonic texts themselves. In his *Contemplations* on 1 Kings 10, concerning the visit of the Queen of Sheba and her testing of Solomon, Hall does not put much weight on the "questions" (Geneva Bible, cf. 1 Kgs 10:3) she may have asked and how Solomon answered. Instead, he takes up the text's own preoccupation (1 Kings 4—5) with what she observed: in Hall's selective paraphrase, "the architecture of his buildings, the provisions of his table, the order of his attendants, [and] the religion of his sacrifices." This episode occurs in the narrative of 1 Kings 3—11 immediately after the lengthy description of how Solomon had built the Temple and his own house subsequent to his being given the gift of wisdom (1 Kgs 5:1—9:25, cf. 9:15). Hall quotes in full, from the Geneva Bible, the Queen's conclusion: "I beleeved not the words till I came, and mine eyes had seene it, and loe the one halfe was not told me." He epitomizes the situation as an insight into wisdom itself:

Her eyes were more fore informers then her eares. Shee did not so much heare as see *Salomons* wisedome in these reall effects. His answers did not so much demonstrate it, as his prudent gouernment.

On the basis of this evidence, Hall contributes a proverbial generalization of his own: "Good discourse is but the froth of wisdome; the pure and solid substance of it is in well-framed actions; if we know these things, happy are we if we doe them."[27] By his interpretation of the narratives about Solomon in 1 Kings 3—11, Hall observes a marked feature within the biblical narrative and, as we shall see, finds confirmation of the same in the shape of the Solomonic books. In my opinion, Hall's observations on this point show a remarkable perception about the intertextual relationship between the shape of the Solomonic books and the presentation of Solomon, a relationship best expressed in the modern period in the debate over the late redaction history and resultant canonical context of ancient Israelite traditions within scripture.

I want to emphasize that modern historical criticism in the centuries after Hall has shown interest mostly in the so-called originating moments prior to biblical wisdom books. From that point of view, the earlier individual proverbs in a certain ancient period and subcollections of proverbs are prebiblical reconstructions, and any pertinent definition of wisdom must derive from general historical criteria related to ancient Near Eastern literature and how those materials are distinctive from other types of contemporary literature. Only in late modernity, especially since the 1970s, have some historical critics adopted genuinely fresh strategies for a description of biblical "books" as whole literary compositions within a larger intertext of scripture. For instance, literary, structuralist, and canonical approaches now invite a different assessment of how Hall conceived of these biblical texts. From a canonical approach, for example, we discover that Hall's identification of biblical wisdom with the "economy" of the household proves not to be an arbitrary or extrabiblical imposition in his reading of these texts. Within the late formation of the Solomonic narrative and books in scripture, the word *house* became a key organizing and defining feature of biblical wisdom regardless of its importance in the prehistory of wisdom traditions that were employed in the formation of these Solomonic books.

We have already noted that immediately after receiving the gift of wisdom, Solomon is portrayed as building houses for himself and for God (cf. 1 Kings 3—9). This pattern parallels the construction of the portable tabernacle in the wilderness by Bezelel and Oholiab to whom God, first, gives a gift of wisdom or skill (Exod 36:2). Similarly, wisdom's building of "a house" (e.g., Prov 9:1; 24:3–4) is a central metaphor in the book of Proverbs, where wisdom is personified as a woman rather than a man.[28] Likewise, the foolish woman's "house," with its trapdoor to Sheol (7:27; cf. 9:13–18) is contrasted with the seven-pillared "house" that the woman wisdom has built (9:1). This same motif in the introductory portion of the book of Proverbs (chapters 1–9) is reasserted, at least editorially, in chapters 10–31 in two places (14:1; 24:3), in the second part of the book devoted entirely to collections of proverbs and other compact wisdom sayings. The effect is to create a metaphorical bridge between the two major parts of the book (chapters 1–9 and 10–31). In 14:1 we are told, once more, "A wise woman buyldeth her house" (Geneva Bible). Elsewhere in the Bible the role of house building belongs exclusively to men, and other activities of the household pertain to women (cf. Prov 24:27). Other individual proverbs throughout the entire book use *house* as a metaphor for the efforts of both righteousness and wickedness (e.g., 3:33; 12:7; 14:11; 15:6; 21:12). Because this latter use of *house* relates only to the word pair "righteous and wicked" rather than to "wisdom and folly," it may represent historically a later editorial level within the formation of the book of Proverbs, within the canonical intertext of scripture.[29]

Though wisdom is not personified as a woman in Ecclesiastes, descriptions of house building and house deterioration constitute the interpretive framework (Eccl 2:1–11 and 12:1–8) around the book's core collection of aphoristic sayings. By implication, wisdom's provenance is analogous to house building and the governance of a house (Eccl 2:1–11). Correspondingly, the human grasp of wisdom requires constant preservation and is vulnerable to deterioration over time. Wisdom, by analogy to such a house and its estate, may fall into ruin over time or waste away and be forgotten after the death of its owner (Eccl 12:1–8). The perishable nature of human wisdom finds its ultimate threat in death, so that the wasting of the body in old age and the ruin of a house both signify at the end of Ecclesiastes the "vanity" of all human wisdom, despite its impressive, temporary powers. Finally, the editorial addition of a summarizing proverb near the end of the

book of the Song of Songs applies, again, the same metaphor to that
Solomonic book (Song of Songs 8:6–7, esp. v. 7b). From a modern
critical perspective, we may conjecture that this use of *house* came to
play a highly constitutive and definitive role in the late biblical
presentation of wisdom, both in the narrative of 1 Kings 3—11 and in
the Solomonic books, whether or not it played any similar role within
the diverse conceptions of wisdom in earlier periods of Israelite
history.[30]

In sum, using a canonical approach, we can see evidence for why
Hall thinks household economics is a key topic of biblical wisdom.
Although the Solomonic traditions themselves lack a Hebrew equiva-
lent for "economics," the Greek and Latinized forms of the word
depend on the same metaphorical use of the word *house* and signify
etymologically the same concern with rules for the management of a
household (Greek, *oikos*).

House, Household, and Family in Hall's Own Day

Alongside these insights into Hall's vision of the biblical text, we
need to consider what were the cultural, social, and political circumstances of the family and its economics that Hall addresses, condones,
or reproves with Solomonic wisdom. In the last decade, a large
number of new studies have begun to shed light on the inner
relationship between house and family and between family members
within the hierarchy of the household.[31] This knowledge gleaned from
diaries, court records, and other ephemeral sources of social research
advances our understanding of the family well beyond the remarkable
and ground-breaking study by Edmund S. Morgan in the 1940s: *The
Puritan Family: Religion and Domestic Relations in Seventeenth Century
New England*. I want to note two dimensions in this research; namely,
attention to the form and function of houses and households as a way
to comprehend political roles within the family, and the increasing
tension that arose between women and men of the period regarding
their respective powers within the social hierarchy of that economic
structure.

First, the prevalence of a rigid demarcation in social roles and codes of behavior in the seventeenth century is confirmed by Morgan's older sociological study, which without any reference to Hall organizes its material into chapters corresponding to the same family dichotomies that Hall presumes in his book: "Husband and Wife" (chapter 2), "Parents and Children" (chapter 3), and "Masters and Servants" (chapter 5). The collection of wisdom sayings together based on their address to particular persons belonging to the same social status occurs in the New Testament books (cf. Eph 5:21–9; Col 3:18–19; and 1 Pet 2:13–3:7), but not in the Solomonic wisdom books. Each dichotomy (e.g., husband and wife) is according to Ramist logic a "relative" rather than an "opposite" because they are "affirmative contraries," each the cause of the other.[32] By these arguments, Ramist logic affirmed a sapiential pursuit of "order" to both the universe and the family, despite the lack of a Hebrew term specifically for "order" in the Solomonic texts.

Hall's description of the economics of the household as a matter of "governance" reflects the same circumstances as found in the impressive study of Alice T. Friedman, *House and Household in Elizabethan England: Wollaton Hall and the Willoughby Family*. When Cassandra Willoughby, Duchess of Chandos, accepts in the 1680s her brother's invitation to come to his aid at the Wollaton Hall estate, she describes his need for her to "manage his household affairs." She calls herself the "Mrs. of Wollaton" and accepts the invitation, "believing that such a government must make me perfectly happy."[33] Similarly, Hall defines his "economics" in the subtitle of this section, "Gouernment of *the* Family" (143).

A second observation is that the identification of a wife's or mistress's role as concerned with the government of the household harbors a potential conflict that became real for many families in Hall's day—that women would want more rights and refuse to allow their husbands absolute approval and control over all these affairs. Women who were sometimes celebrated by their husbands for managing the household finances began to own their own property and a few began to own property despite earlier laws against it.[34] Friedman summarizes this tension between husbands and wives in the Elizabethan period:

The question of women's position in society was particularly pressing among the upper gentry and aristocracy. A number of significant
factors—the presence of a female sovereign, new attitudes toward
the making of wills and property ownership by women, new opportunities for social mobility among men of all classes, Puritan doctrines concerning the marriage bond and the quality of the home
life— conspired to produce what has been described as a widely felt
anxiety about, and within relationships between men and women.
In public, a heated debate about women's "true" role erupted in
popular literature and in books of advice.[35]

Hall's own advice to wives in the light of this background appears
to be a reactionary, proestablishment reaction against these growing
tensions. Even antiestablishment Puritans who opposed the absolute
status of a Roman Catholic or Anglican priesthood, in contrast to
Hall, still viewed social status, especially in the family, as a fixed part
of God's providential orders. Hall's position would find accord with
the opinion of a New England preacher, William Hubbard: "It
appears, whoever is for a parity in any Society, will in the issue reduce
things into an heap of confusion."[36] Nonetheless, as Friedman observes, the Puritan understanding of the marriage bond, as seen in
Hall, strongly advocated love, civility, justice, joy, and lack of conten-
tiousness. These virtues, if given precedence, could challenge the more
simplistic and tyrannical hierarchical conceptions of the order of the
family, subverting the rigid codes of behavior by a call for mutual
respect in the distribution of different duties, responsibilities, and
freedoms to each person within the larger economy of a family.

In a similar manner, the notes of the Geneva Bible to 1 Corinthians
11, about women wearing veils, show some uncertainty about the roles
of women in the family. The annotations repeatedly affirm the "sub-
jection" of the woman who is "one degree beneath the man by the
image of God" and find in verse 8 a biblical proof of the "inequalitie
of the woman, [on the grounds] that the man is the matter whereof
woman was first made."[37] However, in the note on verse 11 about
women and men belonging together, we find reaction against a
tyrannical application of this earlier interpretation:

A digression which the Apostle vieth, least that which hee spake of the superioritie of men, and lower degree of women, in consideration of the policies of the Church, should bee taken as though there were no measure of this inequalitie. Therefore hee teacheth that men have in such sort the preeminence, that God made them not alone, but woman also: and woman was so made of man, that men also are borne by the oneness of women, and this ought to put them in minde to observe the degree of euery sexe in such sort, that mutuall coniunction may be cherished.[38]

By qualifying the "lower degree of women" to its implications "in consideration of the policies of the Church," the practical implications for the subordinate role of woman in the economy of the family are left open to some ambiguity and dispute. Hall argues clearly that in the family the man must be the "head." Still, how this theological and political order of men over women in the family should limit the activities of women in society is a question Hall avoids. His relative silence on this subject is a sign that even he could no longer draw a simple and direct line between the traditional dogmatic position and its contemporary practical consequences for family governance in the seventeenth century.

Likewise, it would do injustice to Hall to regard every silence as a proof that issues untreated were irrelevant to him. The silence of public law in contrast to the adjudication of actual court cases and personal diaries demonstrates that family violence, sexual abuse, incest, and the excessive punishment of children were matters of private, if not public, concern. The Solomonic books do not address most of these family injustices or do so with such discretionary subtlety that we can find them only between the lines. Although these crimes were not overtly discussed, we know from court records and diaries that they did occasionally gain response from the various judiciaries, sometimes with stiff sentences from the local courts.[39] At most, we can say that Hall is no revolutionary in these matters, for he remains silent where the biblical proverbs are silent.[40] A more serious criticism, to which we will return at the end of this essay, is Hall's disregard for a more vigorous case in behalf of the "poor" that he could have easily found in the book of Proverbs.

HALL'S INTRODUCTION TO HOUSEHOLD
ECONOMICS

Hall opens his treatment on the "Oeconomicks" section by assert-
ing categorically, *"The man is the* head, *and guide of the family"* (145).
As a separate opening section, Hall develops this principle by articulating its necessary virtues in wisdom, "stayednesse," and thrift. In the
sections that follow, Hall turns to examine each set of coordinate pairs
that naturally compose the family: husband and wife, parent and
child, master and servant. In stating his initial principle, Hall leaves
the word *head* unitalicized, signifying that it is cited from scripture
rather than his own words. However, neither the Solomonic books
themselves nor the entire Old Testament claims that a husband is the
head of a family, in these terms. This expression must come for Hall
from the New Testament (cf. 1 Cor 11:3; Eph 5:23) and appears to be
the only instance of a citation from the New Testament in this work
by Hall. From a modern perspective, we may argue that the unequal
authority of men over women and children maintained in Proverbs
was typical of peasant economies in the ancient Near East and in
Israel, though it is not explicitly identical with a "headship" hierarchy
of the household found later in Hellenistic culture and accepted in
parts of the New Testament. On this point, Hall has harmonized the
Solomonic description with the household economics he finds in the
New Testament.

When Hall tries to use Proverbs and Ecclesiastes to link wisdom
with this role of the man as "the head" of the house, he faces
repetitions about wisdom *as a woman* who builds a house. The image
of a woman building a house may seem to weaken his argument and
explains why, in my view, he passes over the obvious earlier references
in Proverbs 9:1 or 14:1 to quote here Proverbs 24:3, the only such text
about wisdom's house building that is set in the passive voice:
"Through wisedome an house is builded, and established" (145). This
ambiguity of voice allows Hall to maintain rhetorically his stress
unequivocally on the headship of men over women in the hierarchy
of the household. As further support, Hall cites elsewhere the warning
to men that "the fool shal be seruant to the wife" (146; cf. Prov 11:29).
The citation of Proverbs 24:3, also, confirms how sophisticated is

Hall's literary use of the book of Proverbs. On one level, he easily finds interest within the book regarding the activities of family life. The theme of a house that wisdom builds has become editorially a key topic within the book. Hall sees this aspect of the literature and exploits it. On another level, his concern to affirm a specific formula supportive of man as the head of the family might seem threatened by the role of woman wisdom. In any case, Hall is ingeniously selective in his use of Proverbs, because he is attentive to limitations and possibilities of compelling interpretation within the canonical context itself.

The Husband

This same concern carries over to Hall's next section on the husband. In his paraphrase of Proverbs 12:4, Hall creatively presses its import to make emphatic, once again, the role of a husband as "the head." The biblical text confirms for him that a husband should be "as the heade to which shee is a crowne" (148), despite the Geneva Bible rendering: "A verteous woman is the crowne of her husband." Obviously, because the crown sits on the man's head, Hall sees here the implication of the wife's acceptance of her husband as the head of the household. Hall's insistence that "*The man is the* head, *and guide of the family*" (145) represented one of the most commonly accepted conceptions of the biblical order of the family.[41] The same position, in the same words, occurs in Eve address to Adam in Milton's *Paradise Lost* (Book IV, lines 440–43):

> O thou for whom
> And from whom I was formed flesh of thy flesh,
> And without whom am to no end, my guide
> And head.

Hall's selection of three virtues for the husband betrays his own bias and, to some degree, the predispositions of his own day. The husband should conduct himself wisely, chastely, and both quietly and cheerfully. Each attribute is elaborated with special reference to his relationship to a wife. The first is stated simply as a matter of wise behavior generally so that the man will be "the guide of her youth" (148). The next two find ample support, mostly from Proverbs, about the importance of fidelity and the diminishing of contention in a marriage. Although Hall cites Proverbs 5:18–19 as positive advice for the husband to be satisfied sexually and interpersonally with "the wife of thy youth," most of his advice here touches on the consequences of adultery (cf. 152–53). For example, if someone is hungry and steals, *"it is accepted"* upon repayment sevenfold (152). Not so, adultery, for the rage of a *"wronged husband"* cannot be assuaged (152).

The third virtue for the husband is quietness and cheerfulness. Here, as in the other sections about wives, children, and servants, Hall warns all parties about the corrosive effects of strife and even the need to ignore some offenses, such as words of criticism accidentally overheard or minor misdeeds. Everyone in the family is counseled to seek tranquillity, even at the expense of personally exacting justice or self-vindication. The husband is encouraged to pass over an offense of his wife (Prov 19:11) and to forgive a transgression (Prov 17:9) for the sake of love. There is no direct consideration of the possible abuse by husbands of their wives, but Hall concludes with a citation from Ecclesiastes 9:9, which returns to the theme of the loving community between the husband and wife. The husband should "reioyce," rather than be contentious or unsatisfied with his wife whom he "hath loved all the dayes" of his life (154).

In Hall's warning against a husband's temptation to commit adultery, he quotes Proverbs 6:26 about "the whorish woman" who seeks to destroy a man (151). As a matter of semantics, Hall's interpretation of the proverb confirms the argument of James Kugel that premodern understandings of the two-line saying presupposed that the second line in a two-line saying expands, amplifies, or qualifies the first. Hall inserts between the first and the second line of his citation of the proverb his own words *"and more then that."*[42] Whereas the first line describes how a "whorish woman" will reduce a man's resources to a morsel of bread, the second clarifies the first by expressing the same idea in even more threatening terms: "a Woman will hunt for the precious life of a man" (151). We are also cautioned that a beautiful woman can "take thee with her eie-lids" (151; cf. Prov

6:25).[43] Hall certainly acknowledges that women have some power over men, though it is restricted in these comments to their seductive and potentially destructive influence.

The Wife

Regarding "the wife," Hall initially cites, once again, Proverbs 12:4, which he had altered before in his opening treatment of "the Husband" (148) in order to call attention to the role of the man as the head of the wife. Now he cites it directly from the Geneva Bible—"A Vertuous Wife is the Crowne of her husband"—because it suits his purpose to stress the ideal of "a Vertuous Wife" (155). Therefore, the same verse, read in two different ways by Hall, has served to explain the "relative" nature of these oppositions, husband and wife. The virtues emphasized for the wife are, first, faithfulness to her husband, then, obedience, discretion, providence, and high qualities of being a housewife. His elaboration of unfaithfulness relies extensively on oppositions Hall finds between the depiction of the wanton woman in Proverbs 7 and positive sayings elsewhere in Proverbs. Perhaps worth noting is Hall's assurance to us in his own words, not found in the biblical text itself, that the young man involved with the adulterous woman in Proverbs 7 was in pursuit of illicit sex and was not merely an innocent victim nor merely a naive young man. The man who is seduced in this archetypical paradigm is, for Hall, a man who finds that which he himself foolishly seeks. Hall sets off his advice to be *"carefull and hous-wifelike"* as a separate, fairly extensive subsection (161–165) that relies heavily on Proverbs 31.

Some obvious contrasts exist between his advice to wives as compared with that given to husbands. Husbands were admonished to seek wisdom, not to stray from their wives, and to be thrifty. Hall has stressed for wives, first, their relation to their husbands and the need to be faithful and obedient to them. Second, Hall elaborates some virtues of wisdom common to all human beings— discretion and providence—before turning again to special characteristics of a housewife. Both husbands and wives are warned against temptations to adultery and any inclination to be contentious with each other.

Clearly, the economic sphere of the wife is defined in relation to her obedience to her husband and service to the family, whereas the husband is assigned a wider range of responsibilities and authority.

In his separate treatment of the activities of the housewife, Hall cites every verse in the portrait of the ideal wife found in Proverbs 31 (one verse cited twice, 31:15). His Ramist chart illustrates well how he seeks to clarify an argument in Proverbs 31, requiring him to rearrange certain verses. Near the end, he commends her speech in 31:26 —"she opens her mouth with wisdom"—in a manner comparable to his extensive praise of her skillful actions. As seen in our earlier comments on Solomon in his *Contemplations*, Hall prizes actions more than rhetoric as evidence of wisdom. Her actions are divided between those "in her own person" and those "in the oversight of her family" (vv. 15b + 27, assigning tasks to servants). Her actions "in her own person" include a distinction between, first, "labours" with her own hands (loom and needlework, vv. 13, 15, 17) and, second, "bargains" (purchase, use, and sale of land and other items; vv. 14, 16, 18). In this way, Hall cites every other verse and redistributes them into the distinctions he wants to identify. We see here an emphasis on needlework, which was a principal concern of women in the period, followed by a recognition of other business activities.

What may seen remarkable in this period is v. 16: "She considereth a field, and getteth it" (162). In general, laws in England denied land ownership by wives. Hall may be admitting here a changing pattern in the range of activities permitted for wealthy women in the seventeenth century, as the study by Friedman suggests. When he comes to the wife's liberal provisions for members of the household, Hall reverses the order of the biblical verses so that the first member is "*her husband*, who is knowen in the gates" (v. 23, p. 163), followed by verses aimed at herself, her servants, and the poor (vv. 22, 21, 20). Again, Hall puts stress on the priority of the husband in a fashion even more hierarchically accentuated than in the Old Testament itself. Later, Hall mentions the wife's "oversight" of the family without fully resolving a possible tension with the role of the husband as the head of the family. He simply assumes that the wife's activity belongs to a known set of tasks outside or subordinate to the domain of the man's principal authority in the home.

The tension that often existed between the roles played by husbands and wives in the seventeenth century has been observed by recent studies and demonstrates some of what Hall's advice was intended to prevent. Lisa Jardine has shown that controversial roles of women in contemporary drama reflect this same tension.[44] In Friedman's study of generations in the Willoughby household, she cites a seventeenth-century account by Cassandra Willoughby of conflicts between Lady Willoughby and her husband, Sir Francis, in the late sixteenth century:

> Sir Francis pressed her to be reconciled to her sister, which she refused. He then asked her if in all other things she would be ruled by him. Upon which she answered she would not be ruled by him. Upon which Sir Fowlk Grevell said "Why, madam, will you refuse to be ruled by your husband?" She answer'd she was the Queen's sworn servant and knew not but Sir Francis might command her something against Her Majestie's proceedings, to which Sir Fowlk said that was an evil objection for a wife to lay to her husband.[45]

By playing off the authority of her husband against the greater authority of the Queen, Lady Willoughby could challenge her obligation to obey her husband. In general, Hall's advice was supportive of husbands such as Sir Francis, though the economics of Hall was not explicit enough to offer a practical solution to problems arising from the conflict in the roles of husbands and wives in this period.

From court records in New England, we also know that there were laws against either husbands' or wives' striking each other and against the use of excessively abusive language in reference to each other. Adultery and incest were capital offenses, though usually lesser punishment ensued. Certainly, husbands had an unfair advantage within the home, but Hall and other Protestants hoped to protect the subordination of wives to their husbands from any harsh consequences by an appeal to the "duty" of love in a marriage. Because marriages were seen as rational rather than romantic liaisons, love often was assumed to be the result rather than the cause of that marriage covenant.[46] By Hall's admonitions about charity, love, and joy between husbands and wives, he attempted to address a myriad of individual problems in marriage by an overarching appeal to the human expression of a divine love, as he understood it through scripture.

Parents and Children

In these two sections, and the last on "The Maister, & Servant," Hall begins to talk of "duties" and what one party "owes" the other. Parents owe their children provision, instruction, and correction. By provision, Hall cites only Proverbs and parts of Ecclesiastes concerned with inheritance. We may assume that the ordinary care of children is taken for granted. Hall's lengthy catena of sayings for parents from Proverbs on not sparing the rod may strike us as harsh (167–69). He warns of the weakness of the mother in this regard (cf. Prov 29:15, p. 168). In his concluding citation from Proverbs 19:19, Hall avoids the Geneva Bible and chooses a translation with the assurance, "The sonne that is of a great stomach, shall indure punishment" (168–69). Obviously, correction was more than a form of reprisal for wrong actions, including in it an effort to inure children to face pain and hardships later in life. The second part of the same verse emphasizes the reconciliation by the parent who held the rod when, afterwards, he "yet . . . shalt take him [the child] in hand againe" (169).

The duties of children to parents consisted in obedience, submission to correction, and care for themselves and their parents. Stress is given by Hall to the proverbs about children obeying every command of their parents. Though much of the language in Proverbs is probably honorific, so that the sage teachers are surrogate parents and the children are pupils in school, Hall takes it all at face value as a set of statements of life in the home. Children are told, in Hall's own words, to be *"not obedient to counsell only, but to stripes"* (171). They must not hate their parents on account of this correction (cf. Prov 12:1), for it is "the waie of life" (Prov 6:23, p. 171). There is no hint of the problem of child abuse, either in Proverbs itself or in Hall's interpretation of it. We have every reason to believe it was a hidden injustice in the seventeenth century, rarely admitted or confronted directly by the public.

The Master and Servant

Hall may shock modern sensibility with his opening observation in his own words, *"The seruant is no small commodity to his master"* (172). As support, Hall cites Proverbs 2:9, as follows: "Hee that is despised, & hath a seruant of his own is better then he that boasts (*whether of gentry, or wealth*) & wanteth bread" (172). With a considerably different import, the Geneva Bible offers for the same verse: "He that is despised and is his owne seruant, is better the' he that boasteth him self and lacketh bread." In both England and New England, servants were often single persons assigned to households, and the ability to maintain servants was a sign of a successful family. Hall, also, advises the master that he should *"not bee ouer-rigorous in punishing, or noting offences, sometimes* not hearing his seruant, that curseth him" (173). The unitalicized quotation from Ecclesiastes 7:23 recalls Hall's advice also to husbands that they should pass over some of what they hear from their wives. At a minimum, Hall tries to temper the inequality of social status by advising the ones with the most privileged authority not to be always "over-rigorous" in their response to offenses or injustice to themselves.

CONCLUSIONS

The genius of Hall's interpretation cannot be best appreciated by a search for anticipations of modern historical criticism. Recent literary, canonical, or compositional approaches prove more helpful than standard historical criticism for helping us grasp a vision of the biblical text similar to what Hall possessed. We may acknowledge the "realism" of a biblical text within its own canonical context without being able to ground that realism in a modern reconstruction of "history." Conversely, through our knowledge of standard historical criticism we see that substantial differences, including contradictions, exist between the prehistory of a biblical book and the book's later presentation of ideas, persons, and events.

When ancient prebiblical traditions were caught up in a long complex history of traditions leading to their present place within a "biblical" book, they inevitably participate in a wide range of possible semantic transformations. Within a biblical book, a unit of tradition may have a high degree of retention with its prehistory, or it may be woven into a completely new topical and anachronistic relation with other traditions, or it may be altered radically by redactional expansions. The specific context and scope of a text may invite readings in conformity with or against earlier authors' intents. Nevertheless, such a late modern perspective regarding the semantic complexity of the Bible should only enhance rather than rule out our ability to enter by empathetic imagination into the world of Joseph Hall and his vision of scripture. Our modern eyes peering through his spectacles at the same scriptural text should understand what he confronted in his activity of interpretation; and, at the same time, we should necessarily have a greater acuity of things we could not expect him to see.

Through this investigation of Hall's work on ethics, politics, and economics, I have attempted to show that his vision of the canonical context of the Solomonic books played an important role in both helping and restricting the choices he could make in the course of his scriptural interpretation. We see in this evidence that Hall thinks of the text as having a real voice, articulated through a particular wedding of the human persona of Solomon to his spoken or written words. Moreover, Hall seeks to hear the voice of God behind the voice of Solomon, the wisdom of God within Solomon's wisdom, so that the result of this re-presentation is a collation of words and phrases cast in the present tense instead of the past. When Hall reads and hears scripture, he confronts it as a voiced subject rather than a voiceless object of interpretation. For this reason, we do justice to Hall's effort only when we can sense the semantic pressure that exists between these two subjects, the text and the interpreter. Our attention to the canonical context helps us illuminate some of the evidence of how the text has boundaries—giving rise to a specific semantic arena—within which Hall had to work in order to remain a competent interpreter of the Bible as scripture.

Hall and the English Protestants routinely stated that proper biblical interpretation requires that one must hold text and subject matter together. The subject matter can be shown to be pertinent to the text by its relation to patterns of signification within the text itself.

Protestants argued that the analogy of faith could be seen in these patterns and was essential to guide the reader to the Word of God, the true subject matter of the text. Conversely, the analogy of faith and the subject matter, the Word of God, provided a norm to determine if the actions or words of a biblical figure ought to be taken as an exemplary mode of behavior or belief.[47] A desire to make explicit the relationship between the text and its subject matter underlies Hall's use of rhetorical devices, both his Ramist logic and his appeal to the commonplace topics or *loci*. The reader should ideally be helped by these devices to hear and remember more easily the Bible's own subject matter, though a danger exists similar to that which prompted the Protestant criticism of the Roman Catholic Church. There is a potential domestication of our ability to hear the Bible itself, so that these aids to the reader become a substitute for the Bible itself and serve only to confirm what we already assume to be the tradition of the church. In considering the positive implications for contemporary biblical interpretation of Hall's efforts, I will make three brief observations:

1. In the light of the recent emphasis on praxis, we recognize that Hall, also, placed greater weight on the implementation of wisdom than on its rhetorical expression. He prefers sagacious action over mere words of wisdom. Yet Hall basically supports the status quo; he assumes that the present social order accords with providential design. Although Hall shows concern for benevolence to the poor (e.g., by the wife, p. 163), he fails to take full advantage of warrants within Proverbs to explore the ironic social plight of the poor and the unjust opportunities of the rich. Almost all of these verses occur in his "ethics" under the virtue of "justice" (e.g., Prov 14:31; 19:7, 14; 21:13; 22:7, 9, 16, 22; 28:6; 28:8, 27; 29:7; 30:14) so that very few by comparison belong to his politics (exceptions, 14:21; 19:4; 22:7). The effect is to view the plight of the poor as a circumstance that calls for kindness and generosity without acknowledging the problem engendered by the political system itself and by the self-interest of the wealthy landowners within it.

2. Hall quotes from Song of Songs at three places, twice under "felicity" and once in his "politics." All of these usages (3:9, 10; 6:8) pertain only to Solomon's building activities or to the extent of his

household. Otherwise, Hall hears the Song of Songs as a metaphor based on an analogy between the love of a man for a woman and Christ's love for the church. My point is only that he could have used Song of Songs in its literal sense as a biblical resource for wisdom about human erotic love. Besides the famous proverb of 8:6 ("love is strong as death, passion fierce as the grave"), there are the repeated admonitions: "do not stir up or awaken love until it is ready!" (NRSV; cf. Song of Songs 2:7; 3:5; 8:4). The internal descriptions of the playfulness of erotic love take up in a positive manner the very same language of seduction that in another context leads to negative consequences (cf. Prov 7:6–27).[48] The physical activities are almost identical; but in one context it is a joyous celebration blessed by God, whereas in another it leads to destruction and even loss of life. In other words, nothing in Hall's approach, if transformed into late modern interpretation, would prevent us from viewing the topic of sexuality as one most obviously addressed by wisdom and one that invites Jews and Christians to rival the world in terms of wisdom and folly, justice and injustice.

3. An overview of Hall's understanding of biblical wisdom as a biblical and theological idiom suggests, in my view, some fruitful possibilities for late modern use of the Bible. In his ethics, Hall finds in wisdom rules and precepts leading to happiness (felicity) and the good; in his politics and, again, in his economics, he describes more generally what is astute and moral, underscoring especially the "duties" of various classes of persons. Politics reflects the interaction between persons in a highly segmented society (commonwealth), and each person is taught the duties and social skills requisite to his or her position within the social strata. Economics signifies the proper duties, skillful action, and moral responsibility congruent to each category of persons in the culturally specific hierarchy of the family. This threefold presentation of the aims of Solomonic wisdom according to one major theme (ethics) and two instances of governance (politics and family economics) makes no effort at any systematic statement regarding the nature of wisdom. Hall has already granted that the Bible lacks any adequate attention to knowledge about nature in general that also belongs to wisdom. Hall certainly would agree

that biblical wisdom includes more than he presents here and that the ordering of his presentation, as granted in his preface, invites our criticism. Even with these limitations, we find here what Hall considers to be the essentials, the characteristic achievements of Solomonic wisdom.

Despite all of its limitations, Hall's approach to wisdom illustrates how the biblical tradition invites Jews and Christians to have a profound conversation with the world on matters of ethics, politics, and family economics. This conversation self-consciously brackets out some idiosyncratic religious language integral to the identity of Jewish and Christian faith in order to allow for the maximum family resemblance between such biblical wisdom and wisdom as the world—the Queen of Sheba!—knows it. This strategy adopted by Judaism is inherited by Christianity through scripture. One of its strengths is that it allows for a competitive illumination of wisdom in the world apart from any conception of a "natural theology" to justify itself.[49] Biblical wisdom, in this regard, leaves many issues unaddressed and unresolved, yet still serves Hall in two ways common within the older tradition of interpreting the Solomonic literature. It is a source of divine revelation about reality, and it is, also, a resource for refining the questions that an interpreter brings to the text, even as the Queen of Sheba sought to bring worthy questions to King Solomon. So, biblical wisdom makes an important contribution both to our encyclopedic knowledge of the world and to our hermeneutical ability to perceive the living word of the biblical text itself. This latter aspect of wisdom helps explain why each generation of interpreters must reinterpret the Bible with the full strength of improved questions and better knowledge of their own time and place. Our new and, one might hope, wiser questions asked of the scriptures inevitably hold forth the possibility of our hearing new responses from scripture. Hall expresses this idea in Christian terms at one point in his *Contemplations* on the visit of the Queen of Sheba: "There is much wisedome in mouing a question well, though there bee more in assoiling [answering] it: What use do we make of *Salmons* Teacher, if sitting at the feet of Christ we leaue our hearts either ignorant or perplexed?"[50]

NOTES

1. For consideration of the place of this literature in the lifework of Hall, see the essay in this volume by Richard A. Muller; and Frank Livingstone Huntley, *Bishop Joseph Hall, 1574–1656: A Biographical and Critical Study* (Cambridge, Eng.: D. S. Brewer, 1979), 53–55.

2. Cf. Eugene F. Rice, *The Renaissance Idea of Wisdom* (Cambridge: Harvard University Press, 1958), 1–92.

3. See Barbara Lewalski, *Protestant Poetics and the Seventeenth Century Religious Lyric* (Princeton: Princeton University Press, 1979), 53–71; Elaine Tuttle Hansen, *The Solomon Complex: Reading Wisdom in Old English Poetry* (Toronto: University of Toronto Press, 1988), 41–183; and Beryl Smalley, *Medieval Exegesis of Wisdom Literature*, ed. Roland Murphy (Atlanta: Scholars Press, 1986).

4. Lawrence Boadt, "St. Thomas Aquinas and the Biblical Wisdom Tradition," *The Thomist* 48 (1985): 575–611. Hansen's monograph (see n. 3) can be similarly challenged for some of her preliminary observations in the first chapter, "The Wisdom of Solomon," 12–40.

5. Joseph Hall, "Contemplations," in *The Works of Joseph Hall, Doctor of Divinitie, and Dean of Worcester* (London: 1925), 1271.

6. Whereas the Pentateuch condemns reliance upon foreign prophets, Deuteronomy 4:6–8 proposes that obedience to the revealed Torah should cause other nations to applaud Israel for "wisdom." So, too, the prophet condemns reliance on other nations for security (e.g., Isa. 31:1–3) but portrays Solomon positively ofr his reliance on King Hiram of Tyre for help in securing building supplies for the Temple. Proverbs is the only book in the Bible with overt, titled collections of tradition borrowed from non-Israelite sources (cf. Prov 30:1–4).

7. *The Geneva Bible: A Facsimile of the 1560 Edition* (Madison: University of Wisconsin Press, 1969), 275.

8. On Ramism and Chaderton, see Donald K. McKim, *Ramism in William Perkins' Theology* (New York: Peter Lang, 1987), 37–50 and 44–45, respectively.

9. Ibid., 44.

10. Patrick Collinson, *The Religion of the Protestants: The Church in English Society, 1559–1625* (Oxford: Clarendon Press, 1982), 151–53.

11. Robert Kolb, "Teaching the Text: The Commonplace Method in Sixteenth Century Lutheran Biblical Commentary," *Bibliothèque d'Humanism et Renaissance* 49 (1987): 579.

12. Ibid., 576.

13. Gerhard von Rad, *Wisdom in Israel*, trans. James D. Martin (Nashville: Abingdon Press, 1972), 124–37.

14. Cf. 2 Sam. 23:2; Sid Z. Leiman, *The Canonization of the Hebrew Scripture: The Talmudic and Midrashic Evidence* (Hamden, Conn.: Archon Books, 1976), 14–16; and Peter Schäfer, *Die Vorstellung vom Heiligen Geist in Der Rabbinischen Literatur* (München: Kösel-Verlag, 1972), 94–97.

15. In contrast, for example, to Boadt's observation that "wisdom was thought . . . to put aside all divinely-revealed knowledge in favor of trust in human experience" ("St. Thomas Aquinas," 575).

16. Hall, "Contemplations," 1274.

17. John Cotton, *A Briefe Exposition with Practicall Observations upon the Whole Book of Ecclesiastes* (London, 1654); and Edmund S. Morgan, *The Puritan Family: Religion and Domestic Relations in Seventeenth Century New England* (Boston, Boston Library, 1942; repr. New York: Harper & Row, 1966), 18.

18. F. E. Sparshott, *An Enquiry into Goodness* (Toronto: University of Toronto Press, 1958), 27–45.

19. See Aristotle's *Nicomachean Ethics*; and Paul Lehman, *Ethics in a Christian Context* (New York: Harper & Row, 1963), 167–68, 173–75.

20. Gerald T. Sheppard, "The Epilogue to Qoheleth as Theological Commentary," *CBQ* 39 (1977): 182–89.

21. Harvey H. Guthrie, *Wisdom and Canon: Meanings of the Law and the Prophets* (Seabury, N.Y.: Seabury-Weston Theological Seminary, 1966); and Gerald T. Sheppard, *Wisdom as a Hermeneutical Construct: A Study in the Sapientializing of the Old Testament* (Berlin: Walter de Gruyter, 1980); and Jacob Neusner, *Torah: From Scroll to Symbol in Formative Judaism* (Philadelphia: Fortress Press, 1985).

22. See Gerald T. Sheppard, "Between Reformation and Modernity: The Perception of the Scope of Biblical Books," in William Perkins, *A Commentary on Galatians*, facs. ed., Pilgrim Classic Commentaries Series, ed. Gerald T. Sheppard (New York: The Pilgrim Press, 1989), vii–xiii.

23. Morgan, *The Puritan Family*, 11–17.

24. Richard McCabe, *Joseph Hall: An Study in Satire and Meditation* (Oxford: Clarendon Press, 1982), 39.

25. See Collinson, *The Religion of the Protestants*, 81–82.

26. For a defense of mimetic realism as a key feature in the history of biblical interpretation, see Hans W. Frei, *The Eclipse of Biblical Narrative: A Study in Eighteenth and Nineteenth Century Hermeneutics* (New Haven: Yale University Press, 1974).

27. Hall, "Contemplations," 1271.

28. Cf. Claudia Camp, "Bible and Literature," in *Wisdom and the Feminine in the Book of Proverbs* (Decatur, Ga.: The Almond Press, 1985), 11.

29. R. B. Y. Scott, "Wise and Foolish, Righteous and Wicked," *VTSup* 23 (1960): 146–65.

30. Cf. Gerald T. Sheppard, *The Future of the Bible* (Toronto: United Church Press, 1990), 103–30.

31. Eric Mercer "The Houses of the Gentry," *Past and Present* (1954): 11–32; Eric Barbour Mercer, *English Art, 1553–1625* (Oxford: Clarendon Press, 1962); Eric Mercer and N. Elias, "Structure of Dwellings and the Structure of the Society," in *The Court History* (Darmstadt, 1969; repr. New York, 1983). Mark Girouard, *Life in the English Country House: Social and Architectural History* (New Haven: Yale University Press, 1978).

32. Morgan, *The Puritan Family*, 22–23.

33. Alice T. Friedman, *House and Household in Elizabethan England* (Chicago: University of Chicago Press, 1989), 1.

34. Morgan, *The Puritan Family*, 42–43, states that women could not legally own property in Massachusetts and in England in the seventeenth century, though on occasion they handled the family finances.

35. Friedman, *House and Household*, 7.

36. Quoted by Morgan, *The Puritan Family*, 18.

37. Gerald T. Sheppard, ed., *The Geneva Bible: The Annotated New Testament, 1602 Edition*, facs. ed., The Pilgrim Classic Commentaries Series (New York: The Pilgrim Press, 1989), 85, nn. 2, 4, 7, and 8.

38. Ibid., n. 11.

39. Morgan, *The Puritan Family*, 44–48. For a similar situation a century later, see *Religion and Domestic Violence in Early New England: The Memoirs of Abigail Abbot Bailey*, ed. Ann Taves (Bloomington: Indiana University Press, 1989).

40. Specifically on Hall's conservative views about the roles of women, see T. F. Kinloch, *The Life and Works of Joseph Hall* (London: Staples Press, 1951), 70–72.

41. Morgan, *The Puritan Family*, 25–28; and Lawrence Stone, *The Family, Sex, and Marriage in England, 1500–1800* (London: [publisher], 1977).

42. James Kugel, *The Idea of Biblical Poetry: Parallelism and Its History* (New Haven: Yale University Press, 1981), 51–58, in contrast to the modern assumptions about parallelism in Hebrew poetry that Bishop Lowth popularized at the end of the eighteenth century, *contra* Huntley, *Bishop Joseph Hall*, 55.

43. On Hall's view of women, see n. 40.

44. Lisa Jardine, *Still Harping on Daughters: Women and Drama in the Age of Shakespeare* (New York: Columbia University Press, 1989), with additional bibliography. See also K. Wrightson, *English Society, 1580–1680* (London, 1984), chap. 4; and Friedman, *House and Household*, 6–8.

45. Friedman, *House and Household*, 61.

46. Morgan, *The Puritan Family*, 54–56.

47. Cf. Gerald T. Sheppard, "Interpretation of the Old Testament Between Reformation and Modernity," in William Perkins *A Commentary on Hebrews 11 (1609 Edition)*, facs. ed., Pilgrim Classic Commentaries Series, ed. John Augustine (New York: The Pilgrim Press, 1991), 62–63, and Sheppard, "Between Reformation and Modernity," lxii.

48. Cf. Brevard S. Childs, "Proverbs, Chapter 7, and a Biblical Approach to Sex," in *Biblical Theology in Crisis* (Philadelphia: The Westminster Press, 1970), 184–200.

49. See the Introduction to this volume, n. 6.

50. Hall, "Contemplations," 1271.

Index

Proverbs

Note: The biblical references here reflect the numerical order of the RSV and when the numeration of Hall's work differs, it is recorded after the RSV numeration in square brackets. When a typographical mistake was found in the original numbering, the correct verse numeration was used in the index but it is followed by "(written x)," with x as the inaccurate numerical notation exactly as it appears in the book. When verses are cited by Hall in numerical succession but in reverse order the reference is followed by "(reverse)." Not every typographical error or wrong citation has been detected. Also, at several places, the printer failed to record the numerical citation after the abbreviation "Pr.," for example, see pp. 19, 37, 44, 47, and so forth. This index makes no effort to locate and to identify all of these mistakes or omissions, therefore, its value is heuristic and subject to the many limitations of this particular edition.

The Pilgrim Classic Commentaries
Volumes in the Series
Gerald T. Sheppard, Series Editor

The Geneva Bible
The Annotated New Testament, 1602 Edition
(Facsimile Edition)
with Introductory Essays

The Geneva Bible and English Commentary, 1600–1645, *by Gerald T. Sheppard*
The Geneva (Tomson/Junius) New Testament Among Other English Bibles of the Period, *by Marvin W. Anderson*
"Cleared by Faith": The Use of Scriptural Precedent in English Protestant Defenses of Poetry, *by John H. Augustine*
From England to New England: The Protestant and "Puritan" Movement, 1600–1645, *by Nicholas W. S. Cranfield*

A Commentary on Galatians (*1617 Edition*)
(Facsimile Edition)
by William Perkins
with Introductory Essays

William Perkin's Exposition Among Seventeenth-Century Commentaries, 1600–1645, *by Gerald T. Sheppard*
Reflections on the Reissue of William Perkins' *Commentary on Galatians, by Brevard S. Childs*
Authority and Interpretation in Perkins' *Commentary on Galatians, by John H. Augustine*
Between Reformation and Modern Commentary: The Perception of the Scope of Biblical Books, *by Gerald T. Sheppard*

SALOMONS
Diuine Arts,
Of
1. ETHICKES,
2. POLITICKES,
3. OECONOMICKS:

That is ; the Gouernment

Of { 1. BEHAVIOVR,
2. COMMON-VVEALTH,
3. FAMILIE.

Drawne into Method, out of his
Prouerbs & *Ecclesiastes.*

With an open and plaine Paraphrase, vpon the
SONG *of* SONGS.

By *Ioseph Hall.*

AT LONDON,
Printed by *H.L.* for
Eleazar Edgar, and
Samuel Macham.
1609.

TO THE RIGHT
HONOVRABLE AND
Hopefull Lord, ROBERT,
Earle of Essex, my singular
good Lord, all increase
of Grace & true
Honour,

RIGHT HONOVRABLE,

Hiles I desired to congratu-
late your happy Returne
with some worthy present;
I fel vpon this : which I dare
not only offer, but commend ; the royal-
lest Philosopher and wisest king, giuing
you those precepts, which the Spirit of
God gaue him. The matter is all his;

no-

nothing is mine, but the methode; which
I doe willingly ſubmit to cenſure. In
that he could not erre: In this, I cannot
but haue erred; either in art, or application, or ſenſe, or diſorder, or defeĉt :
yet not wilfully. I haue meant it well,
and faithfully to the Church of God, &
to your Honor, as one of her great hopes.
If any man ſhall cauill that I haue gone
about to correĉt Salomons order, or
to controule Ezekias ſeruants : I complaine both of his charity, and wiſdom;
and appeale more lawefull iudgement:
Let him aſwell ſay, that euery Concordance peruerts the Text. I haue only en-
deuoured to be the common-place-booke
of that great king, and to referre his
diuine rules to their heads, for more eaſe
of finding, for better memory, for readier vſe. See, how that God, whoſe wiſdom
thought good to bereaue mankinde of
Salomons profounde commentaries of
Nature, hath reſerued theſe his diuine
Morals, to out-liue the world; as know-

ing,

ing, that thofe would but feed mans cu-
riofitie, thefe would both direct his life,
and iudge it. Hee hath not done this
without expectation of our good, and
glory to himfelfe: which if wee anfwere,
the gaine is ours. I know how little need
there is, either to intreat your Lo : ac-
ceptation, or to aduife your vfe. It is
enough to haue humbly prefented them
to your hands; and through them to the
Church: the defire of whofe good, is my
good ; yea, my recompence and glory.
The fame God, whofe hand hath led and
returned you in fafetie, from all for-
raine euils : guide your wayes at home,
& gratioufly increafe you in the ground
of all true honor; Goodneffe. My praiers
fhall euer follow you:

VVho vow my felfe
Your Honours,

in all humble and true
duetie,

Iof. Hall.

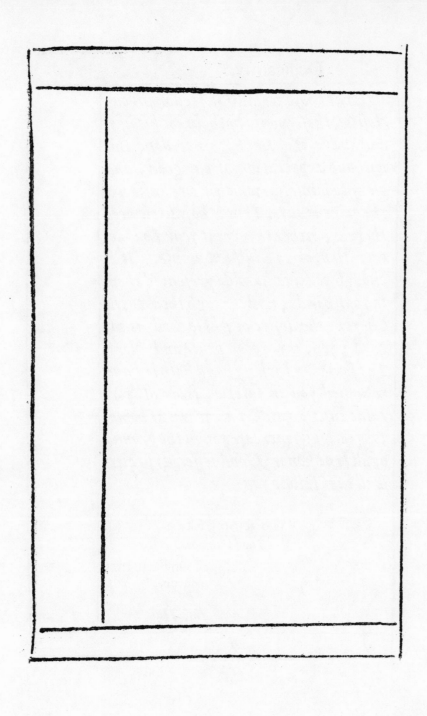

SALOMONS

OECONOMICKS,

or Gouernment of
the FAMILY.

1. { HVSBAND,
     WIFE.

2. { PARENT,
     CHILDE.

3. { MASTER,
     SERVANT.

Anno Domini, 1609.

SALOMONS

Ethickes, or Gouerne-
ment of Behauiour and
Manners.

THE firſt BOOKE.

FELICITY.

§. 1. Of *Ethicks* in common: ⎰ The deſcription,
⎱ The chiefe end, which is *Felicity*.

ETHICKS *is a Doc-*
trine of wiſedom and
knowledge *to liue wel,*
and ot the madneſs and fooliſhneſſe *of vice* : *or* Inſtruction to

Ecc.1.17.

Ecc.7.27.

doe

'r. 1. 3.

Ec. 3. 12.

Ec. 2. 3.

doe wisely by iustice and iudgement and equitie, and to doe
good in our life. *The end wherof
is* to see *and attaine* that *chiefe*
goodnes of the children of men,
which they inioy vnder the sun,
the whole number of the dayes
of their life.

§. 2. Wherein
Felicity is not.

Not in pleasure,

Not in wealth.
For heerein is

1. No satisfaction
2. Increased ex-
   pence,
3. Restlesnesse,
4. Want of fruiti-
   on,
5. Vncertainty,
6. Necessity of lea-
   uing it.

Ec. 2. 1.

VVHich *cōsists* not in ple-
sure; *for* I sayd in mine
heart, Go to now, I will prooue
thee with ioy, therfore take thou

plea-

pleafure in pleafant things; yea, I with-drewe not my heart from any ioy: for my heart reioyced in all my labour : and who could eat, and who could hafte to out-warde things more then I? and beholde, this alfo is vanitie.

Ec. 2. 10.

Ec. 2. 25

Ec. 2. 1.

Not in riches. ¹· For he that loueth filuer fhall not be fatisfide with filuer, and hee that loueth riches fhall be without the fruite of them : this alfo is vanity.

Ec. 5. 9.

²· When riches increafe they are increafed that eate them: and what good commeth to the owners thereof, but the beholding therof with their eies? *yea, much euill*; for *whereas* the fleep of him that trauelleth is fweet, whether he eate little, or much; *contrarily*,

Ec. 5. 10

Ec. 5. 11.

Ec.5.12.

The fatietie of the rich will not suffer him to fleepe; fo there is an euill fickeneffe, which I haue feene vnder the Sunne, riches referued to the owners thereof, for their euill, *and ofter*, *not for*

Ec.6.1.

their good: for there is another euill, which I haue feene vnder the Sunne, and it is frequent a-

Ec.6.2.

mong men; A man to whome God hath giuen riches and treafures, and honour, and he wanteth nothing for his foule, of all it defireth; but God giueth him not power to eate thereof; *and if hee haue that*, *yet how long ?*

Pr.27.24.

Riches *remaine* not alwayes, but

Pr.23.5.

taketh her to her wings as an Eagle, and flyeth to the heauens.

Ec.5.14.

And for their owner, As he came

forth

forth of his mothers belly, hee
shall returne naked, to goe as he
came, and shall beare away nothing of his labour, which hee
caused to pass by his hand: And
this is also an euill sicknesse, that
in all points as hee came, so shall
he goe: and what profit hath he,
that hee hath trauelled for the
winde?

Ec. 5. 15.

§. 3. Not in magnificence
- of estate
  - royaltie,
  - great attendance.
- of works
  - planting,
  - gathering Treasures,
  - building, &c.

NOt *in honor & magnificence.*
I the Preacher haue beene
King ouer Israell in Ierusalem,
and I was great, and increased a-
boue all that were before me in

Ec. 1. 12.

Ec. 1. 16.
Ec. 2. 9.

Ierufalem, *which alfo J fhowed in*
effect; for I made me great works,
I built me houfes, I planted me
vineyards, I made me gardens,
and orchards, & planted in them
trees of all fruites; I made mee
ponds of water, to water therewith the woods that growe with
trees; I got me feruants, & maids,
and had children borne in the
houfe; alfo I had great poffeffi-
on of beeues, and fheep, aboue
all that were before me in Ierufalem; I gathered to me alfo filuer and gold, and the chief treafures of kings and prouinces; I
prouided Men-fingers, & Wo-
men-fingers, and the delights of
the fonnes of men, muficall con-
forts of all kindes : Yea, I King

Ec. 2. 4.

Ec. 2. 5.

Ec. 2. 6.

Ec. 2. 7.

Ec. 2. 8.

S A L O M O N made my selfe a
Palace of the trees of Lebanon;
I made the Pillars thereof of siluer, and the pauement thereof
of golde; the hangings thereof
of purple; whose mids was pa-
ued with the loue of the daughters of Israel: Then I looked on
all my vvorkes that my hands
had wrought, (as who is the
man that will compare with the
King in things which men now
haue done? and on the trauell
that I laboured to doe; and beholde all is vanitie, and vexation
of spirit; and there is no profit
vnder the sunne.

Cant. 3. 9.

Cãt. 3. 10.

Ecc. 2. 11.

Ecc. 2. 12.

Ec. 2. 11.

§. 4. Long life and issue reiected, for
{
certaine end,
vnperfect satisfaction,
remembrance and continuance of darkenesse.
}

Ec. 6. 3.

NOt *in long life, and plentious issue: for* If a man beget an hundreth children, and liue many yeares, and the dayes of his yeares be multiplyed; And his soule be not satisfide with good things, and hee be not buryed, I say that an vntimely fruit is better then he. For he commeth in-to vanity, and goeth into darkenesse, and his name shalbe coue-red with darkenesse: Also, hee hath not seen the sun, nor knowen it; therefore, this hath more rest then the other: And if hee

Ec. 6. 4.

Ec. 6. 5.

had

had liued a thoufand years twife
tolde , and had feene no good;
fhall not all goe to one place?
and howfoeuer , the light furely
is a pleafant thing, and it is good
for the eyes to fee the funne; yet
tho a man liue many yeares, and
in them all he reioice; if he fhall
remember the dayes of darkeneffe , becaufe they are manie,
all that commeth is Vanitie.

§. 5. Knowledge { Tho better then folly;
yet reiec { experience,
ted, vpon { indifferécy of euéts,
imperfection.

NOt *in learning , and humane
knowledge.* I haue giuen my
heart to fearch and find out wifdome, in all things that are done

vnder

Ec. 6.6

Ec. 11.7.

Ec. 11.8.

Ec. 1.13.

vnder the heauen, (this fore trauaile hath God giuē to the fons
of men to humble them therby)
yea, I thought in my heart and
fayd, Beholde I haue amplified
and increafed wifedome, aboue
all them that haue beene before
mee, in *the Court and Vniuerfitie
of* Ierufalem , and mine heart
hath feene much wifedome and
knowledge : for (*when J was at
the wildeſt*) my wifedome remained with mee : Then I fawe, in-
indeede, that there is profit in
wifedome more then in folly ;
as the light is more excellent
then darkeneffe ; For the wife-
mans eyes are in his head, but
the foole walketh in darkeneffe :
but yet, I knowe that the fame

Ec. 1.16.

Ec.2.9.

Ec. 2.13

Ec. 2.14.

condition falleth to them all :
Then I thought in mine heart; *Ec.2.15.*
It befalleth to mee as it befalleth
to the foole; why therefore doe
I labour to be more wife ? For,
what hath the Wife-man more *Ec.6.8.*
then the foole ? There shall bee
no remembraunce of the wife, *Ec.2.16.*
nor of the foole for euer : for
that that now is , in the dayes
to come shall bee forgotten ;
and how dieth the Wife-man? as
dooth the foole : *Besides the im-*
perf Ation of the best knowledge ;
for the eye is not satisfie with *Ec. 1. 8.*
feeing , nor the eare filled with
hea ing : I thought I wil be wife: *Ec.7 25.*
but it wert farre from mee ; it
is farre off, what may it bee ?
and it is a profound deepenefs,

who

who can find it? *yea, so farre is it from giuing contentment, that* in the multitude of wisdō is much griefe, and hee that increaseth knowledge, increaseth forrowe.

Lastly, not in any humane thing: for I haue considered all the workes that are done vnder the funne; and behold, all is vanity & vexation of spirit.

Ec.1.18.

Ec.1.14.

§. 6. Wherein Felicity is
.i. In approuing our selues
to GOD. From hence

- Life,
  - Fauour,
  - Ioy,
  - Blessing
    - Preseruation,
    - Prosperity,
    - Long life, &c.

VVHerein then doth it con-*sist?* Let vs heare the end of all; Feare God, and keep his Commandements; for this

Ec.12.13.

is the whole of Man, *the* whole *dutie*, *the* whole *scope*, *the* whole *happinesse*; *for* Life is in the waie of righteousnesse, and in that path there is no death ; *and attending thereon*, *all* Blessings are vpon the head of the righteous. *Wouldst thou haue fauour?* A good man getteth fauour of the Lord: *Joy?* The righteous shall sing & reioice ; *and* surely to a man that is good in his sight, God giueth wisedome and knowledge and ioie; *so that* the light of the righteous reioyceth, but the candle of the wicked shall be put out: *Preseruation and deliuerance?* Lo, the righteous is as an euerlasting foundation ; *for* the waie of the Lord is strength to the vpright

Pr. 12.24
Pr. 11.19

Pr. 10. 6

Pr. 12.2

Pr. 29.6

'Ec.2.26

Pr. 13.9

Pr. 10.25

Pr. 10.29

man

Pr. 10.30.

Pr. 11 4.

Pr. 12. 13.

Pr. 11. 8.

Pr. 13. 6.

Pr. 15. 6

Pr. 14. 11.

Pr. 10. 27.

Pr. 12. 7
Ec. 8. 12.

man, *fo as* the righteous fhall neuer be remoued ; *and if hee be in trouble*, Riches auaile not in the daie of wrath, but righteoufneffe deliuereth from death ; fo the righteous fhall come out of aduerfitie, and efcape out of trouble, and the wicked fhall come in his ftead : *thus euery way* Righteoufnes preferueth the vp-right in heart ; *Profperitie and wealth* ? The houfe of the righteous fhall haue much treafure, and his Tabernacle fhall florifh. *Long life* ? The feare of the Lord increafeth the daies ; *& not onely himfelfe*, but his houfe fhall ftand ; And though a finner do euill an hundred times, and God prolong his daies, yet know I that it

fhall

ſhall be well to them that feare
the Lord, & do reuerēce before
him; *and laſtly, whatſoeuer good*?
God will grant the deſire of the
righteous, and hee that keepeth
the lawe is bleſſed.

Pr. 10. 2. 4
Pr. 29. 18

§. 7. In the eſtate of wickedneſs

our good things are accurſed
- Wealth,
- Life,
- Fame,
- Deuotiōs; — Prayers, Sacrifices.

Euill inflicted; of
- Loſſe,
- Paine; — Affliction, Death, Damnatiō.

Cbr Ontrarily, ther is perfect miſe-
ry in wickedneſſ. Looke on all
that might ſeem good in this eſtate;
welth. The treſures of the wicked
profit nothing; the L. will not fa-
miſh the ſoule of the righteous,
but he *either* caſteth away the ſub

Pr. 10. 2
Pr. 10. 3

stance of the wicked, *so that* the belly of the wicked shall want, *or els imploieth it to the good of his*: for the wicked shal be a ransome for the iust; & to the sinner God giueth paine to gather, and to heap, to giue to him that is good before God. *The wicked man may be rich*: *but how?* The reuenues of the wicked is trouble. *Life*; The yeares of the wicked shall bee diminished : As the whirle-winde passeth, so is the wicked no more; *for* God ouerthroweth the wicked, and they are not. *Whatsoeuer therefore their hope be*, the wicked shall be cut off from the earth, & the transgressors shall be rooted out; It shall not be well to the wicked,

Pr.13.25.

Pr.21.18.

Ec.2.26.

Pr. 15.6.

Pr.10.27.

Pr.10.25.

Pr.12.7.

Pr.2.22.

Ec.8.13.

neither

neither ſhall he prolõg his daies; he ſhall be like to a ſhadow, becauſe he feared not God; *yea, the very* houſe of the wicked ſhall bee deſtroyed. *Fame. Whereas* the memoriall of the iuſt ſhall be bleſſed, the name of the wicked ſhall rot: *yea looke vpon his beſt indeauours* ; *His Prayers.* The Lord is farre off from the wicked, but heareth the prayer of the righteous: *farre off from accepting. for* Hee that turneth away his eare from hearing the lawe, euen his prayer ſhall bee abhominable; His ſacrifice (*tho well intended*) as al the reſt of his wayes, is *no better then* abhomination to the Lord; how much more when hee brings it with a

Pr. 14. 11.

Pr. 10. 7

Pr. 15. 29

Pr. 28. 9

Pr. 15. 8

Pr. 15 9.

Pr. 21. 27.

wicked minde ? *And as no good,*
so much euill; whether of losse : The
way of the wicked will deceiue
them; their hope shall perish, e-
specially when they dy; their candle shall be put out, their works
shall proue deceitful; *Or of paine;*
for the excellent that formed all
things, rewardeth the foole, and
the Transgressour; *and hee hath*
appointed, that Affliction should
follow sinners : *Follow? yea ouer-*
take them; His own iniquity shall
take the wicked himself, and co-
uer his mouth; and hee shall be
holden with the coardes of his
own sinne : *euen* in the transgression of the euill man is his snare;
so the wicked shall fall in his own
wickednes: *for of it own selfe,* Iniquity

Pr. 12. 26.

Pr. 10. 28

Pr. 13. 9.

Pr. 11. 18.

Pr. 26. 10

Pr. 13. 21

Pr. 5. 22.

Pr. 10. 6.

Pr. 29. 6.

Pr. 11. 5

quitie ouerthroweth the finner : | Pr. 13. 6.

But befides that, the curfe of the | Pr. 3. 33
Lord is in the houfe of the wic-
ked : tho hand ioyne *in* hand, | Pr.
he fhall not be vnpunifhed : be-
holde, the Righteous fhall bee | Pr. 11. 31.
payde vppon earth, how much
more the vvicked and the fin-
ner ? That *then* vvhich the wic- | Pr. 10. 24
ked man feareth fhall come vp-
pon him ; *both,* ᴅ*eath* ; Hee
fhall die for default of inftruc- | Pr. 5. 23.
tion, *and that by his owne hands* :
for, by following euill hee feeks | Pr. 11. 19.
his ovvne death ; *and after that*
damnation ; The vvicked fhall | Pr. 14. 32
bee caft awaie for his malice :
Hell and deftruction are before | Pr. 15. 11.
the L O R D ; and a man of
vvicked imaginations vvill hee | Pr. 12. 2.

Pr.10.29.

Pr.19.29.

condemn; *ſo both in life, in death,*
after it, nothing but Terror ſhall
be for the workers of iniquitie:
where contrarily, The feare of
the Lord leadeth to life, and hee
that is filled therewith ſhall con-
tontinue, and ſhall not be viſited
with euill.

SALO-

SALOMONS
ETHICKES.

The second Booke.

PRVDENCE.

§. 1.Of Vertue in cómon: {Wherein it consisteth. Whereby it is ruled, and directed.

Ertue consistes in the *mean; vice in extreams.* Let thy wayes bee ordered aright ; Turne not to the right hand, nor to the left, but remoue thy foote from euill; *The rule whereof is Gods*

Pr. 4.26.

Pr. 4.27

Pr. 6. 23.

Pr. 30. 5.

Pr. 4. 20.

Pr. 4. 21.

Pr. 4. 22.

Pr. 7. 2.

Pr. 7. 3.

Lawe: for the commandement is a lantern, and inſtruction a light; and euery word of God is pure. My ſon, hearken to my words; incline thine eare to my ſayings; Let them not depart from thine eies; but keepe them in the midſt of thine heart. For, they are life vnto thoſe that finde them, and health vnto all their fleſh. Keepe my commandements and thou ſhalt liue, and mine Inſtruction as the apple of thine eye: Binde them vpon thy fingers, & write them vppon the Table of thine heart.

All Vertue is eyther {
Prudence,
Iustice,
Temperance,
Fortitude.

1. Of Prudence: which comprehends {
Wisdome,
Prouidence,
Discretion.

§. 2. Of wisdome; the {
Description,

Effectes.
It procures {
Knovvledge:
safety {
from sinne,
from iudgemēt.

good direction {
for actions,
for words.

Wealth, Honor, Life.

THe prudent man is he, whose eyes are in his head *to see all things, and to foresee; and* whose heart is at his right hand *to doe all dextrouslie, and with iudgement.* VVisedome dwelles with Pru-

Ec. 2. 14.

Ec. 10. 2.

Pr 8. 12.

C 4   dence,

dence and findeth forth knowledge, and counfels. *And to de-*
fcribe it : The wifedome of the
Prudét is to vnderftand his way ;
his owne ; If thou bee wife , thou
fhalt be wife for thy felfe : *An ex-*
cellent vertue. for Bleffed is the
man that findeth wifedome, and
getteth vnderftandinge : The
merchandife thereof is better
then the merchandife of filuer,
and the gaine thereof is better
then golde : It is more precious
then pearles, and all the things
that thou canft defire are not to
bee compared to her. Length
of dayes are in her right hand ;
and in her left hand riches and
glory: Her wayes are wayes of
pleafure, and all her pathes pro-
                              fperity:

Pr. 14. 8.

Pr. 9. 12.

Pr. 3. 13.

Pr. 3. 14.

Pr. 16. 16

Pr. 3. 15.

Pr. 3. 16.

Pr. 3. 17.

fperitie: Shee is a tree of life to
them that laie holde on her, and
bleſſed is he that receiueth her.
*The fruites of it are ſingular: for,
firſt,* A wiſe heart doth *not only
ſeeke, but* get knowledge, without which the minde is not good;
& the eare of the wiſe, learning;
and not get it onely but lay it vp,
and not ſo onely but workes by it;
and yet more, is crowned with it.
Beſides knowledge, heere is ſafety.
When wiſdome entreth into thy
heart, and knowledge delighteth thy ſoule, then ſhall counſell preſerue thee, and vnderſtanding ſhall keep thee: and deliuer thee from the euil way, and
from the man that ſpeaketh froward things, and from them that

leaue

Pr.3.18.

Pr.15.14.

Pr.18.15.

Pr. 19. 2

Pr.10.14.
Pr.13.16.

Pr.14.18.

Pr. 2. 10.

Pr. 2. 11.

Pr.2.12.

Pr.2.13.

leaue the wayes of righteoufneffe, to walke in the wayes of
darkeneffe : *and as from finne, fo*
Pr. 15.24. *from iudgement.* The way of life
is on hy to the Prudent, to avoid
from heli beneath. *Thirdly, good*
direction. 1. *For actions*; Wifdom
Pr. 8.20. caufeth to walke in the waie of
righteoufnes, and in the mids of
the paths of iudgement : 2. *For*
Pr.16.23. *words*, The hart of the wife guideth his mouth wifely , and ad-
deth doctrine to his lips ; *So that*
Pr. 10.12. the words of the mouth of a wife
man haue grace : *yea, he receiues*
grace from others. Either Inftruct,
Pr. 19.25 *or* reprooue the Prudent, and he
wil vnderftand knowledge. *Not*
to fpeake of wealth ; fhee caufeth
Pr.8.21. them that loue hir to inherit fub-

ſtance, and filleth their treaſures: *ſhe giueth not onely honor* : *for* the wiſdome of a man doth make his face to ſhine, *&* the wiſeman ſhal inherit glory; *but life*. Vnderſtanding is a wel-ſpring of life to him that hath it; *and* he that findeth me (*ſayth wiſdome*) findeth life, and ſhall obtaine fauour of the Lord. *Wherfore* Get wiſdom; get vnderſtanding; forget not, neither decline from the words of my mouth. Forſake her not, and ſhe ſhall keep thee; loue her, & ſhe ſhall preſerue thee. Wiſdom is the beginning; get wiſedome *therfore*, & aboue all poſſeſſions get vnderſtanding: Exalt her and ſhee ſhall exalt thee : Shee ſhall bring thee vnto honour, if thou

Ecc.8.11.
Pr.3.35

Pr.16.22

Pr.8.34

Pr.4.5.

Pr.4.6.

Pr.4.7.

Pr.4.8.

em-

Pr. 4. 9.

embrace her : fhee fhall giue a
goodly ornament to thine head;
yea, fhe fhall giue thee a crowne
of glorie:

§. 3. Of Prouidence $\begin{cases} \text{What fhee is,} \\ \text{What her obiects,} \\ \text{What her effectes,} \end{cases}$

Ec. 8. 5.

PRouidence *is that* wherby the
heart of the wife *fore*-knowe-
th the time, and iudgement; *the
time when it will be;* the iudgemét
how it will bee done: both which

Ec. 8. 6.

are appointed to euery purpofe
vnder heauen: *Not that man can
fore-fee all future things*: No, he

Ec. 8. 7.

knoweth not that, that fhall be ;
For who can tel him when it fhal
be? *not fo much as cócerning him-*

Ec. 9. 12.

felfe. Neither doth man knowe
his time, but as the fifhes are ta-

ken

ken with an euill net, and as the birdes which are caught in the snare; so are the children of men snared in the euill time, when it falleth on them suddenly; yea, the steps of a man are ruled by the Lord; how should a man thē vnderstand his owne way? *but, sometimes hee may*: The prudent man seeth the plague afarre off, and fleeth; *and as for good things*, With the Pismire hee prouideth his meat in summer; *working still according to fore-knowledge; yet not too strictly, and fearefully*; for he that obserueth the wind shall not sowe, and he that regardeth the cloudes shall not reape.

Pr. 20. 24

Pr. 22. 3

Pr. 30. 25.

Ecc. 11. 4

§. 4. Of Difcretion: { what it is,

{ what it worketh { for our acts { for our { fpeeches.

Pr. 16.20.

Pr. 16.23.

D_ífcretion is that whereby_ a man is wife in his bufineffes, _and whereby_ the heart of the wife guideth his mouth wifely, & addeth doctrine to his lips. _For actions_ :

Pr. 14.15.

The Prudent wil confider his fteps, _and make choice of times:_ _for,_ To all things there is an ap-

Ec. 3. 1.

pointed time ; and a time for e-uery purpofe vnder heauen ; a time to plant, & a time to pluck

Ec. 3. 2.

vp that which is planted ; a time to flay, and a time to heale, &c.

Ec. 3. 3.
3. 4.
Ec. 3. 8.

A time of warre and a time of peace : _From hence it is that_ the

Pr. 24. 5.

wife man is ftrong , _and rich_ ; for

by

by knowledge shall the Chambers be fild with precious things *which he knows how to employ wel:* The crown of the wise is their riches ; *from hence, that* his good vnderstanding maketh him acceptable *to others. For speeches,* The tongue of the wise vseth knowledge aright, *&* in the lips of him that hath vnderstanding wisdome is found; & his words haue grace, *both' for the seasonablenes,* A word spoké in his place is like apples of Gold with pictures of siluer, & how good is a word in due seaso! *² for the worth of them,* The lips of knowledge are a precios iewel; *lastly, for their vse :* the lips of the wise shall preserv them, & their toung is helth,

Pr. 14.24

Pr. 13.15

Pr. 15. 2.

Pr. 10.13

Pr 10.12.

Pr. 25. 11.

Pr. 15.23.

Pr. 20.15.

Pr. 14.3.

Pr. 12. 18

and

Pr.16.24.

and with health pleafure; Fayre wordes are as an hony-combe; fweetneffe to the foule; & health to the bones.

§. 5. The extreames
{
  Ouer-wife,
  Foolifh
}
{
  VVho hee is :
  what kinds
  there bee
  of Fooles;
  VVhat fucceffe.
}
{
the meer foole :
the rafh foole:
the wicked fool.
}

Ec.7. 18.

Ec. 7. 19.

Pr. 21.16

Pr. 17. 16

Pr. 15. 2.

HEre are *two extreams: On the right hand*; Make not thy felf ouer-wife, wherfore fhouldft thou be defolate? *on the left*: Neither be foolifh; why fhouldft thou perifh, not in thy time ? The fool *is that man* that wandreth out of the waie of wifdom, which hath none hart, *that is*, is deftitute of vnderftanding, *either to conceiue, or to do as he ought*: *Of which fort*

is

is, 1. *The meere foole;* That foole who when he goeth by the waie, his heart fayleth; whofe folly is foolifhneffe, in whofe hand there is a price *in vaine* to get wifdom, *which* is too high for him *to atain:* *laftly,* In whom are not the lips of knowledge. 2. *The rafh foole,* that is haftie in his matters, that povvreth out all his minde *at once;* which the wife man keepes in, till afterwarde; *that* hafteth with his feet *and therfore finneth.* There is more hope of *the other* foole then of him. 3. *The wicked foole:* That defpifeth wifedome and inftruction, that maketh a mock of finne; to whom it is an abhomination to depart from e-uill; to whom foolifhneffe is ioy,

Pr. 14. 24.

Pr. 17. 16.

Pr. 24. 7.

Pr. 14. 7.

Pr. 29. 20.

Pr. 29. 11.

Pr. 19. 2.

Pr. 29. 20

Pr. 1. 7.

Pr. 14. 9.

Pr. 13. 19

Pr. 15. 21.

Pr.10.23.
Pr. 13.16.
Pr.27.22.
Pr. 26. 11.
Pr.23.9.
Pr.1.22.
Pr. 1.23.

yea, it is his paftime to doe wickedly, *and his practice* to fpread
abroad folly : *And this man is ob-
ftinate in his courfes; fo* r tho thou
bray a foole in a morter among
wheat, brayd with a peftell, yet
wil not his foolifhnes depart from
him : *and tho it feem to depart, yet*
as a dog turneth again to his vo-
mit, fo returns hee to his foolifhnes. *Spare thy labor therfore,* fpeak
not in the eares of a foole, for he
will defpife the wifdome of thy
words. *To thefe faith wifdome,* O
ye foolifh, how long will ye loue
foolifhnes, and the fcornfull take
pleafure in fcorning, and fooles
hate knowledge ? Turne you at
my correction. Lo, I will powre
out my mind vnto you; & make

you

you vnderſtand my words : Becauſe I haue called and ye refuſed,I haue ſtretched out my hãd,
and none would regard; But ye
haue deſpiſed all my counſell,
and would none of my correction ; I will alſo laugh at your
deſtruction, and mocke vvhen
your feare commeth; like ſuddaine deſolation, and your deſtruction ſhall come like a whirl-
winde; when affliction, and an-
guiſh ſhall come vppon you .
Then ſhall they call vppon mee,
but I will not anſwere: they ſhall
ſeeke mee early, but they ſhall
not finde me; Becauſe they hated knovvledge , and did not
chooſe the feare of the Lord ;
they would none of my counſel,

Pr.1.24

Pr.1.25.

Pr.1.26.

Pr.1.27.

Pr.1.28.

Pr. 1. 29.

Pr.1. 30.

but deſpiſed all my correction;
Therefore ſhall they eate of the
fruite of their owne way, and be
filled vvith their owne deuiſes :
and what is that fruit but ſorrow ?
Euen in laughing their heart is
ſorrowfull ; and the end of that
mirth is heauineſſe : *and* like the
noiſe of thornes vnder a pot, ſo
(*ſhort and vaine*) is the laughter
of fools : *what but ſtripes ?* A rod
ſhall be for the back of him that
is deſtitute of vnderſtanding :
yea, it is proper to him. To the
horſe belongeth a whip, to the
aſſe a bridle, & a rod to the fools
backe : *wherewith not onely him-*
ſelfe ſhal be beaten, but the companion of fools ſhal be afflicted :
Laſtly, what but death ? Fooles

Pr. 1. 31.

Pr. 14. 13.

Ec. 7. 8.

Pr. 10. 13.

Pr. 26. 3.

Pr. 10. 8. 10.

Pr. 13. 20.

ſhall

shall dy for want of wit, and remain iu the congregation of the
dead ; *yea* the mouth of the foole
is prefent deftruction ; *and* The
lippes of a foole shall deuoure
himfelfe, *and that which should*
feeme to preferue him, Very eafe
slayeth the foolish, and the profperitie of fooles deftroyeth
them.

Pr.10. 21.

Pr.21. 16.

Pr. 10. 14

Pr.

Pr.1.32

D 3　　SALO-

SALOMONS
ETHICKES.

THE third BOOKE.

JVSTICE.

Iuſtice gives to each his owne;

To God, Pietie: which cōprehends { Feare, Honour and reſpeſt, Obedicnce. } *

To God & man { Fidelitie, Truth { in words, in dealings. } Loue. }

To man only { others { Mercie, Liberalitie. } our ſelues ; Diligēce in our vocations. }

*Honor and Obedience are indeede mixed duties of Iuſtice both to God & man: but becauſe as they belong to mā, they are politick vertues & there hādled ; here we conſider thē onely as due to God.

D 4

1. Of

§. 1. { 1. Of Iustice in generall.
        { 2. Of { what it is
        { the feare of God { what fruits it hath { present
                                    { future

Pr. 15. 21.

Pr. 20. 7

Pr. 16. 17

Pr. 12. 22

Ext to Prudence, is Ju-stice. A man of vnder-standing vvalketh vp-rightly : The iuſt man, *therfore*, is he that walketh in his integrity ; *and* whoſe path is to decline from euill ; *and brieflie*, hee that deales truely , *in giuing each his owne.*

Ec. 8. 13.

Whether to God ; *vnto whome Iuſtice challengeth Pietie* : *which comprehends, firſt*, the feare of the Lord; and this feare of the Lord is to hate euil, as pride, arrogan-cie, and the euill way ; *and* in all

                                 our

our waies to acknowledge God; Pr. 3. 6.
that he may direct our waies; *so
that*, he that walketh in his righ- Pr. 14. 2
teoufnes, feareth the Lord; but
hee that is lewd in his wayes defpifeth him: *which grace, as* it is Pr. 1.7.
the beginning of knowledge, *&
the very inftruction of wifdom, Pr. 15. 33
fo in fome refpect knowledge is the
beginning of it*; *for* If thou calleft Pr. 2. 3.
after knowledge, and cryeft for
vnderftanding; If thou feekeft Pr. 2. 4.
her as filuer, and fearcheft for hir
as treafures; then fhalt thou vnderftand the feare of the Lord, Pr. 2. 5.
and finde the knovvledge of
God; *And this feare giues both
contentment*; Better is a little Pr. 15. 16.
with the feare of the Lord, then
great treafure, and trouble ther-

with

Pr.23.18.

with; *and* 2. *future hope*. Feare the Lord continually : for surely there is an end, & thy hope shall not be cut off. *In which regarde,*

Pr. 14.26

This feare of the Lord is an assured strength *to depende vpon*; *because* his childrē shal haue hope *yea & present health & ioy.* Feare

Pr.3.7.

the Lord, & depart from euil; so

Pr.3.8.

health shall be to thy nauell, and marrowe to thy bones: *and with health, life eternall;* The feare of

Pr. 19.23

the Lord leadeth to life , *yea* is a

Pr.14.27.

welspring thereof, and he that is filled therewith, shall continue, and shall not be visited with euil;

Pr. 28.14

so that Blessed is the man that feareth alway : *whereas on the cōtrary*, He that hardneth his hart,

Pr.30.9.

and denies God , and saith who

is

is the Lord, shall fall into euill.

Pr.28.14.

§. 2.
Honor
- in the best things,
- in the best times.

Obedience
- in attending on his will,
- in performing it.

2. **H**Onor *& respect ; both from the best things*: Honor the Lord, with thy riches, and the first fruits of all thy increase ; so shall thy barnes be filled with abundance, and thy presses shall burst with new wine : *and in our best times ;* Remember now thy Creatour in the dayes of thy youth ; vvhile the euill dayes come not, nor the yeares approach, wherein thou shalt say, I haue no pleasure in them.

Pr.3.9.

Pr. 3. 10.

Ec.12.1.

Pr. 1.33.

Thirdly, Obedience. He that o-
beyeth mee, fhall dwell fafely
(*fayth wifdome*) and be quiet frō
feare of euill: *whether in atten-*

Pr. 4.20.

dance to the will of God; My fon
hearken to my wordes, incline

Pr.4.21.

thine eare vnto my fayings; Let
them not depart from thine eies,
but keepe them in the midſt of

Pr.10.17.

thine heart: *for,* Hee that regardeth inſtruction is in the waie of

Pr. 28.9.

life; *wheras* he that turneth away
his eare from it, his *very* prayer
fhall be abhominable ; *or in exe-*

Pr. 28.7.

cuting of it. He that keepeth the
commandement is a child of vnderſtanding ; *yea* he is bleſſed, *&*

Pr.

thereby keepeth his owne foule ;

Pr.28.4.

where they that forfake the lawe
prayfe the wicked : *and* he that

                defpidespiseth his wayes shall die.

Pr. 19.16

§. 3. Fidelitie { in performances { To God, To man. } in faithfull eproofe. }

OR *whether to* G O D *and man.* 1. F I D E L I T I E: *both, first in performing that wee haue vndertaken*: If thou haue vowed a vowe to God, deferre not to paie it; for he delighteth not in fooles; pay therfore that thou haft vowed; It is better that thou shouldst not vowe ; then that thou shouldst vow, and not paie it: Suffer not thy mouth to make thy flesh to sinne; Neither fay before the Angell that this is ignorance: Wherefore shall God bee angry by thy voice, and de-

Ec. 5. 3.

Ec. 5. 4.

Ec. 5. 5.

ſtroy the worke of thine hands?

Pr. 20. 25   *For,* It is deſtruction to a man, to deuoure that which is ſanctified; and after the vowes to inquire. *Neither this to God onely,*

Pr. 12. 22.   *but to man;* They that deale truly

Pr. 28. 10.   ly are his delight; and the vpright ſhall inherite good things:

Pr. 28. 20   *yea,* The faithfull man ſhall abound in bleſſings; *whereas the perfidious man as he wrongs others*

Pr. 25. 19   (*for* Confidence in an vnfaithfull man in time of trouble, is like a broken tooth, and a ſliding foot) *ſo hee gaineth not in the end, him-*

Pr. 17. 13   *ſelfe;* He that rewardeth euill for good, euill ſhall not depart from his houſe.

Pr. 27. 5.   2. *In a faithfull reproofe:* Open rebuke is better thē ſecret loue:

The

The wounds of a louer are faithful, & the kiffes of an enemy are
pleafant, *but falfe*: fo *that* he that
reprooueth fhal find more thank
at the laft : *and how euer the* fcorner *take it* , *yet* hee that reprooueth the wife, & obedient eare
is as a golde eare-ring , and an
ornament of fine golde.

Pr. 27. 6

Pr.

Pr. 15.12.

Pr. 25. 12

§.4.truth in words
- The qualitie,
- The fruite
  - to himfelfe
  - to others
- The oppofites
  - 1.
    - Lyes,
    - Slaunder.
  - 2.
    - Diffimulation,
    - Flatterie.

Ee that fpeaketh truth will
fhovve Righteoufneffe .
Wherein ? A faithfull VVitneffe
deliuereth foules: but a deceiuer

Pr.12. 17.

Pr. 14.25

fpeaketh

ſpeaketh lyes; *A vertue of no*

Pr.18.21. *ſmall importance:for,* Death and
Life are in the hand of the
tongue; and as a man loues, he
ſhall eate the fruite thereof, *to*
good, or euill; to himſelfe, others:
Pr. 15.4 *Himſelfe*; A wholeſom tongue
Pr. 12. 19 is as a Tree of life, and the lippe
of Truth ſhall bee ſtable for e-
Pr. 10. 20. uer: *others,* The tongue of the
iuſt man is as fined ſiluer, and
Pr.10.21 the lippes of the Righteous doo
feede manie: *therefore* Buy the
Pr. 23.23. truth, and ſell it not; *as thoſe do,*
which eyther 1. *lie,* 2. *ſlaunder,*
3. *diſſemble, or* 4. *flatter.*

§. 5. The Lyer { His fashions,
His manifestation,
His punishment.

A Faithfull witnesse will not lie, but a false record will speake lyes. Of those sixe, yea seauen things that God hateth, *two are*, A lying tongue, *and* a false witnesse that speaketh lyes; *for such a one* mocketh at iudgement, *and* his mouth swallowes vp iniquity; *yea*, a false tong hateth the afflicted. *He is soone perceiued; for* a lying tong varieth incontinently: *& when he is found*, A false witnes shall not be vnpunished, & hee that speaketh lyes shal not escape; *for* the lying lips are abomination to the LORD,

Pr.14.5.

Pr.6. 16.

Pr. 6.17

Pr. 6. 19.

Pr. 19.28.

Pr.26.28

Pr.12.19

Pr. 19. 5

Pr.12. 22.

E   there-

Pr. 21.28.

Pr.25.18.

therefore a false witnesse shall perish: *and who pitties him?* Such a
one is an hammer, a sworde, a
sharpe arrow to his neighbour;
Pr.24.28. he decceiueth with his lippes and
29. sayth, I will do to him as he hath
Pr. 30.7. done to mee. Two things *then*
haue I required of thee, deny me
them not vntill I die &c. Re-
Pr.30.8. mooue farre from me vanitie, &
Pr.19.22. lyes. Let me be a poore man *ra-*
ther then a lyer.

§. 6. The slaunderer

		in misreports,
what his	exercise	in vnseasonable meddling.
	what his entertaynment.	

Pr. 16.27. **T**His wicked man diggeth vp
euil,& in his lips is like bur-
Pr.16.30. ning fire; Hee shutteth his eyes

to deuife wickedneffe : he moo-
ueth his lips, and bringeth euill
to paffe : *and either he inuenteth
ill rumours;*A righteous man hateth lying words:but the wicked
caufeth flaunder and fhame ; *or
els in true reports* he will be foo-
lifhly medling, *and* goeth about
difcouering fecrets; *(where* hee
that is of a faithful heart concealeth matters *) and by this meanes
raifeth difcorde.* Without wood
the fire is quenched, and without a tale-bearer ftrife ceafeth;
for the words of a tale-bearer are
as flatterings, and goe down into the bowells of the belly: *therfore as on the one fide,* thou mayft
not giue thine heart to all that
men fpeake of thee; leaft thou

Pr. 13.5.

Pr. 20.3.

Pr.11.13.

Pr.26.20.

Pr.18.8.

Ec.7.23.

heare thy feruant curfing thee;
fo on the other, *no countenance*
muft be giuen to fuch : *for* As the
North-wind driues away raine;
fo dooth an angry countenance
the flaundering tongue.

Pr.25.23.

§. 7.

The diffembler of foure kindes
- malicious,
- vaineglorious,
- couetous,
- impenitent.

The flatterer
- his fucceffe
  - to himfelfe,
  - to his friend.
- his remedie.

THe *flaunderer and diffembler*
goe togither : He that diffem-
bleth hatred with lying lips, and
hee that inuenteth flaunder, is a
foole ; *There is then a malicious*
diffembler : Hee that hateth will
counterfeit with his lippes, and

10. 13

Pr.26.24.

in

in his heart hee layeth vp deceit; *such one,* Tho he speake fauoura-
bly, beleeue him not; for there are seauen abhominations in his heart. Hatred may be couered with deceit; but the malice ther-of shall (*at last*) bee discouered in the congregation. *There is a vaine-glorious dissembler,* that maketh himself rich & is poore; *and* 3. *a couetous:* There is that makes himselfe poore hauing great riches; *& this both in* 1 *bar-gains:* It is naught, It is naught, sayth the buier; but when hee is gone apart; hee boasteth; *and* 2. *In his entertaynement;* The man that hath an euill eye, as though hee thought in his heart, so will hee saie to

Pr. 26.25

Pr. 26.26

Pr. 13.7.

Pr. 13 7.

Pr. 20.24

Pr. 23.6.

Pr. 23.7

thee, Eate and drinke, but his heart is not with thee : *Laftly, an*

Pr. 28. 13

impenitent ; Hee that hideth his finnes fhall not profper : but hee that confeffeth and forfaketh them fhall haue mercie. *The flat-*

Pr. 27. 14.

terer prayfeth his friend with a loude voyce, rifing early in the morning; *but with what fucceß*? *To himfelfe*; It fhall bee counted to him for a curfe : *To his friend*;

Pr. 29. 5.

A man that flattereth his neighbour, fpreadeth a net for his fteps; *hee fpreadeth and catcheth : For*

Pr. 26. 28.

a Flattering mouth caufeth ruine. *The only remedie then is*; Med-

Pr. 20. 19.

dle not with him that flattereth

Ec. 7. 7.

with his lippes; *for* It is better to heare the rebuke of wife men, then the fong of fooles.

8. Truth

§. 8. Truth in dea-
lings : wherein is
the true-dealers
— Practices — To doe right,
with ioye.
— Reward — Gods loue,
good memoriall.

THe vprightneſſe of the iuſt
ſhall guide them, and direct
their waie; *which* is euer plaine
and ſtraight; *whereas* the waie
of others is peruerted, & ſtrãge.
Yea, as to do iuſtice and iudgement is more acceptable (to the
Lord)then ſacrifice; ſo it is a ioy
to the iuſt *himſelfe*, to do iudge-
ment:all his labour therfore tendeth to life ; hee knovveth the
cauſe of the poore, and wil haue
care of his ſoule: His worke is
right, neither intendeth he anie

Pr. 11. 3.
Pr.11.5.

Pr.15.19.

Pr.21.8.

Pr.21.3.

Pr.21.15.

Pr. 10. 16

Pr. 29. 7.

Pr. 29.10

Pr.21. 8.

Pr.3.29.

euill

euill againſt his neighbour; ſeeing he dwelleth by him without feare; *and what loſeth hee by this?*

Pr. 16. 11.   *As* the true balance, and weight are of the Lord,& al the weights of the bagge are his worke : *So*

Pr. 15. 9.   God loueth him that followeth righteouſneſſe : *and with men*;

Pr. 12. 26.   The righteous is more excellét then his neighbour:*and* Better is

Pr. 28. 6.   the poore that walketh in his vprightneſſe, then hee that peruerteth his wayes, though hee be rich. *Yea finally*; The memo-

Pr. 10. 7.   riall of the iuſt ſhall bee bleſſed.

9. Deceit

The kinds
- Coloured,
- Direct
  - Priuate,
  - Publike.

§. 9. Deceit
- The iudgement attending it.

*C*Ontrary to *this is Deceit: whe-ther in a colour* ; As hee that faineth himself mad, casteth fire-brands, arrowes, and mortall things; *so* dealeth the deceitfull man, & saith, Am I not in sport? *As this* deceit is in the heart of them that imagine euill : *so in their hands are* Diuers weights, and diuers balances : *or direct-ly*, Hee that is partner with a theefe, hateth his owne soule, *and dangerous* are the wayes of him that is greedy of gaine; *much more publiquely*, I haue

Pr.26.18.

Pr.26.19.

Pr.12.20.

Pr.20.10

Pr.29.24.

Pr. 1. 19.

seene

Ec.3.16. ſeene the place of iudgement, where was wickedneſſe ; and the place of iuſtice vvhere was ini-

Ec.3.17. quitie: I thought in mine heart God will iudge the iuſt and the wicked, *yea oft-times ſpeedily* ; *ſo*

Pr.12.27. *as* The deceitfull man roaſteth not what he tooke in hunting : *or*

Pr.20.17. *if he eate it* ; The bread of deceit is ſweet to a man, but afterward his mouth ſhal be filled with gra-uell.

§.9. Loue ⎨ To God, rewarded ⎨ with his loue, / with his bleſſings. To men ⎨ In paſſing by offences, / In doing good to our enemies.

Pr.8.17. **L**Oue to God : I loue them that loue me : and they that ſeeke me early ſhall finde me ; *& with*

me,

me, *bleßings* : I cauſe them that loue me to inherit ſubſtance, and I will fill their treaſures. 2 . *To men,* 1. *Jn paßing by offences*; Hatred ſtirreth vp contentions, but loue couereth all Treſpaſſes, and the ſhame *that ariſes from them : ſo that* hee *onely* that couereth a tranſgreſſion ſeeketh loue. 2. *Jn doing good to our enemies,* If hee that hateth thee bee hungry giue him bread to eate; and if hee bee thirſty, giue him water to drinke. *Here therefore doe offend,* 1. *the contentious.* 2. *the enuious.*

Pr.8.21.

Pr. 10. 12

Pr.12.16.

Pr. 17. 9.

Pr.25.21.

§. 10. The contentious { whether in rayfing ill rumours, or whether by preffing matters too farre.

Pr. 6. 19.

TH*E first* is hee that raifeth contentions among bre-thren: *which once raifed are not fo*

Pr. 18.19.

foone appeafed. A brother offen-ded is harder to win thē a ftrong city : *and* their contentions are like the barre of a palace. *This is*

Pr. 16. 29.

that violent man that deceiueth his neighbour, and leadeth him into the way that is not good, *the way of difcord : whether by ill*

Pr. 18.6.

rumours ; The fooles lips come with ftrife ; *and* as the coale ma-

Pr. 26. 21.

keth burning coales, and wood a fire , fo the contentious man is apt to kindle ftrife ; *and that euen*

among

among great ones, A froward perfon foweth ftrife, *and* a talebea-
rer maketh diuifion among
Princes; *or by preſſing matters too* Pr. 16.28.
farre : When one churneth milk, Pr. 30.32
he bringeth forth butter; and he
that wringeth his nofe, caufeth
blood to come out : fo he that
forceth wrath, bringeth forth
ftrife, *the end wherof is neuer good* :
for if a wife man contend with a Pr. 29.9.
foolifh man, whether he bee an-
gry or laugh, there is no reft.

§. 11. Enuie
- The kinds
  - At our neighbour,
  - At the wicked.
- The effects
  - To others,
  - It felfe.

TH E *ſecond is that iniuſtice*
wherby the foule of the wic-

Pr. 21. 10.

ked wisheth euill, and his neighbour hath no fauour in his eyes;

Pr. 24.'17.

that moueth him to be glad when
his enemie falleth, and his heart
to reioyce when hee stumbleth;
and this is a violent euill. 1. *To it*

Pr. 14. 30.

selfe; A found heart is the life of
the flesh; but enuy is the rotting

Pr. 27. 4

of the bones. 2. *To others;* Anger
is cruell, and wrath is raging: but
who can stand before enuie?
But of all other it is most vniust,
when it is set vpon an euill subiect.

Pr. 24. 20

Fret not thy selfe becaufe of the
malitious, neyther bee enui-

Pr. 3. 31.

ous at the wicked, nor chufe a-
nie of his wayes; neyther let

Pr. 23. 17.

thine heart bee enuious against

Pr. 24. 1.

finners, nor defire to bee with

Pr. 24. 2.

them; *for, as* their heart ima-

gineth

gineth deſtruction , and their
lips ſpeake miſchiefe, *ſo* the fro-
warde is an abomination to the
Lord; and there ſhall bee none
end of the plagues of the euill
man ; and his light ſhall bee put
out .

Pr. 3. 32

Pr. 24.20.

§. 12. Iuſtice
To man on-
ly : Firſt to
{
  others
  1. in
  {
    Mercy
    {
      The qualitie,
      The gaine of it.
    }
  }
}

L Et not mercy and trueth forſake thee : binde them on thy
necke, and write them vpon the
table of thine heart;*this ſuffereth
not* to ſtop thine eare at the cry
of the poore : *yea,* the righteous
man regardeth the life of his

Pr.3.3.

Pr.21.13.

Pr.12.10.

beaſt;

beaſt ; *no vertue is more gainfull*:
for By mercy and trueth iniquity

    Pr.16.6.

    Pr.3.4.

ſhall bee forgiuen ; *and* By this
thou ſhalt find fauor and good
vnderſtanding in the ſight of
God and man : *Good reaſon* ; For

    Pr. 14. 31.

he honoreth God that hath mercy on the poore : *yea he makes*

    Pr.19.17.

God his debter; He that hath mer-
on the poore lendeth to the
Lord, and the Lord will recom-

    Pr.11.17.

pence him : *So that* The mercifull man rewardeth his owne

    Pr.21.21.

ſoule ; *for* Hee that followeth
righteouſneſſe and mercy , ſhall
find righteouſneſſe, and life, and

    Pr. 14. 21

glory ; *and therefore* is bleſſed
for euer.

§. 13. Againſt mercy offend
- 1. Vnmercifulneſſe,
- 2. Oppreſſion,
- Blood-thirſtineſſe.

1 THat *(not onely)* the rich ruleth the poore, but that the poore is hated of his owne neighbour; whereas the friends of the rich are many: *Of his neighbour? Yea* All the brethren of the poore hate him : how much more will his friendes depart from him ? though he be inſtant with wordes, yet they will not.

2. There is a generation, whoſe teeth are as ſwordes, and their iawes as kniues, to eate vp the afflicted out of the

Pr.22.7.

Pr.14.20.

Pr.19.7.

Pr.30.14.

F   earth

Pr. 22.16. earth. Thefe are they that oppreffe the poore to increafe
themfelues, and giue to the rich;
Pr. 22.22. *that* rob the poore, becaufe he is
poore, and oppreffe the affli-
&ted in iudgemét; that take away
Pr. 25.20. the garment in the cold feafon,
& therfore are like vineger powred vpon nitre, or like him that
fingeth fongs to an heauy heart;
Pr. 11.17. That trouble their owne flefh,
and therefore are cruell; *An ordi-*
nary finne. I turned and confi-
Ec. 4. 1. dered all the oppreffions that
are wrought vnder the Sunne;
and behold the teares of the op-
preffed, and none comforteth
them; and the ftrength is of
the hand of thofe that oppreffe
them, & none comforteth them.

None?

None? *Yes surely, aboue.* If in a country thou feeſt the oppreſſion of the poore, and the defrauding of iudgement, and iuſtice, bee not aſtonied at the matter ; for he that is hyer then the hyeſt regardeth, and there bee hyer then they, which will defend the cauſe of the poore, to *cauſe* the oppreſſour to come to pouerty : *in which eſtate* hee ſhall cry and not be heard.

3. *The bloody man is hee which not only* doth hate him that is vpright, *but* laieth wait againſt the houſe of the righteous, and ſpoyleth his reſting place; *yea* that doeth violence againſt the blood of a perſon, *Such as*

Ec. 5. 7.

Pr. 22. 23.
Pr. 22. 16.

Pr. 21. 13.

Pr. 29. 10.

Pr. 24. 15.

Pr. 18. 17.

will

Pr. 1.11. *will say,* Come with vs, wee will lay wait for blood, and lie priuily for the innocent without a cause.

Pr. 1.12. We will swallow them vp aliue like a Graue, euen whole ; as those that goe downe into the

Pr. 1.15. pit; But, my sonne, walke not thou in the way with them: refraine thy foot from their path:

Pr. 1.16. For their feet run to euill, and make haste to blood-shed. Cer-

Pr. 1.17. tainely as without cause the net is spred before the eyes of all

Pr. 1.18. that hath wings: So they lay wait for blood, & lie priuily for their

Pr. 12 10. liues; Thus the mercies of the wicked are cruell : *But shall they*

Pr. 26.2. *preuaile in this?* The causelesse

Pr. 24.16. curse shall not come : The iust man may fall seuen times in a

day,

day, but hee rifeth vp againe, whiles the wicked fhall fall into mifchief ; *Yea into the fame they had deuifed* : Hee that diggeth a pit fhall fall therein; and he that rolleth a ftone , it fhall fall vpon him, *and crufh him to death : for* He that doth violence againft the blood of a perfon, fhall flee vnto the Graue, and they fhall not ftay him.

Pr. 26.27.

Pr. 28.17.

§. 14. The fecond kind of Iuftice to others, is Liberality

- Defcribed,
- Limited,
- Rewarded, { with his owne, with more.

Liberality or beneficēce, *is* to caft thy bread vpon the waters;

Ec. 11.1.

Ec. 11.2.

Pr. 22. 9.

Pr. 3. 27.

Pr. 3. 28.

Ec. 5. 18.

Ec. 11. 3.

to giue a portion to feuen, and alfo to eight ; *in a word*, to giue of his bread to the poore, *and* not to withhold his goods from the owners thereof (1. *the needy*) tho there bee power in his hand to doe it, *and* not to fay to his neighbour, Goe and come againe, to morrow I will giue thee, if hee now haue it; *Not that God would not haue ʋs inioy the comforts he giues ʋs,* our felues; *for,* to euery man to whom God hath giuen riches and trea-fures, and giueth him power to eate thereof, and to take his part, and to inioy his labours, this is the gift of God ; *but* if the clouds bee full, they will powre out raine vpon the earth,

and

and yet they shall bee neuer the emptier. The liberall person shall haue plentie, and he that watereth, shall also haue raine : *yea not onely* hee that giueth to the poore, shall not lacke, *but* shall finde it after many daies ; *whereas* he that hideth his eies, shall haue manie curses : *but,* There is that scattereth and is more increased ; *thus* Hee that hath a good eye is blessed of God.

Pr. 11.25.

Pr.28.27.
Ec. 11.1.

Pr.11.24

Pr.22.9.

§. 15. The extreams whereof are { Couetousnes { The descripon of it, The curse. Prodigalitie.

THe *couetous* is he, that is gree dy of gaine, that hauing an

Pr.1.19.
Pr.23.6.

Pr.21.26.
Pr.23.4.

Pr.11.24.

Pr. 28. 8.

Ec.4.8.

euill eie, *and* coueting still gree-
dily, trauelleth too much to bee
rich ; *and therefore both* spareth
more then is right, *and* increaseth his goods by vsury and interest ; There is one alone, & there
is not a second, which hath neither sonne, nor brother ; yet is
there none end of his trauell,
neither can his eyes bee satisfied
with riches, neither doth hee
thinke for whom doe I trauaile
and defraud my soule of plea-
sures. *This man is* ⱱnſatiable,
like to The horse-leeches two
daughters, which cry still, Giue,
Giue : *eſpecially in his deſires* ;
The Graue and deſtruction can
neuer bee full ; ſo the eyes
of a man can neuer bee ſatiſ-
fied:

Pr. 30.15.

Pr.27.20.

fied : All the labour of man is
for his mouth , and yet the
foule is not filled : *yea this is the*
curſe that God hath ſet vpon him;
He that loueth ſiluer ſhall not be
ſatisfied with ſiluer : and he that
loueth riches ſhal be without the
fruite thereof ; *and whereas* the
riche mans riches are his ſtrong
Citie, hee that truſteth in riches
ſhall fall, *and by his* ſparing commeth ſurely to pouertie. *All this*
while hee ſets his eyes on that
which is nothing, *and* dooth but
gather for him, that will be mercifull to the poore : *wherefore,*
Better is a little with right, then
great reuenues without equitie.
Giue mee not pouerty, nor riches: feed me with foode conue-

nient

Marginal references: Ec. 6.7; Ec. 5.9; Pr. 18. 11; Pr. 11. 28; Pr. 11. 24; Pr. 23. 5; Pr. 28.8; Pr. 16. 8; Pr. 30. 8

Pr. 30.9
nient for mee, leaſt I be full and
denie thee, and ſaie, vvho is the
Lord : or leaſt I bee poore and
ſteale, & take the name of God
in vaine.

§. 16. Pro-
digality in
{
Too much ex-
pence: whereof
{
The quality,
The ende.
}
Careleſneſs of his eſtate.
}

Pr. 12.9
Pr. 21.17
Pr. 28.7
Pr. 28.19
Pr. 6.12

Pr. 6.14.
THE prodigall is the man that
boaſteth of falſe liberalitie,
that loueth paſtime, and vvine
and oyle, that feedeth gluttons,
and followeth the idle; The vn-
thriftie man and the wicked man
walketh with a froward mouth;
Lewde things are in his heart,
he imagineth euill at all times;

Ther-

Therefore (*also*) shall his destruction come speedily, and he shall bee destroyed suddainely vvithout recouerie ; *and in the meane time,* The riches of vanity shall diminish ; *so that* hee shall be a man of want ; *yea* filled with pouertie , *and* a shame to his Father ; *Of this kinde also is hee that is otherwise carelesse of his estate:* Be not thou of them that touch the hand , nor among them that are surety for debts : If thou hast nothing to paie ; vvhy causest thou that he should take thy bed from vnder thee.

Pr.6. 15

Pr. 13. 11

Pr. 21. 17
Pr. 28. 19

Pr. 23. 7

Pr. 22. 26

Pr. 22. 27
See more of this rule in the two last pag. of *Politicks,* following.

§. 17. Di-
ligence
{
  what it is,

  how profitable in
}
{
Health,

wealth & abúdance

Honour.
}

Pr.16.26

I *Vstice to a mans selfe, is Diligence; for* hee that trauelleth,
trauelleth for himselfe: *The diligent is he, who,* all that his hand
shall finde to doe, dooth it with
all his power. I haue seene (*indeed*) the trauell, that God hath
giuen the sons of men, to humble them thereby, *that* all things
are full of labour, man cannot
vtter it; *But* what profit hath he
that worketh, of the thing wherin hee trauelleth? *Much euerie
way: first, Health:* The sleep of
him that trauelleth is sweete,

Ec. 9. 10

Ec. 3. 10

Ec. 1.8

Ec. 3. 9.

Ec. 5. 11.

whe-

whether hee eate little or much;
Secondly, *wealth* : Open thine
eyes, and thou shalt be satisfied
with bread: *yea*, The hand of the
diligent maketh rich , and his
soule shal be fat: *and not sufficien-*
cy only ; *but* in all labour there is
abundance, but the talke of the
lippes bringeth want : *yet more,*
the riches that the diligent man
hath , are precious. 3. *Honour.*
A diligent man shall stand before kings , and not before the
base sort ; *and* The hand of the
diligent shall beare rule, but the
idle shall bee vnder tribute.

Pr. 20.13

Pr.10.4

Pr.13.4

Pr.14.23

Pr.12.27

Pr.22.29

Pr.12.24

§. 18. Slouthfulneſs $\left\{\begin{array}{l}\text{The properties,}\\\text{The danger of it.}\end{array}\right.$

Ec. 4. 5

Pr. 19. 24

Pr. 26. 24

Pr. 6. 10

Pr. 15. 19

Pr. 22. 13
Pr. 26. 13.

THe ſlouthfull, *is he that* fol-deth his hands, and eateth vp his owne fleſh; That hideth his hand in his boſome, and will not pull it out againe to his mouth; that turneth on his bed, as a dore turneth on his hinges, *and ſaith,* Yet a little ſleepe, a little ſlumber, a little folding of the hands to ſleepe. *Euery thing that hee ought to doe is trouble-ſome,* The waie of the ſlouth-full man is an hedge of thornes (*which hee is loath to ſet ſoote in*): There is a lion without (*ſaith he*) I ſhall be ſlaine in the ſtreet: *who*

al-

although herein hee bee wiſer in his owne conceit, then ſeauen men that can render a reaſon : Yet (*the truth is*)he that (*ſo much as*) followes the idle, is deſtitute of vnderſtanding. Hee luſteth (*indeed*) *& affecteth great things,* but his ſoule hath nought ; ſo, The verie deſire of the ſlouthfull ſlayeth him, for his hands refuſe to worke. And *not onely* he that is ſlothfull in his worke is bro-ther to him that is a great vva-ſter; but he that ſleepeth (*and* Slothfulneſſe cauſeth to fall a-ſleepe) in harueſt, is the ſonne of confuſion : *and* Hee that vvill not plovve, becauſe of winter; ſhall begge in Sommer, and haue nothing : Loue not

Pr. 26.16

Pr. 12.11.

Pr. 13.4

Pr. 21.25

Pr. 18.9

Pr. 10.5

Pr. 19.15.

Pr. 20.4

Pr. 20.13

ſleepe

ſleepe *therfore*, leaſt thou come to pouertie ; *for, what is it, that hence commeth not to ruine?* For, *the houſe* : By ſlouthfulneſs the roofe of the houſe goeth to decay, and by idlenes of the hands, the houſe droppeth thorough. *For the land*; I paſſed by the field of the ſlouthfull, & by the vineyard of the man deſtitute of vnderſtanding ; And loe, it was all growen ouer with thornes, and nettles had couered the face of it; and the ſtone wall thereof was broken downe. Then I behelde and conſidered it well; I looked vpon it, and receiued inſtruction; *ſo in euery reſpect* the ſlouthfull hand maketh poore. Go to the Piſmire *therefore* thou ſluggard,

Ec. 10.18

Pr. 24. 30

Pr. 24. 31

Pr. 24. 32

Pr. 10. 4

Pr. 6. 6

gard, and behold her waies, and
bee wife: For, fhee hauing no
guide, Gouernour, nor Ruler,   *Pr. 6. 7*
prepareth her meate in fummer,   *Pr. 6. 8*
and gathereth her foode in har-
ueft; How long wilt thou fleepe   *Pr. 6. 9*
O fluggard? when wilt thou a-
rife out of thy fleepe? Yet a lit-
tle fleepe, yet a little flumber,   *Pr. 24. 33*
yet a little folding of the hands
to fleepe: Therfore thy pouer-   *Pr. 6. 11*
ty commeth as a fpeedie Tra-
ueller, and thy neceffitie as an
armed man.

G   SALO-

SALOMONS ETHICKES.

THE fourth BOOKE.

Temperance & Fortitude.

Temperance is the moderation of our desires: whether

- in Diet; Sobrietie.
- in words & actions
  - Modestie,
  - &
  - Humilitie.
- in affectiōs,
  - continencie,
  - refraining of anger.

§. 1.

- Temperance in diet,
- excesse: how dangerous to
  - Bodie,
  - Soule,
  - Estate.

HE *temperate in dyet, is hee* that refrayneth his appetite, *that* looks not on the wine when it is red, *that*

Pr. 25.28

Pr. 23.31

G 2   puts

Pr. 23. 2.
Pr. 23. 1.
Pr. 25. 16

Ec. 3. 13.

Ec. 5. 17

Ec. 9. 7

Ec. 3. 22

puts his knife to his throat, when hee sits with a Ruler; *that* when he findes honie, eates but that vvhich is sufficient for him; least hee should be ouer-full: *It is true,* that a man eateth, and drinketh, and seeth the commoditie of all his labour; this is the gifte of God: *yea,* this I haue seene good, that it is comely to eate and to drinke, and to take pleasure in all his labour vvherein hee trauelleth vnder the Sunne, the vvhole number of the dayes of his life vvhich G O D giueth him; for this is his portion; *God allowes vs to eate* our bread vvith ioy, and drink our wine with a cheerfull heart, and there is nothing

better

better then this, *yea* there is no profite but this : *But not* that a man ſhould bee giuen to his appetite; that hee *ſhould* ſeeke in his heart to drawe his fleſh to vvine; *or that* vvhatſoeuer his eyes deſire hee ſhould not with-holde it from them : *Such a man* vvhen hee is full, deſpiſeth an hony-comb; whereas to the hungrie, euery bitter thing is ſweet; *and in his exceſſe is outra-geous: One of the* three things, yea foure, for which the earth is mo-ued, and cannot ſuſtaine it ſelf, is a foole vvhen hee is filled vvith meate. *Neither doth this proſper, with himſelfe. For his bodie*; The ſatietie of the rich, vvill not ſuffer him to ſleepe:

Ec.2.24.

Pr.23.2

Ec.2.3.

Ec.2.10

Pr.27.7

Pr.30.21

Pr.30.22

Ec.5.11

Pr.23.29 To whome is woe? to whome is
sorrow? to whom is murmuring?
to whom are woundes without
cause?and to whō is the redneſſe
Pr.23.30 of the eyes ? Euen to them that
tarry long at the wine; to them
that goe and ſeeke mixt wine :
Pr. 23.31. *For his ſoule* ; Looke not on the
wine when it is red, and ſhoweth
his colour in the cuppe, or go-
Pr.23.32. eth downe pleaſauntly. In the
ende thereof, it will bite like a
ſerpent, and hurt like a cocka-
Pr. 23.33. trice : Thine eyes ſhall looke vpon the ſtrange woman, and thy
lippes ſhall ſpeake lewd things :
Pr.23.34. And thou ſhalt bee as one that
ſleepeth in the midſt of the ſea,
and as hee that ſleepeth in the
top of the maſt : They haue ſtri-
ken

ken mee (shalt thou say) but I
was not sicke : they haue beaten
mee, but I knewe not vvhen I a-
wooke ; therefore will I seeke it
yet still : *For his estate*, He is like
a Citie which is broken downe,
and without walles : Keepe not
companie *therefore* vvith drun-
kards, nor with gluttons ; for the
glutton and drunkard shall bee
poore, and the sleeper shall bee
cloathed with ragges ; *and in all
these*, Wine is a mocker, & strong
drinke is raging, and vvhosoe-
uer is deceiued thereby is not
vvise.

Pr. 23. 35

Pr. 25. 28

Pr. 23. 20

Pr. 20. 1

```
                                    ┌ what it requires: ┌ few,
                          ┌ In words ┤                   ┤ sea-
                          │          └ that they be      ┤ sona-
                          │                              └ ble.
               ┌ Modestie ┤                   ┌ argues
               │          │          ┌ what it ┤ wisedome,
               │          └ In actions.│ profits └ giues safetie.
     §. 2. ────┤
               │                      ┌ Loquacitie,
               └ Contrarie to it, ────┤ Ill speech,
                                      └ Immoderate mirth.
```

Pr. 17.27

Pr. 10. 19

Pr. 17.27.
Pr.18.4.

Pr. 10.31.

Pr. 10.21.

pr.12.14 ⎱
Pr. 13.2 ⎰

THe modest (for wordes) is a
man of a pretious spirit,
that refraineth his lippes, *and*
spareth his words. The wordes
of a *modest man are* like deepe
waters, and the welspring of wisdome like a flowing riuer: *but
when he doth speak, it is to purpose;
for,* The mouth of the iust shalbe
fruitfull in wisdom: & the lips of
the righteous do feed many, *yea
himself;* A man shalbe satiate with

good things by the fruite of his
mouth;*&* with the fruit of a mans
mouth his belly shal be satisfied:
but still hee speaketh sparingly;
A wise man concealeth knowledge, and a man of vnder-
standing will keepe silence:
which as it argues him wise (for
euen a foole when hee holdeth
his peace is counted wise; and
hee that stoppeth his lippes, as
prudent); *so it giues him much*
safetie. Hee that keepeth his
mouth, and his tongue, keepeth
his soule from affliction; *yea,* he
keepeth his life; *where contrari-*
ly, The mouth of the foole is in
the multitude of wordes, it babbleth out foolishnesse; *as it is*
fedde with it: *neither* hath hee

Pr.18.20.

Pr.12.23.

Pr.11.12.

Pr.10.19 ⎫
Pr.17.28 ⎭

Pr.21.23.

Pr.13.3.

Ec.5.2.
Pr.15.2.

Pr.15.14.

Pr.18.2.

any

any delight in vnderſtanding, *but* that which his heart diſcouereth ; *and while he bewrayeth it,* The heart of fooles publiſheth *his* fooliſhneſſe : *And as* he multiplieth words, *ſo* in many words there cannot want iniquity : his mouth *(ſtill)* babbleth euill things; *for either* he ſpeaketh froward things, *or* how to lie in wait for blood, *or* in the mouth of the fooliſh is the rod of pride ; *And what is the iſſue of it ?* He that openeth his mouth , deſtruction ſhall bee to him. And hee that hath a naughty tongue ſhall fall into euill ; *for, both* it ſhall be cut out, *and* the frowardneſſe of it is the breaking of the heart. *Laſtly,* A fooles mouth is his owne de-

ſtruction,

Pr.12.23.

Ec.10.14.

Pr. 10.19.

Pr.11.28.

Pr.15.32.

Pr. 12.6.

Pr.14.3.

Pr.13.3.

Pr.17.20.

Pr.10.31.

Pr.15.4.

Pr. 18.7.

ſtruction, and his lips are a ſnare for his ſoule.

    For Actions : The modeſt ſhall haue honour : *And tho wee need not ſay,* Of laughter, thou art mad, & of ioy, what is this thou doeſt ; *yet* Anger is better then laughter, for by a ſadde looke the heart is made better. The heart of the wiſe, *therefore*, is in the houſe of mourning, but the heart of fooles is in the houſe of mirth. Reioyce then, O yong man, in thy youth, and let thine heart cheere thee in the dayes of thy youth, & walke in the wayes of thine heart, and in the ſight of thine eyes; but know, that for all theſe things God will bring thee to iudgement.

Pr. 11. 16.

Ec. 2. 2.

Ec. 7. 5.

Ec. 7. 6.

Ec. 11. 9.

3. Humi-

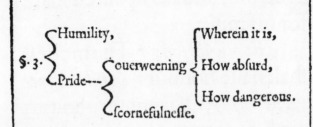

<table>
<tr><td rowspan="2">§. 3.</td><td>Humility,</td><td></td><td></td></tr>
</table>

Humility,

Pride --- { ouerweening { Wherein it is, How abſurd, How dangerous.

ſcornefulneſſe.

Pr. 29. 23.

Pr. 30. 2.

Pr. 30. 3.

Pr. 11. 2.

Pr. 13. 31.

Pr. 16. 19.

NExt to the *modeſt*, *is* the humble in ſpirit ; *Hee ſaith,* Surely, I am more fooliſh then a-man, & haue not the vnderſtan-ding of a man in me ; for I haue not learned wiſedome, and haue not attained to the knowledge of holy things: *But doth he want it ere the more? No* : With the lowly is wiſedome, *and* The eare that hearkeneth to the corre-ctions of life, ſhall lodge among the wiſe : Better it is, *therefore,* to bee of an humble mind with

the

the lowely, then to diuide the
fpoyles with the proud : *for be-*
fore honour goeth humilitie; Pr.15.33
and hee that confeſſeth and for- Pr.18.12
faketh his ſinnes, ſhall haue mer- Pr.28.13.
cy ; *yea*, the humble of ſpirit ſhall Pr.29.23.
inioy glory : *and* the rewarde of Pr.22.24.
humilitie, & the feare of God, is
riches, and glory and life.

Contrary whereto; There is a
generation, whoſe eyes are hau- Pr.30.13.
tie, and their eye-lids are lift vp ;
There is a generation that are Pr.30.12.
pure in their owne conceit, and
yet are not waſhed from their
filthineſſe. *Yea*, All the wayes of
a man are cleane in his own eies : Pr.16.2.
but the Lord pondereth the Pr.21.2.
ſpirits; *and not ſo onely*, *but* Many
men will boaſt of their goodnes; Pr.20.6.

but

Pr.25.27.

Pr. 27.2.

but It is not good to eate much honie, fo to fearch their owne glory is not glory ; Let another man prayfe thee, and not thine owne mouth; a ftranger and not thy owne lips: *This ouer-weening is commonly incident to great men.*

Pr.28.11.

The rich man is wife in his owne conceit, but the poore that hath vnderftanding can trie him : *Hence it is, that he affeEts fingu-*

Pr. 18.1.

larity; According to his defire, he that feparates himfelf, will feeke, and occupy himfelfe in all wife-dome: *but* Seeft thou a man *thus*

Pr.16.12.

wife in his owne conceit, there is more hope of a foole then of him: yea, *he is a foole in this*: In

Pr. 14. 3.

the mouth of the foolifh, is the

Ec. 7.25.

rod of pride; I thought, I will be

wife

wife, but it went farre from me;
it is farre off, what may it bee? *Ec. 7. 26.*

and that, a wicked foole; A hautie *Pr. 21. 4.*
looke, and a proud heart which
is the light of the wicked is fin:
If *therefore* thou haft bene foo- *Pr. 30. 32.*
lifh in lifting vp thy felfe, and if
thou haft thought wickedly, lay
thy hand vpon thy mouth, *for*
God hateth an hauty eye; *yea he* *Pr. 6. 17.*
fo hateth it, that al that are proud *Pr. 16. 5.*
in heart, are an abomination to
the Lord: and tho hand ioyne in
hand, they fhall not be vnpunifhed; *and what punifhment fhall*
he haue? The Lord will deftroy *Pr. 15. 25.*
the houfe of the proud man; *and*
his very pride is an argument of
his ruine: Before deftruction the
heart of a man is haughty : Pride *Pr. 18. 22.*

Pr.16.18.

goeth before deſtruction, and an hie mind before the fall : *Before it ? yea with it* : When pride commeth, then cōmeth ſhame . *Now the height of pride is ſcorneſulneße.* Hee that is proud and haughty, ſcornefull is his name, who worketh in the pride of his wrath;and *this man* deſpiſeth his neighbour,and *therefore* is deſtitute of vnderſtanding: when the wicked commeth, then commeth contempt ; and with the vile man is reproche ; *but of all, him that reproues him* : Hee that reproueth a ſcorner, purchaſeth to himſelfe ſhame, and hee that rebuketh the wicked, getteth himſelfe a blot; *therefore* Iudgements are prepared for the ſcor-

Pr.11.2.

Pr.21.24.

Pr.11.12.

Pr.18.3.

Pr.9.7.

Pr.19.29.

ners,

ners, and ftripes for the backe of
fooles ; *fo, as others are hurt by
his finne ; for* a fcornefull man
bringeth a whole citie into a
fnare : *fo they fhall bee likewife
bettered by his iudgement* ; when
the fcorner is punifhed, the foolifh is wife.

Pr.29.8.

Pr.21.11.

§. 4. Continency $\left\{\begin{matrix} \text{of Luft,} \\ \text{of Anger,} \end{matrix}\right\}$ with their cōtraries.

OF *the firft kind, is* hee that
drinkes the waters of his
owne cifterne ; that defires not
the beautie of *a ftranger* in his
heart ; neither lets her take him
with her eye-lids : *contrarily, the
incōtinent* is he that delights in a
ftrange woman, & imbraces the
bofome of a ftranger; or fhe that

Pr. 5.15.

Pr.6.25.

Pr.5.20.

Pr. 2.17.	forfakes the guide of her youth, and forgetteth the couenant of
Pr. 23.28.	God ; fhee lyeth in wait for a pray, and fhee increafeth the trangreffers amongft men. For
Pr. 23.27.	a whore is as a deepe ditch,& a ftrange woman as a narrow pit:
Ec. 7.28.	*Yea*, I finde more bitter then death the woman whofe heart is
See more of this viee, *Oecon.*fect.2. & 3.	as nets and fnares, and whofe hands as bands: hee that is good before God fhall bee deliuered from her, but the finner fhall be taken by her.
Pr. 16 32.	*Of the fecond, is* he that is flow
Pr. 14.29.	to anger, flow to wrath; whofe
Pr. 19.11.	difcretion differreth his anger, and whofe glory is to paffe by an offence : *which moderation,*
Pr. 14. 29.	*as it argues him to bee* of great

wife-

wifedome *(for* wife men turne away wrath *)fo it makes* him better then the mightie man, *and procures him iuſt honour* ; *for* It is the honour of a man to ceafe from ſtrife: *cõtrary to which, is* he that is of an haſty ſpirit to be angry; *which as it proues him fooliſh*: (for anger reſteth in the boſom of fooles, *and* he that is haſtie to anger, *not onely* committeth folly , *but* exalteth it) *So it makes him dangerous* : Anger is cruell, and wrath is raging ; *and* a furious man aboundeth in tranſgreſſions: *wherefore* make no friendſhippe with an angry man, leaſt thou learne his wayes, and receiue deſtruction to thy ſoule.

Pr.29.8.

Pr. 16.23.

Pr.20.3.

Ec.7.11.

Ec.7.11.

Pr.14.17

Pr.14.29

Pr.27.4.

Pr.29.22.

Pr.22.24.

Pr.22.25.

§. 5. Fortitude { In generall, / The speci-als of it; } { Confidence, / Patience { in Gods afflictiõs, / in mens iniuries. } }

Pr. 18.14.

Pr. 28.1.

Pr. 24.10.

Pr. 29.25.

Pr. 18.14.

Pr. 28.1.

Pr. 3. 5.

Fortitude is that, whereby The spirit of a man susteines his infirmities; *which makes* the righteous bold as a lyon : *contrarily the weake of strength* is he that is faint in the day of aduersitie ; *whose* feare bringeth a snare vpon him ; *and that*, *desperate* : A wounded spirit who can beare? *which is often caused through guiltinesse*: The wicked fleeth, when none pursueth him. *Confidence is, to* trust in the Lord with all thine heart, and not to leane

to thine owne wifedome ; *but*
in all thy wayes to acknowledge   Pr.3.6.
him , *and* to commit thy works   Pr.16.3.
to the Lord , *and to* haue hope   Pr.14.32.
in thy death : *and tho in other*
things, The hope that is defer-   Pr.13.12.
red is the fainting of the heart ;
yet in this, hee that trufteth in   Pr.28.25.
the Lord fhall bee fatte ; *for*,
from hence, not onely his thoughts   Pr.16.3. ⎱
and wayes are directed , *but he*   Pr.3.6. ⎰
receiueth fafetie , and protection;
He is a fhield to thofe that truft   Pr.30.5.
in him. The horfe is prepared
for the day of battaile, but fal-   Pr.21.31.
uation is of the Lord. *Yea*,
The name of the Lord is a   Pr.18.12
ftrong tower : the righteous
runneth to it, and is exalted.
So that, Hee that trufteth in   Pr.16.20.

the Lord, he is bleſſed; *whereas* Hee that truſteth in his owne heart, is a foole: *and it is a vaine thing,* to boaſt thy ſelfe of to morrow; for thou knoweſt not what a day will bring forth.

Patience is, not to refuſe the chaſtening of the Lord, neither to be grieued with his correcti- on: *The patient man,* in the day of wealth, is of good comfort, and in the day of affliction conſide- reth, God alſo hath made this contrary to that, that man ſhould finde nothing after him *whereof to complaine: knowing that* the Lord correcteth whom hee lo- ueth; *and that* the patient abi- ding of the righteous ſhall bee gladneſſe: *Contrarily,* The heart

of

Pr. 28. 26.

Pr. 27. 1.

Pr. 3. 11.

Ec. 7. 16.

Pr. 3. 12.

Pr. 10. 28

of the foole, fretteth againſt the
Lord; he is careleſſe and rageth:
but to what purpoſe? Man cannot
ſtriue with him that is ſtronger
then he: *Yea rather,*the man that
hardeneth his necke when hee is
rebuked, ſhall ſuddenly bee deſtroyed, and cannot bee cured:
*in reſpect of mens iniuries,*He ſaith
not, I will recompence euill; but
waits vpon the Lord, and he ſhall
ſaue him. *In which regard,* the
patient in ſpirit *that ſuffers,* is
better then the proud of ſpirit,
that requites.

Pr.19.3.

Ec. 6.10.

Pr.29.1.

Pr.20.22.

Ec. 7.10.

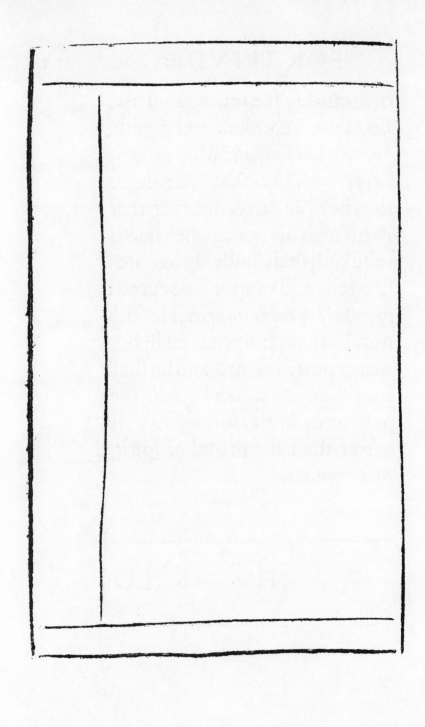

SALOMONS
POLITICKS,

Or

Common-wealth :

1. BOOKE.

His {
KING,
COVNSAILOR,
COVRTIER,
SVBIECT.

Anno Domini, 1609.

SALOMONS
POLITICKES,
or Common-wealth:

And, firſt, H I S K I N G.

§. 1. Degrees { muſt be and are { ſubordinate, hyeſt { not many, but one. } } and thoſe from God.

IN all well ordered gouerments there are degrees,
An hyer then the hyeſt,
and yet an hyer then
they : *and theſe, of Gods appointment ; not onely in the inferiour rankes,* The rich & poore meet,

Ec. 5.7

Pr. 22.2

and

and the Lord is the Maker of them all: *but in the supreame: By me Kings raigne (saith Wisdom) and Princes decree Iustice : and not they only, but* the Nobles & all the Iudges of the earth; *so, it is a iust wonder, that* The grashoppers haue no King; yet they goe forth by bands. *And as no King is a iudgement ; so, many : for* Becaufe of the Transgreſſion of the land, there are many Princes *many, not only in frequent fuccesſion, but in focietie of regiment.*

Pr. 8. 15

Pr. 8. 16

Pr. 30. 27

Pr. 28. 2

§. 2. In a King are deſcribed

- Quality of his perfon
  - Naturall,
  - Morall.
- Actions.

A King muſt be hie; *as in place, so in bloud:* Bleſſed art tho

Ec. 10. 17

O

O Land, vvhen thy King is the ſonne of Nobles; *not of any ſer-uile condition ; for, nothing can bee more* vncomely, then for a ſeruant to haue rule ouer Prin-ces: *and it is a monſter in State,* to ſee ſeruants ride on horſes, and Princes (*of blood*) to walke as ſeruants on the ground; *nei-ther more monſtrous, then intole-rable.* There are three things for vvhich the earth is mooued, yea foure which it cānot ſuſtein : *whereof one is,* A ſeruant when he reigneth.

Pr.19. 10

Ec.10.17

Pr.30. 21

Pr. 30. 22

	Negatiue; what one he may not be:	Not lasciuious, Not riotous, Not hollow and dissembling, Not childish, Not imprudent, Not oppressing.
§. 3. Morall qualities	Affirmatiue.	

ANd as his bloud is heroicall, so his disposition; *not lasci-uious.* What, O son of my de-sires, giue not thy strength to women, nor thy wayes: *But why* should he withhold from his eies whatsoeuer they can desire, and withdrawe his heart from anie ioy? *why may he not haue* all the delights of the sonnes of men: as women take captiue; as Queens and Concubines, and Damosels without number? This is to de-stroy Kings; He shall finde more

Pr. 31. 23

Ec. 2. 10.

Ec. 2. 8

Cant 6 7.
Pr. 31. 3

bittter then death the vvoman Ec.7.28
whofe hart is as nets and fnares.
Not riotoufly excessiue; whether in
wine: *for* It is not for Kings to Pr. 31.4
drink wine, nor for Princes ftrõg
drinke: *What, not at all? To him*
alone is it not faide, Goe eat thy Ec. 9. 7.
bread with ioy, and drinke thy
wine with a cheerefull heart?
who fhould eat or drink, or haft Ec. 2.25.
to outwarde things more then
hee? *Not immoderately*: fo as he
fhould drinke and forget the de- Pr. 31. 5
cree, and change the iudgement
of all the Children of affliction:
Or in meat ; *for*, Woe be to thee Ec. 10. 16.
ô Land, when thy Princes eate
in the morning: and if he be not Pr.23.2
the mafter of his appetite, his
daintie meates will prooue de- Pr 22. 3

Pr. 17.7

ceiueable. *Not hollow, not double in speeches, in profession* : The lip of excellencie becomes not a foole; much leſſe, lying talke a Prince: *Not childiſh;* Wo to thee,

Ec. 10.16.

O Land, whoſe King is a child: *not ſo much in age, which hath ſometimes proued ſuccesſull; but in condition : Not imprudent, not op-preſſing; two vices conioined* : A

Pr. 28.16

Prince deſtitute of vnderſtanding is alſo a great oppreſſour; *And to conclude, in all or any of theſe, not wilfully inflexible* : A

Ec. 4. 13

poore and wiſe childe is better then an old & fooliſh king, that will no more be admoniſhed.

§. 4 Affirmatiue;
what one he muſt be :

To others { Iuſt, Mercifull, ſlow to anger, Bountifull.

In himſelfe { Temperate, Wiſe, Valiant, Secret.

Ontrarily, *he muſt be Tempe-rate.* Bleſſed art thou, O Land, vvhen thy Princes eate in time, for ſtrength and not for drunkenneſſe : *Iuſt and righteous; for* falſe balances (*eſpecially in the hand of gouernment*) are an abo-minatiõ to the Lord: but a perfit weight pleaſeth him ; *A vertue beneficial, both' to himſelf (for* the throne is eſtabliſhed by Iuſtice) *&*[2] *to the State.* Iuſtice exalteth a Nation ; *then which, nothing doth*

Ec.10.17

Pr.11. 1

Pr.16.12

Pr.14.34

more binde and cheare the hearts of the people: *for,* When the righteous are in authority the people reioice, but when the wicked beares rule the people figh: *and with truth & iuftice, muft mercy be ioined infeparably; for* Mercy and truth preferue the King : and his Throne fhall be eftablifhed, *alfo,* by mercy. *And all thefe muft haue wifdome to menage them* : By it, Princes rule, *& are terrible to the ill-deferuing.* A wife King fcattereth the wicked, & caufeth the wheele to turn ouer them. *To all thefe muft bee added bountie ;* A Prince that hateth couetoufnefs fhall prolong his daies; *where cõtrarily,* A man of gifts deftroieth his country : *andyet further, a cõ-*

r. 29.2.

Pr. 20. 28

Pr. 8. 16.

Pr. 20. 26

Pr. 28. 16

Pr. 29. 4.

queſt of his owne paſſions; a prince-
ly victory: for He that is ſlowe to
anger, is better then the mighty
man; and he that ruleth his owne
minde better then hee that vvinneth a Citie ; *becauſe of all other,*
The kings wrath is like the roa-
ring of a lion : *and what is that*
but the meſſenger of death ? *and*
if it may be, a conqueſt of all others,
through valour. There are three
things that order well their going, yea foure are comely in going : *wherof the laſt and principall*
is, A King againſt whom no man
dares riſe vp : *Laſtly, ſecrecy in*
determinations. The heauen in
height, and earth in deepneſſe,
and the kings heart can no man
(*no man ſhould*) ſearch out : *ney-*

Pr. 16. 32

Pr. 19. 12

Pr. 30. 29

Pr. 30. 31

Pr. 25. 3

I 2   *ther*

Pr. 21. 1.

ther should it be in any hands, *but* the Lords ; *who* as he knowes it, *so* hee turnes it whitherfoeuer it pleafeth him.

§. 5. His actions
- common,
- speciall to his place:
  - To iudge righteoufly
    - 1. according to the truth of the caufe.
    - 2. according to ỹ diftreffe of the partie, vnpartially.
  - remit mercifully.

HIs actions muft fute his dif po- fit ion; which muft be vniuer-

Pr. 16. 12

fally holy : for, It is an abhomina- tion to Kings (*of all other*) to cõ- mit wickednefs. *Which holineffe alone is the way to all peace*: When

Pr. 16. 7.

the waies of a man pleafe the L. he wil make his enimies at peace

with

with him : *Peculiarly to his place;* *he muſt firſt iudge his people*: a king that ſitteth in the throne of iudge ment, chaſeth away all euill with his eyes; & by this, he maintains his country: *& while hee doth ſit there,* A diuine ſentéce muſt be in the lips of the king, & his mouth may not tranſgreſs in iudgemēt. *for,* A king that iudgeth the poor in truth, his throne ſhall be eſtabliſhed for euer : *Neither may his eare be partially open: which diſpoſition ſhalbe ſure to be fed with reports; for,* Of a Prince that harkeneth to lyes, al his ſeruants are wicked: *nor his mouth ſhut; eſpecially in caſes of diſtreſſe* : Open thy mouth for the dumbe in the cauſe of all the children of de-

Pr. 20. 8

Pr. 29. 4

Pr. 16. 10

Pr. 29 14.

Pr. 29 12.

Pr. 39.8

I 3   ſtruction

31.9.

ſtructiõ : open thy mouth, iudge righteouſly, & iudge the afflicted & the poore : *yet, not with ſo much regard to the eſtate of perſõs,*

Pr. 17. 26   *as the truth of the cauſe; for* Surely it is not good to condemne the iuſt *in what-euer condition;* nor that Princes ſhould ſmite ſuch for equity: *wherin he ſhal wiſely ſearch*

Pr. 25. 1   *into all difficulties* . The glorie of God is to paſs by infirmities, but the kings honour is to ſearch out a thing ; *yet ſo, as he is not ſeldome mercifull in execution,* Deliuering

Pr. 24. 11.   them that are drawne to death, and preſeruing them that are drawne to be ſlaine : *Theſe obſer-*

Ec. 8. 9   *ued, it cannot be, that* man ſhould rule ouer man to his hurt.

SALOMONS
COVNSAILOR.

Sect. 6.
Coūsaile
- For the soule
  - How giuē:
    - The necessitie of it,
    - The qualitie
      - wise,
      - righteus
      - pleasant.
  - How receiued.
- For the State.

AS *where no soueraigntie, so*
vvhere no counsell is, the
people fall; *and contrarily,* where
many Counsellers are, there is
health ; *and more then health,*
Stedfastnes: *Counsel for the soule,*
Where no vision is, the people
perish : *which requires both holi-*
neße and wisedome : The fruit of
the righteous is as a tree of life,
and hee that vvinneth soules is

Pr. 11. 14

Pr. 24. 6

Pr. 15. 22

Pr. 29. 18

Pr. 11. 30

wise

is vvife ; *and* the more vvife the Preacher (*is*) the more hee tea-cheth the people knovvledge, and caufeth them to heare, and fearcheth forth, and prepareth many parables:*&* *not only* an vp-right writing (*& ſpeaking*) euen the word of truth; *but* pleaſant words *alſo*; *ſo that* the ſweetneſs of the lips increaſeth doctrine;*&* *not more delightfull,then effectual*: *for,* The wordes of the wiſe are like goades, and nayles faſtned by the maſters of the aſſemblies, that are giuen by one Paſtour : *which againe,of euery hearer, chal-lenge due reuerence & regard;who* muſt take heed to his foot, when he entreth into the houſe of God, and bee more neere to heare,

then

Marginal references: Ec. 12.9   Ec. 12.10   Pr. 16.21   Ec. 12.11   Ec. 4.17

thé to giue the sacrifice of fooles :
for, He that despiseth the word,
shall be destroyed : but hee that
feareth the commaundement,
shall be rewarded.

Pr.13.13.

§. 7. In a Coun-
sellour of State,
or Magistrate, is
required

Wisdom,
  Discussing of causes,
  Prouidence, and
  working according to
  knowledge.

Pietie,

Iustice, and
freed from
  Partialitie,
  Bribes,
  Oppression.

Without Counsell, all our
thoughts (*euen of policie &*
state) come to nought: but in the
multitude of Counsellors is stedfastnes: *& no lesse in their goodnes*;
i. in their wisdom, which *alone* giv's
strength *to the owner*, aboue ten
mighty princ.that are in the city;

Pr.15.22.

Pr.24.5.

Ec. 7.2.

a ver-

a vertue, *which tho* it refteth in
the heart of him that hath vnderftanding, *yet* is knowne in the
mids of fooles. *For* wifedome
is in the face of him that hath
vnderftanding, *and in his lippes*:
for, *howfoeuer* he that hath knowledge fpareth his words, *yet* the
tongue of the wife vfeth knowledge aright; *and* the foole cannot open his mouth in the gate;
*and therefore is vnfit for authori-
tie.* As fnowé in fummer, and
raine in harueft; fo is honor vn-
feemely for a foole. *And tho it
bee giuen him* ; *how ill it agrees ?*
As the clofing vp of a precious
ftone in an heape of ftones, fo is
he that giues glory to a foole.
From hence, the good Iufticer both

care-

Pr. 14. 33.

Pr. 17. 24.

Pr.

Pr. 15. 2.

Pr. 24. 7.

Pr. 26. 1.

Pr. 26. 8.

carefully heareth a cause, knowing,
that He which answereth a mat-   Pr.
ter before he heare it, it is a folly
and shame to him; *and that rela-*
ted on both parts; for Hee that is
first in his owne cause is iust :   Pr.18.17.
then commeth his neighbour
and maketh inquirie of him;
and deepely sifteth it : else he loseth
the truth; for The counsel of the   Pr.20.5.
heart of a man is like deepe wa-
ters: but a man that hath vnder-
standing will draw it out. *From*
hence, is his prouidence for the
common good; not onely in seeing
the plague, and hiding himselfe,   Pr.22.3.
but in deliuering the city : *and as*   Ec.9.15.
hee foreseeth, so hee worketh by   Pr.13.16
knowledge : *and not in peace on-*
ly; as, The words of the wise are   Ec.9.17.

more

more heard in quietneſſe, then the cry of him that ruleth among fooles; *but in warre* : A wiſe man goeth vp into the city of the mighty, and caſteth downe the ſtrength of the cõfidence thereof. *For,*wiſedome is better then ſtrength, *yea* then weapons of warre : I haue ſeene this wiſdome vnder the ſun, and it is great vnto mee ; A little citie and fewe men in it, and a great king came againſt it, and compaſſed it a-bout, and builded forts againſt it; and there was found, in it, a poore and wiſe man, and he de-liuered the city by his wiſdome: *neither can there be true wiſedome in any Counſellour, without piety.* The wiſe man feareth, & departs from

Pr. 21. 22.

Ec. 9.16.

Ec. 9.18.

Ec 9.13.

Ec. 9.14.

Ec. 9.15.

Pr. 14.16.

from euill; *being well assured, that* there is no wisdome, nor vnder-standing, nor counsel againſt the Lord; *& that,* Man cānot be eſta-bliſhed by wickednes: *and indeed how oft doth God so diſpose of eſtats that* the euil ſhal bow before the good, & the wicked at the gates of the righteus? *neither is this more iuſt with God, then acceptable with men : for,* when the righteous re-ioice, there is great glory, *&* whē they are in authority the people reioice; *cōtrarily,* whē the wicked comes on, *and* riſes vp, *&* beares rule, the mā is tried; the goodliide thēſelues, & all the people ſigh: *&* the righteous man falling down before the wicked, is like a trou-bled Well, and a corrupt ſpring.

Pr. 21. 30.

Pr. 12. 3.

Pr.

Pr. 28. 12.

Pr. 29. 2.

Pr. 28, 12.

Pr. 28. 28.

Pr. 29. 2.

Pr. 25. 26.

Nei-

Neither is iustice leſſe eſſentiall, then either; for to do iustice and iudgement is more acceptable to the Lord, then ſacrifice : To know faces, *therefore (in a iudge)* is not good ; for that man will tranſgreſſe for a peece of bread; *much leſſe to* accept the perſon of the wicked, to cauſe the righteous to fall in iudgement : Hee that ſaith to the wicked thou art righteous, him ſhall the people curſe, and the multitude ſhall abhorre him : *Yea yet hyer;* Hee that iuſtifieth the wicked, & condéneth the iuſt, both are an abomination to the Lord. *Wherefore, howſoeuer* The wicked man taketh a gift out of the boſome, to wreſt the wayes of iudgemét;

and

Pr.

Pr.28.21
Pr.24.23

Pr.18.5.

Pr.24.24.

Pr.17.15.

Pr.17.23.

and commonly, A mans gift inlar- | Pr. 18. 16.
geth him, *and leadeth him (with*
approbation) before great men:
yet he knoweth, that the reward | Ec. 7.9.
deſtroyeth the heart ; *that the*
acceptance of it is but the robbery | Pr.21.7.
of the wicked; which ſhall de-
ſtroy them, becauſe they haue
refuſed to execute iudgement:
he hateth gifts,*then,*that he may | Pr.15.27.
liue, *and* it is a ioy to him to doe | Pr.21.15.
iudgement : *He doth ʋnpartial-*
ly ſmite the ſcorner, *yea ſeuerely* | Pr.19.25.
puniſh him, *that the wickedly* | Pr. 21. 11.
fooliſh may beware and become
wiſe. *And wheras* Euery way of | Pr.21.2.
a man is right in his owne eyes,
and a falſe record will ſpeake | Pr. 14.5.
lies, and vſe deceit; *he ſo* maketh | Pr. 12.17.
inquirie, *that* a falſe witnes ſhall | Pr. 18.17. / Pr. 19.5.

Pr. 19. 9.

Pr.

Pr. 14. 31.

Pr. 22. 22.

Pr. 24. 26.

not be vnpunished : and he that
speaketh lies shall perish: *Lastly,
his hand is free from oppression of
of his inferiors: which as* it makes
a wise man mad; *so the actor of it,
miserable* : *for* Hee that oppres-
seth the poore, reproueth him
that made him: *and* if the afflicted bee opprest in iudgement,
the Lord will defend their cause,
& spoile the soule that spoyleth
them; *and vpon all occasions , he
so determineth, that* they shal kisse
the lippes of him that answereth
vpright words.

SALOMONS
COVRTIER

§. 8. Muſt be
- Diſcreet,
- Religious,
- Humble,
- Charitable,
- Diligent,
- Faithfull.

IN the light of the Kings countenance is life, and his fauour
is as the cloud of the latter
raigne, *or* as the deaw vpon the
graſſe : *which that the Courtier
may purchaſe;he muſt be* 1.Diſcreet:
The pleaſure of a king is in a
wiſe ſeruant, but his wrath ſhall
bee towards him that is lewd;
2. *Religious, both in heart*, Hee
that loueth pureneſſe of heart
for the grace of the lips the king
ſhalbe his friend: *& in his actions,*

Pr. 16.15

Pr.19. 12.

Pr.14.35.

Pr.22.11

K   He

Pr. 11.27.

Hee that seeketh good things getteth fauour; *in both which,*

Pr. 12.26.

the righteous is more excellent then his neighbour: *and besides*

Pr. 22.4.

these, humble; The reward wher-

Pr. 15.33.

of is glory: *for,* before glory goeth humilitie. *He dare not there-*

Pr. 25.6.

fore boast himselfe before the king, *and* thrust himselfe ouer-

Pr. 25.7.

forward in the presence of the Prince, whom his eyes doe see:

Pr. 25.15.

whom if he see moued, he pacifieth by staying of anger, *and* by a soft answer breaketh a man of bone; *not aggrauating the faults of o-*

Pr. 17.9.

thers: He that couereth a transgression seeketh loue; but hee that repeateth a matter separateth the Prince. *To these,* he is diligent, taking heed to the mouth

Ec. 8.2.

of

of the King; *& therfore worthily*
ſtandeth before kings, and not
before the baſe ſort: *and withall,*
true and faithfull; when he vnder-
takes anothers ſuite he lingers not:
knowing, that The hope that is
differred is the fainting of the
heart; *andtho* A bribe *or* reward
is as a ſtone pleaſant in the eyes
of them that haue it, and proſpe-
reth whither ſoeuer it turneth,
(*for,* euery man is a friend to him
that giueth gifts) : *yet he accoun-*
teth the gathering of treaſures
by a deceitfull tongue, to be vanitie, toſſed too and fro, of them
that ſeeke death.

Pr. 22.29

Pr. 13. 12.

Pr. 17.8.

Pr. 19. 6.

Pr. 21.6.

SALOMONS
SVBIECT.

§. 9. His Duety to {
His Prince; { Reuerence,
Obedience.

Fellow Subiects.

Pr. 14.28.

*E*very gouernment presupposeth *Subiects.* In the multitude of the people is the honour of the King ; and for the want of people, commeth the destruction of the Prince : *Of whom God requires, in respect of the Prince, Reuerence, Obedience ;* That they

Pr. 19.6.
Pr.29.26.

should reuerence, and seeke the face of the Prince ; not cursing the King, *so much* as in their

Ec. 10.20.

thought,

thought, nor the rich in their bedchâber; *but* fearing the Lord, and the King, and not meddling with the feditious, which onely feeke euill. *For, as* the foule of the heauen fhall cary the voice, and the mafter of the wing declare the matter: *fo (for reuenge)* a cruell meffenger fhall be fent againft them; their deftruction fhall arife fuddenly, and who knoweth their ruine? *For their due homage therefore and obedience to lawes,* they take heede to the mouth of the King, and the word of the oath of God; *and if a law bee enacted, they violate it not, nor ftriue for innouation.* Hee that breakes the hedge, a ferpent fhall bite him. He that

Pr. 24. 21.

Pr. 17. 11.

Ec. 10.20

Pr. 17. 11.

Pr. 24.22.

Ec. 8.2.

Ec. 10.8.

Ec. 10.9.

re-

Ec. 10. 9. remoueth ftones, fhall hurt him-felfe thereby : and hee that cut-teth wood fhall bee in danger thereby. *And if they haue offen-* *Ec. 8.3.* *ded,* they hafte not to goe forth of the princes fight, nor ftand in an euill thing : for he will doe what-euer pleafeth him ; *but ra-* *Ec. 10.4.* *ther* if the fpirit of him that ru-leth rife vp againft them , by gentleneffe pacifie great finnes.

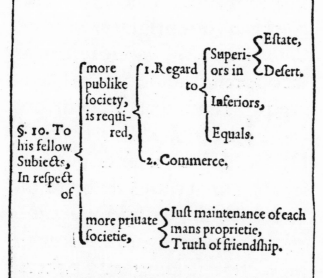

§. 10. To his fellow Subiects, In respect of
- more publike societie, is required,
  - 1. Regard to
    - Superiors in
      - Estate,
      - Desert.
    - Inferiors,
    - Equals.
  - 2. Commerce.
- more priuate societie,
  - Iust maintenance of each mans proprietie,
  - Truth of friendship.

IN respect of themselues, he requires due regard of degrees: whether of superiors. The rich ruleth the poore ; *and* as the fining potte is for siluer, and the fornace for golde, so is euery man tryed according to his dignitie ; *so as* they that come from the holy place be

Pr.22.7.

Pr.27.21.

Ec.8.10.

K 4   not

not forgotten in the city where they haue done right: *or whether of inferiors ; for*, A poore man, if he oppreffe the poore, is like a raging raine that leaueth no food ; *yea (leffe then oppreffion)* He that defpifeth his neighbour is *both* a finner and deftiture of vnderftanding: *or laftly, of equals; & therin, quiet & peaceable demeanure*, not ftriuing with others caufeleffe; *not to begin coentions, for*, The beginning of ftrife is as one that openeth the waters; therefore ere it bee meddled with, hee leaueth off : *and being prouoked*, debateth the matter with his neighbor. *And as* he goes not forth haftily to ftrife : *fo much leffe doth hee take part*

Pr.

Pr.11.12
Pr.14.21

Pr.3.30.

Pr.17.14.

Pr.25.9.

Pr.25.8.

in impertinent quarrells: He that paſſeth by, and meddleth vvith the ſtrife that belonges not to him, is as one that takes a dog by the eare; *and* one of the ſixe things that God hates, is he that rayſeth vp contentions among neighbours.

Pr. 26. 17

Pr. 6. 16
19.

Secondly, mutuall commerce, and interchange of commodities; without which, is no liuing: The abundance of the earth is ouer all: and the King conſiſts by the field that is tilled. *The huſband-man therefore muſt* till his land, that hee may bee ſatisfied with bread; *for,* much increaſe commeth by the ſtrẽgth of the Oxe: *and moreouer, he* muſt ſell corn, that bleſſings may be vpõ him;

Ec. 5. 8

Pr. 28. 19

Pr. 14. 4

Pr. 11. 26

which

which if he withdrawe, the people shall curse him ; *so that* , the
slothfull man vvhose field is o-
uergrowen with thornes, and
nettles, *is but an ill member: And
againe* , the Merchant must
bring his wares from farre; *and
each so trade with other, thatboth
may liue.* They prepare bread
for laughter, & wine comforts
the liuing, but siluer answereth
to all. *For lesse publicke society, is
required due reseruation of proprietie*; not to remoue the ancient boundes which his fathers
haue made; not to enter into
the field of the fatherless; *for,*
he that redeemeth thē is mighty; *not* to increase his riches by
vsury and interest; not to ha-

P.24.30.31

Pr.31.14.

Ec.10.19

Pr. 22.28

Pr. 23. 10

Pr.23.11.

Pr.

sten

sten ouer-much to be rich : *for* | Pr.23.4

such one knoweth not that po- | Pr.28. 22

uerty shall come vpon him ; *&*

that an heritage hastily gotten | Pr.28.20 {

in the beginning, in the ende | Pr.20.21 }

thereof, shall not bee blessed:

and that in the meane time,

The man that is greedie of | Pr. 15.27

gaine troubleth his own house.

2. *Truth of friendship .* A man | Pr. 18.24

that hath friendes, ought to

showe himselfe friendly : for a

friend is neerer then a brother;

Thy owne friend *therefore*, and | Pr.27. 10

thy fathers friend forget thou

not : *for whether hee reprooue*

thee; The woundes of a louer | Pr. 27.6

are faithfull: *or whether hee ad-*

uise ; As Oyntment and Per- | Pr.27.9

fume reioyce the heart, so doth

the

the sweetnesse of a mans friend
by hearty counsell : *or whether*

<!-- margin: Pr.27. 17 -->
he exhort; Iron sharpens iron, so
doth a man sharpen the face of
his friend ; *and all this, not in the*
time of prosperity onely, as com-

<!-- margin: Pr.19.4. -->
monly , Riches gather manie
friends, and the poore is sepa-
rated from his neighbour : *but*

<!-- margin: Pr. 17.17 -->
contrarily, A *true* friend loueth
at all times, & a brother is born
for aduersitie; *in all estates ther-*

<!-- margin: Pr. 27. 19 -->
fore, as the face in the water answers to face, so the hart of man
to man ; *who yet, may not bee too*

<!-- margin: Pr.25.17. -->
much pressed : Withdrawe thy
foot from thy neighbors house,
least he be wearie of thee, and

<!-- margin: Pr.27. 10 -->
hate thee ; neither enter into
thy brothers house in the daie

of

of thy calamitie : *nor againe, too forward in profering kindnesse to his owne losse*; A man destitute of vnderstanding toucheth the hand, and becommeth suretie for his neighbour : If *therefore* thou art become surety for thy neighbour (*much more* if thou haue striké hands with the strāger) thou art snared with the wordes of thine owne mouth, thou art euen taken with the words of thine owne mouth. Doe this now my sonne, seeing thou art comne into the hand of thy neighbour (*not* hauing taken a pledge for thy suretiship) goe and humble thy selfe and solicit thy friends , Giue no sleepe to thine eyes, nor

Pr. 17. 18

Pr. 6. 1. 2. &c.

Pr. 6. 3

Pr. 27. 13

Pr. 6. 4

slum-

Pr.6. 5.

slūber to thine ey lids. Deliuer thy self as a Doe from the hand of the hunter, & as a bird from the hand of the fowler; *& take it for a sure rule* , He that hateth suretiship is sure.

Pr.11. 15

SALO-

SALOMONS
POLITICKS,

Or

Common-wealth:

1. BOOKE.

His {
KING,
COVNSAILOR,
COVRTIER,
SVBIECT.
}

Anno Domini, 1609.

SALOMONS
OECONOMICKS,
Or FAMILY.

§. 1. The head of the Family: in whome is required { Wisedome, Stayednesse, Thrift.

He man is the head, *and guide of the family* ; *Jn whom* wisdome is good with an inheritance: *for* Through wisedome an house is builded, and established : *which directs him to doe all things in due order;*

Ec.7.13

Pr.24.3

L   *first*

Pr. 24. 27

firft, to prepare his worke without, and then after to builde his houſe ; *and there-with, ſtayednes.* *For,* as a bird that wandreth frõ her neaſt, ſo is a man that wandreth from his owne place ; *and (which is the chief ſtay of his eſtate) thriftineß; for,* He that troubleth his owne houſe (*by exceſſe*) ſhall inherit the winde : and the foole ſhalbe ſeruant to the wiſe in hart: *for which purpoſe, he ſhall finde, that* The houſe of the righteous ſhall haue much treaſure, while the reuenues of the wicked is but trouble : *or if not much ; yet,* Better is a little with the feare of the Lord, then great treaſure and trouble therewith : *Howſoeuer, therefore, let him bee content with his eſtate :*

Pr.

Pr. 11. 29

Pr. 15.6

Pr. 15.16

Let the lambes be sufficient for his cloathing; and let the goates bee the price of his fielde. Let the milke of his goates bee sufficient for his foode, for the food of his family, and the sustenance of his maydes : *and if hee haue much reuenue; let him looke for much expence.* For, When goods increase, they are increased that eat them: and what good commeth to the owners therof, but the beholding therof vvith their eyes ?

Pr.27.26

Pr.27.27

Ec.5.10

THE HVSBAND:

§. 2.
Who muſt beare himſelf {
wiſely,
chaſtly,
quietly, and cheerefully.

Pr. 18. 22

HE that findeth a vvife, fin-deth a good thing, and re-ceiueth fauour of the Lord: *Who muſt therefore behaue himſelfe,* 1. *wiſely,as* the guide of her youth: as the heade to which ſhee is a crowne : 2. *chaſtely.* Drink the water of thy owne Ciſtern, and the riuers out of the midſt of thine owne Well. *The matrimoniall loue muſt be pure, and cleare, not muddy and troubled;* Let thy fountaines flowe forth, and the riuers of waters in the Streets;

Pr. 2. 17.

Pr. 12. 4.

Pr. 5. 15

Pr. 5. 16

the

the sweet & comfortable fruits of
blessed marriage, in plentifull is-
sue : But let them bee thine a-
lone, and not the strangers with
thee. *This loue abides no part-*
ners : for, this vvere to giue
thine honour vnto others, and
thy strength to the cruell ; so
should the stranger be filled with
thy strength , and (*as the sub-*
stance will be with the affections)
thy laboures should bee in the
house of a stranger; and thou
shalt mourne (*which is the best*
successe heereof) at thine ende,
vvhen thou hast consumed (*be-*
sides thy goods) thy flesh, and thy
body, *and say* : How haue I hated instruction, and mine heart
despised correctiõ. I was almost

Pr. 5. 17

Pr. 5. 9.

Pr. .5. 10

Pr. 5. 11

Pr. 5. 12

Pr. 5. 14

L 3   plunged

plunged into all euill, *of sinne and torments* ; and that *which is most shamefull*, in the midst of the assembly, *in the face of the world*.

Pr. 5. 18

Let *therfore* that thy owne fountaine be blessed, and reioice with the wife of thy youth : Let her

Pr. 5. 19

be as the louing Hinde, and pleasant Roe : let her breasts satisfie thee, at all times, and erre thou

Pr. 5. 20

in her loue continually; For why shouldst thou delight my sonne, in a strange woman ; or (*whether in affection, or acte*) embrace

Pr. 5. 21

the bosome of a stranger ? For, the vvayes of man are before the eyes of the Lord, and hee pondereth all his pathes : *and if thy godlesnesse regarde not that, yet for thy owne sake*, Desire not

her

her beautie in thy heart , neyther let her take thee with her
eie-lids; for, becaufe of the who-
rifh woman, a man is brought to
a morfell of bread, *yea to the ve-*
ry huskes: *and more then that*; a
VVoman will hunt for the precious life of a man. *Thou fayeft,*
thou canft efcape this actuall de-
filement. Can a man take fire
in his bofome , and his cloa-
thes not bee burnt ? Or can a
man goe vpon coales, and his
feete not bee burnt ? So, hee
that goeth in, to his Neighbours Wife , fhall not bee innocent, vvhofoeuer toucheth
her : *This Sinne is farre more*
odious then thefte : *For*, men
doo not defpife a Thiefe when

Pr. 6. 25

Pr. 6. 26.

Pr. 6. 26

Pr. 6. 27

Pr. 6. 28

Pr. 6. 29

Pr. 6. 30

L 4   hee

hee ſteales to ſatisfie his ſoule, becauſe hee is hungrie . But if

Pr. 6. 31 hee be found, hee ſhall reſtore ſeauen folde, or he ſhall giue all the ſubſtance of his houſe; *and it*

Pr. 6. 32 *is accepted* . But, hee that commits adultery with a woman, is mad: he that would deſtroy his owne ſoule, let him doe it: *For,*

Pr. 6. 33 he ſhall finde a wounde and diſhonour, and his reproache ſhall neuer bee put avvaie : *Neither is the daunger leſſe then the ſhame.*

Pr. 6. 34 For, ielouſie is the rage of a man: therefore *the wronged husband* will not ſpare, in the day of ven-

Pr. 6. 35 geance. Hee cannot beare the ſight of any raunſome; neither will he conſent to *remit it* , tho thou multiplie thy giftes. And

tho Stollen waters be ſweet, and
hid bread be pleaſant *to our cor-*
rupt taſte; yet, *the adulterer*
knowes not that the dead are
there : and that her gueſts are
in the deepes of hell , that her
houſe tendeth to death ; *And*
how ſoeuer her lips drop as an hony-combe, and her mouth is
more ſoft then oyle ; yet the end
of her is bitter as wormewood,
& ſharpe as a two edged ſword :
her feete goe downe to death,
and her ſteps take hold of hell :
yea, The mouth of the ſtrange
woman is a deepe pit, *and* hee
with whom the Lord is angry
ſhall fall into it.

   3. *Quietly and louingly* : *for,*
Betteris a dinner of green herbs

Pr.9.17.

Pr.9.18.

Pr.2.18.
19.
Pr. 5.3.

Pr. 5.4.

Pr.5. 5.

Pr.23.27.

Pr. 22.14.

Pr. 15.17.

where

Pr.17.1.

where loue is, then a ftalled oxe, and hatred therewith. *Yea*,Better is a dry morfell, if peace be with it; then an houfe full of facrifices with ftrife. *And if he find fometime cauſe of blame* ; The difcretion of

Pr.19.11.

a man differreth his anger , and his glory is to paffe by an of-

Pr. 17.9.

fence : *and onely* He that couereth a tranfgreffion , feeketh

Ec.9.9.

loue : Reioyce with thy wife, whom thou haft loued all the dayes of the life of thy vanitie, which God hath giuen thee vnder the Sunne. For, this is thy portion in this life, and in the trauels wherein thou laboureft vnder the Sunne.

The

THE WIFE.

§. 3. She muſt be

{
1. Faithfull to her husband;
   Not wanton.

2. Obedient,

3. Diſcreet,

4. Prouident and houſ-wiſe-like.
}

A Vertuous Wife is the Crowne of her husband : Who ſhall finde ſuch a one? for her price is farre aboue the pearles. *Shee is true to her huſbands bedde*; ſuch as the heart of her husband may truſt to, *as knowing that ſhe is tied to him* by the couenant of God;*not wanton and vnchaſte:ſuch one* as I *once* ſaw from the window of my houſe : I looked through my window, &

Pr.12.4.

Pr.31.10.

Pr.31.11.

Pr.2.17.

Pr.7.6.

Pr.7.7.

ſaw a-

Pr. 7.7.
among the fooles, & confidered
among the children a yong man
Pr. 7.8.
wanting wit, who paffed through
the ftreete by her corner, and
went toward her houfe, in the
Pr. 7.9.
twi-light, in the euening, when
the night began to bee blacke
and darke, *fo as hee thought him-*
Pr. 7.10.
felfe vnfeene ; and behold there
met him *(the fame he fought for)*
a woman with an harlots fafhi-
on, *and* clofe in heart, *as open in*
Pr. 7.11.
her habite. She is babbling and
peruerfe ; whofe feete *(contrary*
to the manner of all modeft wiues,
Pr. 11. 16.
which onely attaine honour)
Pr. 7.11.
cannot abide in her houfe ; *but*
Pr. 7.12.
are euer gadding. Now fhee is
without *the gates*, now in the
Pr. 23.28.
ftreetes, and lyeth in wayte in

euery

euery corner ; *or at the leaft* , fit- | Pr.9.14.
teth at the doore of her houfe,
on a feat in the hie places of the
city : fo fhe (*not ſtaying to be foli-* | Pr. 7. 13.
cited) caught him *by the necke,*
and kiffed him , *and* with an im-
pudent face, faid vnto him , I | Pr.7.14.
haue the flefh of peace offrings,
(*both good cheere , and religion*
pretended) this day haue I paid
my vowes : therefore I came | Pr.7.15.
foorth, *on purpoſe* to meete thee,
that I might earneftly feeke thy
face, *of all others* ; and now , *how*
happy am I that I haue found
thee . I haue decked my bedde | Pr.7.16.
with ornaments, with curtaines,
and ftrings of Egypt. I haue per- | Pr.7. 17.
fumed my bedde with myrrhe,
aloes, and cinnamon, *that wee*

may

may lie sweet ; Come goe, let vs take our fill of loues, vntill the morning, let vs take our pleasure in dalliance ; *feare nothing* , For my husband is not at home, hee is gone a iourney farre off, *neither needest thou to doubt his returne* ; *for* he hath taken with him a bagge of siluer, and will come home at his set day : *sooner hee cannot*; *thus shee said* : *what followed ?* By the abundance of the sweetnesse of her speech, shee caused him to yeeld : and with the flatterie of her lippes , she intised him ; and straight wayes hee followes her as an oxe goeth to the slaughter, and as a foole to the stockes for cor-

re&ion,

Pr.7.18.

Pr.7.19.

Pr.7.20.

Pr.7.21.

Pr.7.22.

rection, till a dart strike through
his liuer, *the seate of his lust* : *or
as a birde hasteneth to the
snare, and knoweth not that it
is against his owne life* : thus
*shee doeth, and when her hus-
band returnes,* shee wipeth her
mouth, and saith I haue not
committed iniquitie. (2.) *She
is duetifull and obedient* ; by a
soft answere appeasing wrath :
not hatefull; *for whom,* a whole
world is mooued ; *not stub-
borne, not quarellous* : *for,* the
contentions *(and brawlings)*
of a wife, are like a continuall dropping in the day of
raine; *a discomfort to the husband, a rotting to the house.*
So, It is better to dwell in a

Pr.7.23.

Pr.30.20.

Pr.15.1.

Pr.30.23.
21.

Pr.19.13 }
Pr.27.15 }

Pr.25.24.

cor--

corner of the houfe top, then
with a contentious woman in a
wide houfe. *And tho, for fociety,*
Ec.4.9.   Two bee better then one; *yet*
Pr.27.19.   It is better to dwell *alone* in the
wildernefle, then with a con-
tentious, and angry woman.
For, herein as his griefe cannot be
auoyded, fo his fhame cannot bee
Pr.27.16.   *conceiued.* For, Hee that hideth
her, hideth the winde; and fhe
is as oyle in his right hand, that
vttereth it felfe.

4. The

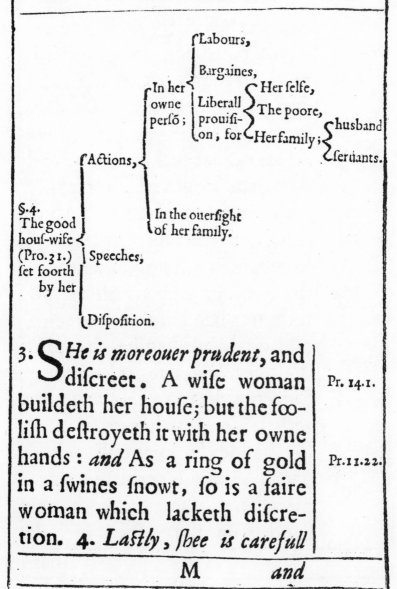

§.4.
The good
houſ-wife
(Pro.31.)
ſet foorth
by her

Actions,

- In her owne perſõ;
  - Labours,
  - Bargaines,
  - Liberall prouiſion, for
    - Her ſelfe,
    - The poore,
    - Her family;
      - husband
      - ſeruants.
- In the ouerſight of her family.

Speeches,

Diſpoſition.

3. **S**He is moreouer prudent, and diſcreet. A wiſe woman buildeth her houſe; but the fooliſh deſtroyeth it with her owne hands : *and* As a ring of gold in a ſwines ſnowt, ſo is a faire woman which lacketh diſcretion. 4. *Laſtly, ſhee is carefull*

Pr. 14.1.

Pr.11.22.

M   *and*

and houf-wifelike; fo as She will

Pr. 31.12. doe her husband good, and not euill, all the dayes of her life : *For, as for her actions,in her owne perfon, whether you looke to her*

Pr. 31.13. *labours ;* Shee feeketh wooll and flaxe, and laboureth cheerefully

Pr. 31.15. with her hands. She rifeth while

Pr.31.17. it is yet night : She girdeth her loynes with ftrength,and ftreng

Pr.31.19. theneth her armes. Shee putteth her hands to the wheele ; and her hands handle the fpindle : *or whether,to her bargaines;*

Pr.31.16. She confidereth a field,and getteth it, and with the fruit of her handes fhe planteth a vine-

Pr. 31.14. yard. Shee is like the fhippe of merchants, fhee bringeth her food from farre ; fhee feeleth

that

that her merchandife is good,
her candle is not put out by
night : fhee maketh fheets & fel-
leth them, and giueth girdles vnto the merchants ; *or whether, to
her liberall prouifion* ; *For her
husband*, who is knowen in the
gates (*by her neate furnifhing*)
when hee fits with the Elders of
the land ; 2. *For her felfe*, Shee
maketh her felfe carpets : fine
linnen & purple is her garment ;
3. *For her feruants*, Shee feareth
not the fnow for her family, for
all her familie is clothed with
fcarlet ; 4. *For the poore*, Shee
ftretcheth out her hands to the
poore, and putteth foorth her
hands to the needy ; *For her
ouerfight of her familie*, fhe gi-

Pr.31.18.

Pr.31.24.

Pr.31.23.

Pr.31.22.

Pr.31.21.

Pr.31.20.

M 2   ueth

Pr. 13.15.	ueth the portion to her houfe-hold, and the ordinary *(or ftint of work)* to her maids: fhe ouer-
Pr. 13.27.	feeth the wayes of her houfe-hold, and eateth not the bread of idleneffe. *For her fpeeches;*
Pr. 31.26.	fhe openeth her mouth with wifedome, and the lawe of grace is in her tongue. *Laftly,*
Pr. 31.25.	Strength and honour is her clothing, and in the latter day fhee fhall reioyce. *So worthie fhee is in all thefe, that* her owne
Pr. 31.28.	children *cannot containe, but* rife vp and call her bleffed; *and* her husband fhall prayfe her,
Pr. 31.29.	*and fay,* Many daughters haue done vertuoufly, but thou fur-
Pr. 31.30.	mounteft them all: Fauour is deceitfull, and beautie is vani-

ty,

tie; but a woman that feareth
the Lord, fhee fhall be praifed:
Since therefore fhee is fo well deferring, Giue her of the fruit of her
owne hands, and let her owne
workes prayfe her.

Pr. 31. 31.

PARENTS:

§. 5. Who owe to their children
{ Prouifion,
Inftruction,
Correction.

P *Arents and Children are the
next payre ; which doe giue
much ioy to each other :* Childrens
children are the Crowne of the
elders, and the glory of the
children are their fathers : *To
which purpofe, the* Parent *oweth to the* Childe, 1. Prouifion.

Pr. 17. 6.

Pr.13.22. | A good man shall giue inheri-
tance to his childrens children.

Ec.2.18. | All the labour, wherein hee hath
trauelled, he shall leaue to the
man that shall be after him. And

Ec. 2, 19. | who knoweth whether hee shall
be wise or foolish: yet shal he rule
ouer all his labour wherein *hee*
hath laboured, and shewed himselfe wise, vnder the sunne. *Here*
are therefore two große vanities,

Ec. 4.8. | which I haue seene: *the one,* There
is one alone, & there is not a se-
cond, which hath neither sonne
nor brother : yet is there none
end of his trauell, neither can his
eye be satisfied with riches ; neither *doth he thinke,* for whom do
I trauell, and defraud my soule of
pleasure. *The other, contrary* ;

riches referued to the owners thereof for their euill. And thefe riches perifh in his euill bufinefs; and he begetteth a fonne, and in his hand is nothing. 2. Inftructiō *and good education* : *for* , He that begetteth a foole (*whether natu- rally, or by ill breeding*) begetteth himfelfe forrow : and the father of a foole can haue no ioy. *And therefore* , Teach a child in the trade of his way: and when he is olde , hee fhall not depart from it. 3. Correction : He that fpareth his rodde , hateth his fonne: but he that loueth him, chafteneth betime ; for foolifh- neffe is bound in the heart of a child : the rodde of corre- ction fhall driue it from him:

Ec.5.12.

Ec.5.13.

Pr.1.8.

Pr.17.21.

Pr.22.6.

Pr.13.24.

Pr.22.15.

M 4 *yea*

yea, there is yet great benefit of due

Pr. 29. 15 *chasticement; for,* The rodde and correctiou giue life : but a child set at libertie makes his mother (*who is commonly faulty this way*) aſhamed ; *yea, more them ſhame, death and hell follow to the child* vpon indulgence:(*onely*) If thou

Pr. 23. 13 ſmite him with the rod, hee ſhall not die : if thou ſmite him with

Pr. 25. 14 the rod, thou ſhalt deliuer his ſoule from hell. *Tho thy* ſonne

Pr. 4. 3. *therefore* be tender and deare in

Pr. 29. 17 thy ſight ; Correct him, and hee will giue thee reſt, and will giue pleaſures to thy ſoule :

Pr. 19.18. *wherefore,* Chaſten him while there is hope ; and let not thy ſoule ſpare, to his deſtruction.

Pr. 19.19. The ſonne that is of a great ſto-

mach

mach, fhall indure punifhment :
and tho thou deliuer him, yet
thou fhalt take him in hand a-
gaine.

CHILDREN:

§. 6. Their duties;
- obedience to
  - inftructions,
  - cōmandements.
- fubmiffion to correction.
- care
  - of their Parents eftate,
  - of their owne carriage.

A Wife Sonne reioyceth the
Father , *and* The Father
of the righteous fhall greatlie
reioyce ; *vvhereas*, The foolifh is the calamitie of his Parents : *Contrarilie*, if thou bee

Pr.15.20
Pr.10. 1.
Pr. 23. 24

Pr.19.13.

a

Pr. 29. 3
Pr. 23. 25

Pr. 13. 1

Pr. 1. 8.

pr. 23. 22 }
Pr. 6. 20 }

Pr. 30. 11

Pr. 20. 20.

Pr. 15. 20.

pr. 30. 17

a wife fonne, *or loueſt wiſdome,*
thy father & thy mother ſhall be
glad, and ſhe that bare thee ſhall
reioice. *Such a one is, firſt, Obe-*
dient ; for, A wiſe fon will heare
and obey the inſtruction of his
father, and not forſake his mo-
thers teaching ; *yea, in euery com-*
mand, he will obey him that be-
got him, and not deſpiſe his mother when ſhe is olde; *not vpon a-*
ny occaſion curſing his parents (as
there is a generation that doth):
for, He that curſeth his father, or
mother, his light ſhall be put out
in obſcure darkneſs; *not mocking*
& ſcorning them ; for, The eye
that mocketh his father, and deſpiſeth the inſtruction of his mother, the rauens of the vally ſhall

picke

picke it out, and the young Eagles eate it : *and not obedient to counsell only, but to stripes*; Hee that hateth correction is a foole: and he that regardeth it, is prudent. *For,* those corrections that are for instruction, are the waie of life : *therfore,* hee that hateth them shall die. *Secondly, Carefull both* [1] *of their estate* : He that robbeth his father & mother, and saith it is no transgression, is a companion of a man that destroieth; *and* [2] *of his owne carriage* : *for* a lewde and shamefull childe destroyeth his father, and chaseth away his mother. Let therefore euen the childe showe himselfe to bee knowen by his dooings, whether his worke be pure and

Pr. 12. 1

Pr. 15. 5

Pr. 6. 23

Pr. 15. 10

Pr. 28. 24

Pr. 19. 26

pr. 20. 11

right

Pr.23.16.

right: *so* his fathers reynes shall reioice, when he speaketh *& doth* righteous things.

The MAISTER, & SERVANT.

§. 7.
- The master must be
  - Prouident for his seruant:
  - Not
    - too seuere,
    - too familiar.
- The seruant must be
  - faithfull,
  - diligent.

Pr. 12. 9.

THe *seruant is no small commodity to his master.* Hee that is despised, & hath a seruant of his own is better then he that boasts (*whether of gentry, or wealth*) & wanteth bread. *The master, therefore, must prouide* sufficiency of foode for his family, and sustenance for his maydes : *who also*

Pr.27.27.

as hee may not bee ouer-rigorous in
punishing, or noting offences; some-
times not hearing his feruant , | Ec.7.23
that curfeth him: *fo not too famili-*
ar;for he that delicately bringeth | Pr.29. 21
vp his feruant from his youth, at
length he wil be as his fonne. *He*
muft therefore be fometimes feuere,
more then in rebukes; (For, A fer-
uant will not bee chafticed with | Pr.29.19.
words : and tho he vnderftand,
yet he will not regarde) *yet fo,*
as hee haue refpeƈt euer to his good
deferuings. A difcreet feruant | Pr.17.2.
fhall rule ouer a levvde fonne :
and he fhall diuide the heritage
among the brethren. *Jn anfwer*
whereto , the good feruant muft
bee faithfull *vnto his mafter;* As | Pr.25.13
the colde of fnovve in time of

harueft

harueſt, ſo is a faithful meſſenger to them that ſend him, for he refreſheth the ſoule of his maſter.

Pr.13.17.

A wicked meſſenger falleth into euil: but a faithfull ambaſſadour is preſeruation ; *and* [2] *diligent ,*

Pr.27.23.

Whether in his charge; Be diligent to knowe the eſtate of thy flock (*or rather,* the face of thy cattel) and take heed to the heardes: *or*

Pr. 27.18

in his attendance , Hee that keepeth his fig-tree ſhall eate of the fruite of it: ſo hee that *carefully* waiteth on his maſter, ſhall come

Pr. 10. 26

to honour; *where contrarily , in both theſe ,* As vinegar to the teeth , and ſmoke to the eyes: ſo is a ſlouthfull meſſenger to them that ſend him.

FINIS.

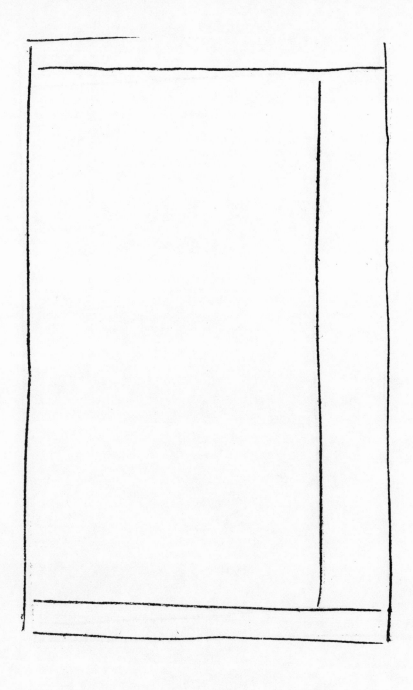

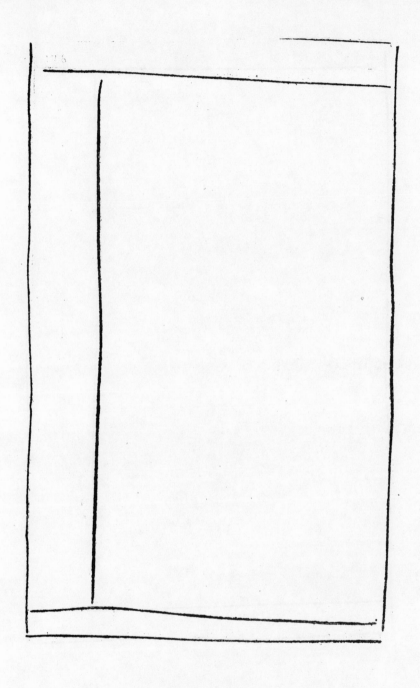

AN
OPEN AND
plaine Paraphrase,

vpon the
SONG OF SONGS,

Which is

SALOMONS.

By Ios. HALL.

Anno Domini, 1609.

TO THE RIGHT

HONOVRABLE, MY
Singular good Lord & Patron,
EDVVARD Lord *Denny*,
Baron of Waltham, *All*
Grace & Happinesse.

RIGHT HONOVRABLE:

Hen I would haue with-
drawen my hand from di-
uine Salomon : the hea-
uenly elegance of this his
best Song drewe me vnto it; *and would
not suffer me to take off mine eies*, *or pen.
Who can read it with vnderstanding*, *&
not bee transported from the world*;

from himſelfe? and be any other where,
ſaue in heauen, before his time? I had
rather ſpende my time in admiration,
then Apology: Surely, heere is nothing
that ſauours not of extaſie, and ſpirituall rauiſhment; neither was there euer
ſo high and paſſionate a ſpeculation de-
liuered by the ſpirit of God, to mankind:
which by how much more diuine it is, by
ſo much more difficult: It is wel, if theſe
myſteries can be found out by ſearching.
Two things make the Scriptures hard:
Prophecies, Allegories; both are met in
this: but the latter ſo ſenſibly to the wea-
keſt eyes, that this whole Paſtoral-mari-
age-ſong (for ſuch it is) is no other then
one Allegory ſweetly continued: where
the deepeſt things of God are ſpoken in
riddles, how can there be but obſcurity
& diuers conſtruction? All iudgements
will not (I know) ſubſcribe to my ſenſes;
yet I haue beene fearefull and ſpiritually nice in my choice, not often diſſenting

from all interpreters; alwaies, from the vnlikeliest. It would bee too tedious to giue my account for euery line : let the learned scanne and iudge. What-euer others censures be, your Honours was fauourable; and (as to all mine) full of loue and incouragement. That, therefore, which it pleased you to allow from my penne, vouchsafe to receiue from the Presse; more common, not lesse deuoted to you. What is there of mine that doth not ioy in your name, and boast it selfe in seruing you? To whose soule and people, I haue long agone addicted my selfe, and my labours; and shall euer continue

Your Lordships, in all hum-

ble & vnfained dutie,

IOS. HALL.

SALOMONS
Song of Songs, pa-raphrafed.

CHAP. I.

Dialog. *The Church, to* CHRIST.

O H that he would be-ftovve vpon me the comfortable teftimo-nies of his loue, and that hee would vouchfafe me yet a nee-rer coniunction with himfelfe; as in glory hereafter, fo for the meane time in his fenfible gra-ces. For, thy loue, O my Sa-

1 *Let him kiffe me, with the kiffes of his mouth; for, thy loue is better then wine.*

N 4　　uiour

uiour, and these fruites of it, are more sweet vnto me, then all earthly delicates can bee to the bodily taste.

Yea, so wonderfully pleasant are the sauours of those graces that are in thee, wherewith I desire to be indued; that al, whom thou hast blessed with the sense thereof, make as high and deare account of thy Gospell, vvhereby they are wrought, as of some precious oyntment, or perfume: the delight whereof is such, that (heereuppon) the pure and holy soules of the faithfull, place their whole affection, vpon thee.

2. Because of the sauour of thy good ointmēts, thy name is as an ointmēt powred out: therfore the Virgins loue thee

Pull me therefore out from the bondage of my finnes: deliuer mee from the world, and doe thou powerfully incline my will, and affections toward thee: and in fpight of all tentations, giue mee ftrength to cleaue vnto thee ; and then both I, and all thofe faithfull children thou haft giuen me, fhall all at once with fpeede and earneftneffe walke to thee, and with thee: yea, when once my royall and glorious husband hath brought mee both into thefe lower roomes of his fpirituall treafures on earth, and into his heauenlie chambers of glorie,

3. Draw me, we will runne after thee: the king hath brought me into his chā-bers, we will reioyce, & be glad in thee: we will remē-ber thy loue, more then vine, the righteous doe loue thee.

then

then will we reioyce and bee
glad in none, but thee; which
ſhalt be all in all to vs: then will
wee celebrate and magnifie
thy loue, aboue all the pleaſures we found vpõ earth; for,
all of vs thy righteous ones,
both Angels and Saints, are inflamed with the loue of thee.

4. I am black
O daughters
of Ieruſalẽ,
but comely :
If I be as the
tents of Ke-
dar, *yet I am*
as the cur-
taines of Sa-
lomon.

Neuer vpbraid mee (O ye
forraine congregations) that I
ſeeme in outward appearance
diſcoloured by my infirmities,
and duskiſh with tribulations:
for, what ſoeuer I ſeeme to you,
I am yet inwardly wel-fauoured in the eyes of him, whom I
ſeeke to pleaſe ; and tho I bee
to you blacke like the tents of
the Arabian ſhepherds: yet to

him

him and in him, I am glorious and beautiful, like the curtains of *Salomon.*

Looke not therefore difdainefully vpon me, becaufe I am blackifh, & darke of hew: for, this colour is not fo much naturall to me ; as caufed by that continuall heate of afflictions wherewith I haue bene vfually fcorched : neither this, fo much vpon my owne iuft defert, as vpon the rage and enuie of my falfe brethren, the World: who would needs force vpon me the obferuation of their idolatrous religions, and fuperftitious impieties ; through whofe wicked importunitie, and my owne

5. Regard yee me not, becaufe I am blacke : for the fun hath looked vpon me; the fons of my mother were angry againft me: they made me keeper of the vines : but I kept not mine owne vine.

weake-

weakeneſſe, I haue not ſo intirely kept the ſincere truth of God committed to me, as I ought.

Now therfore,thatI am ſome little ſtarted aſide from thee, O thou whom my ſoule notwithſtanding dearely loueth, ſhew me,I beſeech thee,where, and in what wholeſome & diuine paſtures thou (like a good ſhepherd)feedeſt,&reſteſt thy flockes with comfortable refreſhings, in the extreamity of theſe hot perſecutiōs: for,how can it ſtand with thy glory, that I ſhould through thy neglect, thus ſuſpiciouſly wander vp and downe, amongſt the congregations of them that both

6. Shew me, O thou whom my ſoule loueth,where thou feedeſt, where thou lieſt at noon: for why ſhold I be as ſhee that turneth aſide to the flockes of thy companions?

command & practife the worfhip of falfe gods.

CHRIST, *to the Church.*

IF thou know not, ô thou my
Church, whō I both efteeme
and haue made moft beutifull
by my merits, and thy fanctification: ftray not amongft thefe
falfe worfhippers, but follow
the holy fteps of thofe bleffed
Patriarchs, Prophets, Apoftles,
which haue bin my true & ancient flocke; who haue both
knowen my voice, & followed
me : & feed thou my weake &
tender ones with this their fpirituall food of life, far aboue
the carnall reach of thofe o-
ther falfe teachers.

7. If thou know not, O thou the faireft among women, get thee foorth by the fteps of the flocke: & feed thy Kids aboue the tents of the fhepherds.

Such

Such is mine eſtimation of thee, O my Loue, that ſo farre as the choiſeſtEgyptian horſes of Pharaoh,for comely ſhape, for honourable ſeruice, for ſtrength and ſpeed,exceed all other, ſo farre thou excelleſt all that may be compared with thee.

Thoſe parts of thee, which both are the ſeats of beauty, and moſt conſpicuous to the eye, are gloriouſly adorned with the graces of my ſanctifi-cation ; which are for their worth as ſo many precious borders of the goodlieſt ſtones,or chaines of pearle.

And tho thou be already thus ſet forth : yet I and my father

ther haue purposed a further
ornament vnto thee, in the
more plentifull effusion of our
spirit vpon thee : which shalbe
to thy former deckings, in
stead of pure gold curiously
wrought with specks of siluer.

borders of gold, with studs of siluer

The Church.

BEhold (O yee daughters)
euen now, whiles my Lord
and King seemes farre distant
from me, & sits in the throne of
heauen amongst the compa-
nies of Angels (who attend a-
round vpon him) yet now doe
I find him present with mee in
spirit; euen now, the sweet influence of his graces, like to
some precious ointmét, spreds

11. While the king was at his repast, my spiknard gaue the smell thereof.

it felfe ouer my foule ; and returnes a pleafant fauour into
his owne nofthrils.

12. *My wel-
beloued is as
a bundle of
myrrhe vnto
me, lying be-
tweene my
breafts.*
And tho I bee thus delight-
ful to my Sauiour, yet nothing
fo much as he is vnto me: for
loe, as fome fragrant poman-
der of myrrhe, laid betweene
the brefts, fends vp a moft cōfortable fent; fo, his loue, laid
clofe vnto my heart, doth ftill
giue me continual & vnfpeak-
able refrefhings.

13. *My wel-
beloued is as
a clufter of
Cypers vnto
me among
the vines of
Engeddy.*
Or if any thing can bee of
more excellent vertue, fuch
fmell as the clufters of cypers-
berries, within the fruitfulft,
pleafantft, & richeft vineyards,
& gardēs of Iudæa, yeeld vnto
the paffengers; fuch and more

de-

delectable doe I finde the fauour of his grace to me.

CHRIST.

NEither doeſt thou on my
part loſe any of thy loue,
O my deare Church : for, behold; in mine eies, thus clothed
as thou art with my righteouſneſſe, oh how faire & glorious
thou art ; how aboue all com-
pariſon glorious and faire!
thine eies (which are thy ſeers,
Prophets, Apoſtles, Miniſters)
and thoſe inward eyes, whereby thou ſeeſt him that is inui-
ſible, are full of grace, chaſtity,
ſimplicitie.

14. My Loue
behold thou
art faire,
thine eyes are
like the doues

O Nay

The Church.

15. *My wel-
beloued, be-
hold, thou art
faire & plea-
sant: also our
bed is greene.*

NAy then (O my sweet sa-
uiour and spouse) thou a-
lone art that faire and pleasant
one indeed , from whose fulnesse I confesse to haue receiued al this little measure of my
spiritual beauty : and behold,
from this our mutuall delight,
& heauenly coniunctiõ, there
ariseth a plentifull and flori-
shing increase of thy faithfull
ones, in all places, & through
all times.

16. *The
beames of our
house are ce-
dars, our gal-
leries are of
firre.*

And behold, the congrega-
tions of Saints, the places
where we do sweetly conuerse
and walke together, are both
firme and during (like cedars

amongst

amongſt the trees) not ſubiect through thy protecting grace to vtter corruptiõ; & through thy fauourable acceptation and word (like to galleries of ſweet wood) full of pleaſure and contentment.

CHAP. II.

Chriſt.

THou haſt not without iuſt cauſe magnified mee, O my Church : for, as the faireſt & ſweeteſt of all floures which the earth yeeldeth, the roſe & lilly of the valleyes, excell for beautie, for pleaſure, for vſe, the moſt baſe and odious weeds that growe; ſo doth my

1. *I am the Roſe of the field, and the Lillie of the valleyes.*

grace, to al them that haue felt the sweetnesse thereof, sur-passe all worldly content-ments.

2. *Like a lilly among the thorns, so is my Loue a-mong the daughters.*

Neither is this my dignitie alone : but thou O my spouse (that thou mayest bee a fit match for mee) art thus excel-lent aboue the world, that no lilly can bee more in goodly shew beyond the naked thorn, then thou in thy glory thou receiuest from me, ouer-loo-kest all the assemblies of aliens and vnregenerates.

The Church.

3. *Like the Apple-tree among the trees of the*

ANd (to returne thine owne praises) as some fruitful & wel-growen Apple-

tree

tree, in comparifon of all the barren trees of the wild foreft: fo art thou(O my beloued fauiour)to me, in comparifon of all men,and angels; vnder thy comfortable fhadowe alone, haue I euer wont to find fafe fhelter againft all mine afflictions, all my tentations and infirmities, againft all the curfes of the Law, and dangers of iudgement, and to coole my felfe after all the fcorching beames of thy fathers difpleafure, and(befides)to feed and fatisfie my foule with the foueraigne fruite of thy holy word,vnto eternall life.

Hee hath gratioufly led me by his fpirit, into the midft of

foreft, fo is my wel-beloued among the fonnes of men: vnder his fhadow had I delight, & fate down; and his fruit was fweet vnto my mouth.

4. He broght me into the wine cellar,

and loue was his banner ouer me.

the myſteries of godlineſs;and hath plentifully broached vnto me the ſweet wines of his Scriptures, & ſacrament. And looke how ſoldiers are drawn by their colours,from place to place, and cleaue faſt to their enſigne : ſo his loue,which he ſpred forth in my hart, was my only bāner,wherby I was both drawen to him, directed by him,and faſtened vpon him.

5. Stay me with flagons, and comfort me with apples: for, I am ſicke of loue.

And now, O ye faithfull E-uangeliſts,Apoſtles,Teachers apply vnto me,with all care & diligence,all the cordiall pro-miſes of the Goſpel: theſe are the full flagons of that ſpirituall wine,which only can cheere vp my ſoule ; theſe are the

apples

apples of that tree of life, in the middeſt of the garden, which can feed me to immortalitie . Oh come and apply theſe vnto my heart: for, I am euen ouercome with a‚ longing expectation and deſire of my delayed glory.

And whileſt I am thus ſpiritually languiſhing in this agony of deſire ; let my Sauiour imploy both his hands to relecue mine infirmitie: let him comfort my head & my heart, my iudgement and affections (which both complaine of weakeneſſe) with the liuely heate of his gratious imbracements : and ſo let vs ſweetly reſt together.

6. His left hand be vnder my head: and let his right hand imbrace mee.

7. *I charge you O daughters of Ierusalem, by the roes & by the Hinds of the field, that ye stirre not vp, nor waken my Loue, vntill he please.*

In the meane time, I charge you (O all yee that professe any friendship or affinitie with mee) I charge you, by whatsoeuer is comely, deare, and pleasant vnto you, as you will auoid my vttermost censures, take heed how you vexe and disquiet my mercifull Sauior, & greeue his spirit, and wrong his name, with your vaine and leud cōuersatiō;& do not dare by the least prouocation of your sin to interrupt his peace

8. *It is the voice of my wel-beloued: behold he cō-meth leaping by mountains and skipping by the hils.*

Loe, I haue no sooner called, but hee heares and answeres me with his louing voice: neither doth he only speak to me afar, but hee comes to me with much willingnes & celeritie;

ſo willingly, that no humane reſiſtaunce can hinder him, neither the hillocks of my leſſer infirmities, nor the mountaines of my groſſer ſinnes (once repented of) can ſtaie his merciful paſe towards me.

So ſwiftly, that no Roe, or Hinde, can fully reſemble him in this his ſpeed & nimbleneſs: and loe, euen now, before I can ſpeak it, is he come neere vnto me; cloſe to the doore and wall of my heart. And tho this wall of my fleſh hinder my full fruition of him : yet loe, I ſee him by the eye of faith, looking vpon me; I ſee him as in a glaſſe; I ſee him ſhining glorioully, through the

9. My welbeloued is like a Roe, or a youg Hart: loe, hee ſtandeth behinde our wall, looking forth of the windowes, ſhewing himſelfe through the grates.

grates

grates and vvindowes of his Word and Sacraments, vpon my foule.

And now, mee thinkes, I heare him fpeake to mee in a gracious invitation & fay , Arife (O my Church) rife vp , whether from thy feeurity, or feare : hide not thy head anie longer, O my beautiful Spoufe for danger of thine enemies : neither fuffer thy felfe to bee preffed with the dulnefs of thy nature, or the careleffe fleepe of thy finnes; but come forth into the comfortable light of my prefence, and fhew thy felf cheerefull in me.

For beholde, all the cloudie winter of thy afflictions is paf-

10. My VVelbeloued fpake, & fayd vnto me, arife my Loue, my faire one, and come thy way

11. For, behold winter is paft, the

fed

fed, all the tempefts of tentations are blowen ouer; the
Heauen is cleare, and novv
there is nothing that may not
giue thee caufe of delight.

Euerie thing novv refem-
bles the face of a fpirituall
Spring; all the fweete flovv-
ers and bloffomes of holy profeffion put forth, and fhewe
themfelues in their opportunities : now is the time of that
heauenly melodie, which the
cheerefull Saints and Angells
make in mine eares ; vvhile
they fing fongs of deliuerance
and praife me with their Alle-
luiahs and fay, Glory to God
on hie, in earth peace, good-
will towards men.

rain is chan-
ged and gone
away.

12. The
flowers ap-
peare in the
earth: the
time of the
finging of
birds is come,
and the voice
of the turtle
is heard in
our land.

What

13. The fig-tree hath broght forth her young figs and the vines with their small grapes haue caft a fauor: arife my Loue, my faire one, and come away.

What speake I of bloſſoms? beholde, thoſe fruitfull vines, and fig-trees of my faithfull ones, whome my husbandry hath carefully tended & dreſ-ſed, yeeld forth both pleaſant (tho tender) fruits of obedi-ence, and the wholſome and comfortable ſauours of better deſires : wherefore, now O my deare Church, ſhake off all that dull ſecuritie, where-with thou haſt beene held; and come forth, and inioy me.

14. My Doue, thou art in the hoales of the rocke, in the ſecret places of the cliftes: ſhewe mee thy

O my beautifull, pure, and chaſte ſpouſe, which like vnto ſome ſolitary doue haſt long hid thine head in the ſecret & inacceſſible clifts of the rocks, out of the reache and know-

ledge

ledge of thy perfecutours ; how-euer thou art concealed from others, fhew thy felfe in thy works and righteoufneffe, vnto me : and let me be euer plied with thy words of imploration, and thankefgiuing: for thy voice (tho it be in mourning) and thy face (tho it bee fad and blubbered) are exceedingly pleafing vnto me.

fight, let mee heare thy voice: for thy voice is fweet and thy fight comely.

And in the meane time (O all yee that wifhe vvell to my Name and Church) do your vtmoft indeauour , to deliuer her from her fecret enemies (not fparing the leaft) who either by hereticall doctrine, or profane conuerfation, hinder the courfe of the Gofpell; and

14. Take vs the foxes, the litle foxes which deftroy the vines: for our vines haue fmall grapes.

per-

peruert the faith of many; e-
fpecially of thofe, that haue
newly giuen vp their names to
me, and are but newly entred
into the profeſſion of godli-
neſſe.

16. *My*
VVelbeloued
is mine, & I
am his: hee
feedeth amõg
the Lillies.

My beloued Sauior is mine,
through my faith; and I am
his through his loue : and we
both are one, by vertue of
that bleſſed vnion on both
partes; whereby wee mutu-
ally inioy each other, with all
ſufficient contentment. And
how worthily is my loue placed vpon him, who leadeth
mee forth into pleaſant paſtures;and at whoſe right hand
there is the fulneſſe of ioy for
euermore?

Come

Come therefore (O my Sauiour) and vntill the day of thy glorious appearance fhall fhine forth to the world, wherin our fpirituall marriage fhall be confummate, and vntill all thefe fhadowes of ignorance, of infidelity , of troubles of confcience , and of outwarde tribulations be vtterly difperfed, and chafed away; come and turne thee to me againe: thou which to the carnall eyes of the world feemeft abfent; come quickly and delay not: but,for the fpeed of thy return be like vnto fom fwift Roe, or Hind, vpō thofe fmooth hills of *Gilead* , which *Iordan* feuers from the other part of *Iury.*

17. *Vntill the day break and the fhadowes flee a-way; returne my VVelbeloued,& be like a Roe or a young Hart vpon the moū taines of Be-ther.*

Chap.

CHAP. III.

1. *In my bed, by night I sought him that my soule loued: I soght him, but I found him not.*

MY securitie told me that my Sauior was neer vnto my soule, yea with it, and in it: but vvhen by serious and silent meditation I searched my owne heart, I found that (for ought my ovvne sense could discerne) hee was farre off from me.

Then thought I vvith my selfe, Shall I lie still contented with this want? No, I wil stirre vp my selfe: and the helpe I cannot finde in my selfe, I will seeke in others ; Of all that haue been experienced in all kinde of difficulties : of all

2. *I will rise therefore now, and goe about in the Citie by the streetes, and by the open places, and will seek him that my soule*

deep

deep Philofophers, of the wifeft and honefteft worldlings, I will diligently enquire for my Sauiour : amongeft them I fought him, yet could receiue no anfvvere to my fatisfaction.

oueth: I foght him, but I found him not.

Miffing him there, I ran to thofe vvife and carefull Teachers, whom God hath fet, as fo many watch-men vpon the walles of his Ierufalem, vvho fooner found me then I could aske after them; to whome I fayde, (as thinking no man coulde bee ignoraunt of my loue) Can you giue mee no direction where I might finde him, vvhome my foule loueth?

3, The watchmen that went about the City, found me: to whom I fayd, haue you feen him whom my foule loueth?

P   Of

4. *VVhen I had paſt a little from them, then I found him vhõ my ſoule loueth: I took holde on him, and left him not, till I had brought him vnto my mothers houſe vnto the chã-ber of hir that conceiued me.*

Of whome when I had almoſt left hoping for comfort, that gracious Sauiour vvho would not ſuffer mee tempted aboue my meaſure, preſented himſelfe to my ſoule: Loe then, by a newe act of faith, I laide faſt holde vpon him, and will not let him anie more part from my ioyfull embracements; vntil both I haue brought him home fully into the ſeate of my conſcience, and haue won him to a perpetuall cohabitation with mee; and a full accompliſhment of my loue, in that Ieruſalem which is aboue, which is the mother of vs all.

CHRIST.

NOw that my diftreffed Church hath beene, all the Night long of my fee-ming abfence, toyled in fee-king mee, I charge you (O all that profeffe anie friend-fhip with mee) I charge you by whatfoeuer is comly, deare, and pleafant vnto you, that (as you will anfwere it) you trouble not her peace vvith anie vniuft or vnfeafona-ble fuggeftions ; vvith vn-charitable contentions, with anie Nouelties of doctrine ; but fuffer her to reft fweete-lie , in that diuine truthe,

5. I charg ye ô daughters of Ierufalem, by the roes, & by the Hinds of the fielde , that yee ftirre not vp nor wake my loue vntill fhee pleafe.

P 2   which

vvhich fhee hath receiued, and this true apprehenfion of mee vvherein fhee reioyceth.

Oh who is this, how admirable ? hovv louely ? vvho but my Church, that afcendeth thus gloriouflie out of the vvildernefle of the world, vvherein fhee hath thus long vvandered, into the bleffed manfions of my fathers houfe; all perfumed vvith the graces of perfect fanctification, mounting right vpward into her glorie, like fome ftraight pillar of fmoake, that arifeth from the moft rich and pleafant compofition of odours that can be deuifed.

6. Who is fhe that commeth vp out of the wildernefs, like pillars of fmoke perfumed with myrrh and incenfe, & with al the chief fpices?

The

The Church.

IAm afcended; and loe how glorious is this place where I fhall eternally inioy the prefence and loue of my Sauiour; hovv farre doth it exceede the earthlie magnificence of S A L O M O N : about his bedde doe attende a guard of threefcore choyfeſt men of Ifrael.

All ſtout VVarriers, able and expert to handle the ſword; which, for more readineſſe, each of them weares hanging vpon his thigh, fo as it may be haſtily dravven vp-

7. *Behold his bed better then* Salomons: three-ſcore ſtrong men are roũd about it, of the valiant men of Ifrael.

8. They all handle the ſword, and are expert in wai euery one hath his ſword vpõ his thigh, for the fear by night.

pon anie ſuddaine daunger: but about this heauenlie pauilion of my Sauiour, attend millions of Angelles, ſpirituall Souldiers, mightie in power, readie to bee commaunded ſeruice by him.

The Bride-bed that S A-L O M O N made (ſo much admired of the World) vvas but of the Cedars of Lebanon.

The Pillars but of ſiluer, and the bed-ſteed of golde; the Teſter or Canopie but of purple; the couerlet wrought vvith the curious and painefull needle--vvorke of the maydes of I E R V S A L E M: but this celeſtiall reſting place of

9. King Salomon made himſelf a bed of the trees of Lebanon.

10. Hee made the pillars therof of ſiluer, and the ſteed thereof of gold, the hangings thereof of purple, whoſe midſt was in-layde with the loue

my

my G O D is not made with
hands, not of anie corrup-
tible metall, but is full of
incomprehenfible light, fhining euermore vvith the glorious prefence of G O D.

of the daugh-
ters of Ieru-
falem.

And as the outward ftate,
fo the maiefty of his perfon is
aboue all comparifon. Come
forth(O ye daughters of Sion)
lay afide all priuate and earthly affections, looke vpon king
S A L O M O N as hee fits folemn-
lie crovvned in the daie of
his greateft royaltie and tri-
umph, and compare his high-
eft pompe vvith the diuine
magnificence of my Sauiour;
in that daie vvhen his bleffed

11. Come
forth yee
daughters of
Sion, and
beholde the
King Sa-
lomon with
the crowne
wherwith his
mother crow-
ned him in the
day of his ma-
riage, and in
the day of the
gladneffe of
his heart.

marriage ſhall bee fully per-
fited aboue, to the eternall
reioycing of himſelfe, and
his Church; and ſee vvhether
there bee any proportion betwixt them.

CHAP. IIII.

CHRIST.

1. Behold, thou art faire my Loue, be-holde thou art faire, thine eyes are like the doues within thy locks, thine haire is like

OH how faire thou art and comely, my deer Spouſe; how inwardely faire with the giftes of my Spirit; how faire outwardly in thy comely ad-miniſtration, and gouernmēt: thy ſpirituall eyes of vnder-ſtanding, and iudgement, are

full

full of puritie, chaftitie, fimpli-
citie; not wantonly caft forth,
but modeftly fhining amidft
thy locks: all thy gratious profeffion and all thy appendances, and ornaments of expedient ceremonies, are fo comely
to behold, as it is to fee a flock
of well-fed goates grafing vpon the fruitfull hils of Gilead.

a flocke of goats which looke downe from the mountaines of Gilead.

Thofe that chew and pre-
pare the heauenly food for thy
foule, are both of gratious fim-
plicitie, and of fweete accordance one with another; hauing all one heart, and one
tongue: and both themfelues
are fanctified, & purged from
their vncleanneffes, and are
fruitfull in their holy labours

2. Thy teeth are like a flock of fheepe in good order, which goe vp from the wa-hing: which euery one bring out twinnes, and none is bar-ren among them.

vnto others; so that their doctrine is neuer in vaine, but
is still answered with plentifull
increase of soules added to
the Church.

3. *Thy lips are like a thred of scarlet, and thy talke is comely; thy temples are within thy locke as a peece of a pomgranate.*

Thy speech (especially in
the mouth of thy teachers) is
both gratious in it selfe, and
such as administers grace to
the hearers; full of zeale and
feruent charitie, full of gra-
uitie and discretion: and that
part of thy countenance,
which thou wilt haue seene
(tho dimly and sparingly) is
full of holy modesty and bashfulnesse; so blushing, that it
seemeth like the colour of
a broken peece of pomgra-
nate.

Those,

Those, who by their holy authority suftaine thy gouernment (which are as some ftraight and ftrong neck to beare vp the head)are like vnto Dauids hie tower of defence, furnifhed with a rich armory ; which affords infinite wayes of fafe protection , and infinite monuméts of victory.

Thy two teftaments (which are thy two ful & faire breafts whereby thou nurfeft all thy faithfull chidren) are as two twinnes of Kiddes : twinnes, for their excellent and perfect agreement, one with another, in all refemblances: of Kiddes, that are daintily fed among the fweete flow-

4. *Thy necke is as the towre of Dauid, built for defence: a thoufand fhields hang therein, & all the targets of the ftrong men.*

5. *Thy two brefts are as two yong Kids that are twins, feeding among the Lillies.*

ers,

ers, for the pleasant nourish-
ment, which they yeeld to all
that sucke thereof.

6. *Vntill the day breake and the shadowes fly away, I will go into the moū-taine of myrrh, and to the mountain of incense.*

Vntill the day of my gratious appearance shall shine
foorth, and vntill all these shadowes of ignorance, infideli-
tie, afflictions, be vtterly and
suddenly dispersed, O my
spouse, I will retire my selfe
(in regard of my bodily presence) into my delightfull and
glorious rest of heauen.

7. *Thou art all faire my loue, & there is no spot in thee.*

Thou art exceeding beau-
tifull, O my Church, in all the
parts of thee: for, all thy sinnes
are done away, and thine iniquitie is couered, and loe I
present thee to my father
without spot, or wrinkle, or

any

any such deformitie.

And now, (O thou which I professe to haue married to my selfe in trueth and righteousnesse) thou shalt be gathered to me from all parts of the world : not onely from the confines of Iudea, where I planted and found thee, but from the remotest and most sauage places of the nations; out of the company of infidels, of cruell & bloody persecutors, who like Lyons and Leopards haue tyrannized ouer thee, & mercilessely torn thee in pieces.

Thou hast vtterly rauisht me from my selfe (O my sister and spouse; for so thou art,

8. *Come with me from Lebanon, my spouse, euen with me from Lebanon, and looke from the top of Amanah, from the toppe of Shenir and Hermon, frō the dens of the Lyons, & frō the mountaines of the Leopards.*

9. *My sister my spouse, thou hast rounded my*

both

hart with one of thine eies: and with a chaine of thy necke.

both ioyned to me in that spirituall vnion, and coheire with mee of the same inheritance, and glory) thou haft quite rauifht my heart with thy loue: euen one caft of one of thine eyes of faith ; and one of the ornaments of thy fanctification wherewith thou art decked by my fpirit, haue thus ftricken mee with loue : how much more , when I fhall haue a full fight of thee, and all thy graces,fhall I bee affected towards thee.

O how excellent , how precious , howe delectable are thofe loues of thine, O my fifter , my fpoufe ; how farre furpafsing all earth-

10. *My fifter, my fpoufe; how faire is thy loue,how much better*

ly

lie delicates ; and the fauour of thofe diuine vertues, wher-with thou art indued, more pleafing to my fent, then all the perfumes in the world.

is thy loue the wine, and the fauour of thine oint-ments then all fpices?

The gratious fpeeches that proceede from thee, are as fo many droppes of the honie-combe that fall from thy lippes: and whether thou exhort, or confeffe, or pray, or comfort, thy words are both fweete and nourifhing ; and the fauour of thy good workes, and outward con-uerfation, is to mee as the fmell of the woode of Lebanon to the fenfe of man.

11. Thy lippes, my fpoufe, drop as hony-combs : honie and milke are vnder thy tongue, & the fauour of thy garments is as the fauour of Lebanon.

My

My sister, my spouse, is as a garden or orchard full of all varietie of the heauenly trees, & flowers of grace; not lying carelesly open, either to the loue of strãgers, or to the rage of enemies, which like the wild Bore out of the wood, might root vp, & destroy her choise plants: but safely hedged and walled about, by my protecti-on, and reserued for my de-light alone; she is a spring and Well of wholesome waters, from whom flowe foorth the pure streames of my word; but, both inclosed and sealed vp: partly, that shee may the better (by this closenesse) pre-serue her owne naturall taste,

and

and vigor, from the corruptions of the world ; and partly, that she may not be defiled & mudded by the profane feete of the wicked.

Thou art an orchard, yea a paradise, whose plants (which are thy faithfull children that grow vp in thee) are as pomgranate trees ; the apples whereof are esteemed, for the largenesse, colour and taste, aboue all other: or (if I would feede my other senses) the plentifull fruites of thy holie obedience (which thou yieldest vnto mee) are for their smell as some composition of Cipresse, Spikenard, Saffron, sweete Cane, Cinamon, In-

13. Thy plants are as an orchard of pomegranats with sweete fruits: as Cipers, Spikenard, euen Spikenard & Saffron, Calamus and Cinamō, with all the trees of Incense, Mirrh & Aloes with all the chief spices.

cense

cenſe, Myrrhe, Aloes, and whatſoeuer elſe may bee de-uiſed, vnto the moſt perfect ſent.

14. *O fountaine of the gardens, O well of liuing waters & the ſprings of Lebanon.*

Thou art ſo a ſpring in my garden, that the ſtreames which are deriued from thee, water all the gardens of my particular congregations, all the world ouer : thou art that fountaine, from whoſe pure head iſſue all thoſe liuing waters, which who-ſo drinketh, ſhall neuer thirſt againe ; euen ſuch cleare currents, as flow from the hill of Libanus, which like vnto another Iordan, water all the Iſrael of God.

The Church.

IF I be a garden, as thou saiſt (O my Sauiour) then ariſe, O all ye Souerain winds of the ſpirit of God, and breath vpon this garden of my ſoule ; that the ſweet odours of theſe my plants, may both be increaſed, and may alſo bee diſperſed a-farre, and carried into the no-ſthrils of my wel-beloued : & ſo let him come into this his owne garden (which his owne hand hath digged, planted, wa-tered) and accept of the fruit of that ſeruice & prayſe, which hee ſhall inable mee to bring forth to his name.

15. Ariſe O North, & come O South, and blowe on my garden, that the ſpices thereof may flow out : let my wel-belo-ned come to his garden, and eate his pleaſant fruit

Q 2 CHAP.

CHAP. V.

CHRIST.

1. *I am come into my garden, my fifter, my Spoufe: I gathered my myrrh with my fpice; I eate my hony with my hony comb, I drank my wine with my milk: eate O my friends drinke, and make you merry O wel-beloued.*

BEholde, according to thy defire, I am come into my gardé, O my fifter, my fpoufe; I haue receiued thofe fruites of thine obedience which thou offereft vnto mee, with much ioy and pleafure. I haue accepted not onely of thy good workes, but thy indeauours & purpofes of holineffe : both which are as pleafant to mee, as the honie and the honiecombe. I haue allovved of the cheerefulneffe of thy feruice, and the wholefomneffe

of

of thy doctrine. And ye, O my
friends, whether bleſſed Angells, or faithfull men, partake
with mee in this ioie ariſing
from the faithfulneſſe of my
Church : cheere vp and fill
your ſelues, O my beloued,
with the ſame ſpirituall dain-
ties vvherevvith I am refre-
ſhed.

The Church.

WHen the world had caſt
mee into a secure ſleep,
or ſlumber rather (for my hart
was not vtterly bereaued of a
true faith, in my Sauiour) e-
uen in this darkeneſſe of my
minde, it pleaſed my gracious Redeemer not to neglect

*2. I ſleepe,
but my heart
waketh: it is
the voice of
my VVelbelo-
ued that knoc-
keth, ſaying,
open vnto me
my ſister, my
Loue, my
doue, my vn-*

defiled : for mine head is full of dew, & my locks with the drops of the night.

mee ; hee came to mee, and knocked oft, and called importunately at the doore of my heart, by his word and chaſtiſements, and ſaid ; Open the doore of thy Soule, O my ſiſter, my deare, chaſte, comely, vnſpotted Church: let me come in,& lodge & dwell with thee,in my graces ; ſhut out the world, and receiue me with a more liuely act, and renouation of thy faith. For loe, I haue long waited patiently for this effect of thy loue, and haue indured all the iniuries both of the night, and weather of thy prouocations, that I might at laſt inioy thee.

I an-

I answered him again, pleading excuses for my delay; Alas Lord, I haue now, since I left my forward profession of thee, auoyded a great number of cares and sorrowes: must I take them vp againe to follow thee? I haue liued cleane from the soile of these euils : and shall I now thrust my selfe into daunger of them?

3. I haue put off my coat: how shal I put it on? I haue washed my feet : how shall I defile them.

When my Sauiour heard this vnkind answere of delay: hee let his hand fall from the key-hole, which he had thus before without successe labored about; & withdrew himself from soliciting mee any more: whereupon my hart & bowels

4. My wel-beloued put his hand from the hole of the doore; & my bowels yearned toward him.

yearned within mee for him, and for the remorse of my so long foreslowing his admittance vnto me.

5. *I rose vp to open to my wel-beloued, and my hands did drop down myrrhe, and my fingers pure myrrhe vpon the handles of the barres.*

And now I rouzed vp my drousy hart (what I could) that I might in some cheerefull manner desire to receiue so gratious a Sauior: which when I but indeauoured, I found that hee had left behind him such a plentifull blessing (as the monument of his late presence) vpon the first motions of my heart, as that with the very touch of them I was both exceedingly refreshed, and mooued to further indignation at my selfe for delaying him.

I ope-

I opened to my beloued Sauiour: but my Sauiour had now (in my feeling) withdrawen himselfe, & hid his countenance from me, holding me short of those gracious offers, and meanes which I had refused; and now I was almost past my selfe with despaire, to remember that sweete inuitation of his, which I neglected: I sought him therefore in my thoughts, in the outward vse of his ordinances, and of my earnest praiers; but he would not as yet be found of me, or let mee finde that I was heard of him.

. Those which should haue regarded me, and by their vigilancy

6. I opened to my Welbeloued: but my Welbeloued was gone and past; mine hart was gone when hee did speak: I soght him but I could not find him; I called him, but hee answered mee not.

7. The watch-men that went

about the City found mee, they smote me and wounded me: the watch men of the walls tooke away my vaile from me.

gilancy haue fecured me from danger, proued mine aduerfaries : inftead of comforting mee, they fell vpon mee, and wounded mee with their falfe doctrines, drawing me on into further errours, fpoyling mee of that puritie and finceritie of profeffion, vvherewith as with fome rich & modeft vaile I was formerly adorned, and couered.

8. I charge you ô daughters of Ierufalem, if you finde my welbeloued, that you tell him, I am ficke of loue.

I aduife you folemnely, O all ye that wifh well to me (for I care not who knowes the vehemencie of my paffion) if you fhall finde my Sauiours prefence in your felues before me, praie for the recouerie of his loue to mee; and bemone

my

my estate to him, tel him how I languish with the impatient desire of his loue, & presence to be restored vnto me.

O thou which art the most happie, most gracious, & most glorious of all creatures, the chosen of the liuing God; what is thy welbeloued whom thou seekest, aboue al other the sons of men? what such eminency is there in him aboue all saints and angells: that thou art both so far gone in affectiō to him; and doest so vehemently ad-iure vs to speake vnto him for thee?

My welbeloued (if you know not) is of perfect beautie; in vvhose face is an exact mix-

9. O the fairest among women, what is thy welbelo-ued, more thē another wel-beloued? what is thy welbe-loued, more then another louer, that thou dost so charge vs?

10. My welbeloued is white & rud-dy, the stan-derdbearer of ten thousand.

ture

ture of the colours of the pu-
reſt & healthfulleſt complex-
ion of holineſſe : for, he hath
not receiued the ſpirit by mea
ſure; and in him the god-head
dwells bodily ; he is infinitely
fairer, then all the ſonnes of
men; & for goodlineſs of perſon may beare the ſtandard of
comelineſſe and grace amõgſt
tenne thouſand.

11. *His
head is as fine
gold, his locks
curled, and
black as a ra-
uen.*

The deitie which dwelleth
in him, is moſt pure and glorious: and that fulneſſe of grace
which is communicated to his
humane nature is wondrouſly
beautifull, and ſo ſets it forth,
as the black curled lockes doe
a freſh and welfauoured countenance.

His iudgement of al things, and his refpect to his Church (which are as his eyes)are full of loue, and full of pittie, fhining like vnto doues wafhed in water, yea in milke, fo as there is no fpot, or blemifh to bee found in them: and they are withall fo fully placed; as is both moft comely and moft expedient for the perfect fight of the eftate, and neceffities of his feruants.

12. *His eies are like doues vpon the riuers of waters, which are wafht with milke, and remaine in their fulneffe.*

The manifeftation of himfelfe to vs in his word, is fweet to our fpirituall feeling, as an heape of fpice, or thofe flowers that are vfed to make the beft perfuming oyntmēts are to the other fenfes: his hea-

13. *His cheeks are as a bed of fpices and as fweete flowers, and his lips like lillies dropping downe pure myrrhe.*

uenly

uénly inſtructions and promiſes of his Goſpel are vnſpeakably comfortable, and plentious, in the grace that is wroght by them.

His actions, and his inſtruments (which are his hands) are ſet forth with much port & maieſtie, as ſome precious ſtone beautifies the ring wher in it is ſet : the ſecret counſells of his breaſt, and the myſteries of his wil are moſt pure and holy, and full of excellent glory.

All his proceedings are firm and ſtable ; and withall, as pillars of marble ſet in ſockets of tryed golde ; ſo as they are neither ſubiect to vvauering,

14. His hands as rings of gold ſet with the chriſolit; his belly like white I- uory couered with ſaphirs.

15 His legs are as pillars of marble, ſet vppon ſockets of fine golde : his countenance as Le-

nor

nor to anie danger of infirmitie and corruption : the fhewe and carriage of his whole perſon whereby he makes himſelf knowen to his choſen , is exceeding goodly,& vpright like to the ſtreight and lofty Cedars of Lebanon.

His mouth out of which , proceedeth innumerablebleſſings & cōfortable promiſes, is to my ſoule euen ſweetneſſe it ſelfe; yea(what ſpeak I of anie one part?) as you haue heard in theſe particulars, hee is as ſweets : there is nothing but comfort in him; and there is no comfort but in him ; and this (if ye would know) is my welbeloued ; of ſo incompa-

banon, excel lent as the Cedars.

16. His mouth is as ſweet things, & he is wholy delectable : this is my welbeloued, and this is my louer, O daughters of Ierufalem.

rable

rable glory and worthinesse, that ye may easily discern him from all others.

Forraine Congregations.

17. *O the fairest among women, whether is thy Welbeloued gon? whither is thy Welbeloued turned aside, that we might seeke him with thee*

SInce thy Welbeloued is so glorious, and amiable (O thou which art for thy beauty worthie to bee the Spouse of such an husband) tell vs (for thou onely knowest it; and to seek Christ without the church we knowe is vain)tel vs where this Sauiour of thine is to bee sought; that we (rauished also with the report of his beautie) may ioin with thee in the same holy studie of seeking after him.

CHAP. VI.

MY Welbeloued Sauiour (if you vvould knowe this alfo) is to bee fought and found in the particular affemblies of his people, which are his garden of pleafure, wherin are varieties of all the beds of renued foules; which both he hath planted, and dreffed by his continuall care, and wherin hee walketh for his delight; feeding and folacing himfelfe vvith thofe fruites of righteoufneffe, and new obedience, which they are able to bring forth vnto him.

And now loe, whatfoeuer

1. My welbeloued i gone down in to his garden to the beds of fpices, to feed in the gardens and to gather lillies.

2. I am my welbelo-

R   hath

ueds., and my welbeloued is mine, who feedeth amõg the Lillies.

hath happened crofs to me, in my fenfible fruition of him; in fpight of al tentations, my beloved Sauior is mine through faith; and I am his through his loue; and both of vs are by an infeparable vnion knit together; vvhofe coniunction and loue is moft fweete, and happy :for, all that are his, he feedeth continually with heauenly repaft.

CHRIST.

3. Thou art beautifull my Loue as Tirzah, comly as Ierufalẽ, terrible as an army with banners.

NOtwithftanding this thy late blemifh of neglecting me, O my Church: yet ftil in mine eies, throgh my grace; vpon this thy repẽtance, thou art beautifull, like vnto that

neat

neate and elegante Citie of
Tirzah, and that orderly building of Ierusalem, the glorie
of the world: and with this thy
louelinesse, thou art awefull
vnto thine aduersaries, throgh
the power of thy censures, and
the maiestie of him that dwelleth in thee.

Yea, such beautie is in thee,
that I am ouercome with the
vehemencie of my affection
to thee : turne away thine eies
a while from beholding mee ;
for, the strength of that faith,
whereby they are fixed vpon
me, rauishes me from my selfe
vvith ioy. I doe therefore a-
gain renew thy former praise ;
that thy gracious profession,

*4. Turne
away thine
eyes from me,
for they ouer-
com me : thine
haire is like a
flocke of goats
which looke
downe from
Gilead.*

and all thy appendances & ornaméts of expedient ceremonies, are so comely to behold, as it is to see a flock of wel-fed goates grasing vpon the fruitfull hills of Gilead.

5. *Thy teeth are like a flock of sheep which goe vp from the washing, which euery one bring out twins, and none is barren among them.*

Thy Teachers, that chew & prepare the heauenly foode for thy soule, are of sweet accordance one vvith another, hauing all on e heart, and one tongue; and both themselues are sanctified & purged from their vncleannesses, and are fruitfull in their holy labours vnto others: so that their doctrine is neuer in vaine, but is still aunsvvered vvith plentifull increase of soules to the Church.

That part of thy countenaunce which thou wilt haue seene (tho dimmely and sparingly) is full of holy modestie and bashfulnesse ; so blushing, that it seemeth like the colour of a broaken peece of Pomgranate.

Let there be neuer so great a number of people and nations of Churches and assemblyes, vvhich challenge my name and loue, and perhaps by their outwarde prosperitie may seeme to plead much interest in mee, and much worth in themselues:

Yet thou onely art alone my true and chaste Spouse, pure and vndefiled in the

6. *Thy Temples are within thy lockes as a peece of a Pomgranate.*

7. *There are threescore queenes, and fourescore concubines, and of the damsels, without number.*

8. *But my Loue is alone and my vndefiled, shee is*

R 3 truth

the onely daughter of hir mother, & she is deare to her that bare hir: the daughters haue seen hir, and coūted hir blessed, euen the queenes and the cōcubines and they haue praised hir.

truth of thy doctrine, and the imputation of my holinesse; thou art shee, whome that Ierusalem vvhich is aboue, (the mother of vs all) acknovvledgeth for her only true, and deare daughter. And this is not my commendation alone, but all those forraine assemblyes, vvhich might seeme to bee riualles vvith thee of this prayse, doe applaude and blesse thee in this thine estate, and saie; Blessed is this people, whose God is the Lord.

9. Who is shee that looketh forth as the morning, faire as the

And admiring thy goodlinesse shall say; Who is this that lookes out so freshlie as the morning nevve risen; which

trom

ᵗrom thefe vveake beginnings is grovven to fuch hie perfection, that nowe fhee is as bright, and glorious, as the funne in his full ftrength, and the moone in a cleare skie; and vvithall is fo dreadefull thorough the maieftie of her countenance, and povver of her cenfures, as fome terrible armie, vvith enfignes difplayed, is to a vveake aduerfarie.

Thou complayneft of my abfence, (O my Church): there vvas no caufe; I meant not to forfake thee: I did but onelie vvalke dovvne into the vvell--dreffed Orcharde of thine affemblyes, to

moone, pure as the funne, terrible as an armie with banners.

1 0. I went downe to the dreffed Orchard, to fee the fruits of the vally, to fee if the vine budded, and if the Pomgranates flourifhed.

R 4   recre-

recreate and ioy my felfe, with the viewe of their forvvard-neffe : to fee the happie pro-greffe of the humble in fpi-rit, and the gracious begin-nings of thofe tender foules, vvhich are newly conuerted vnto mee.

ii. I knew nothing, my foule fet mee as the charets of my noble people.

So earneftly did I long to reuifit thee, and to reftore comfort vnto thee; that I hafted I knevve not vvhich vvaie : and vvith infenfible fpeede, I am come backe, as it were vppon the fwifteft cha-riots, or the vvinges of the vvinde.

12. Return, return, ô Shu-lamite: re-turne, return,

Now therefore returne(O my Spoufe, the true daughter of Ierufalem) returne to mee,

return

returne to thy felfe and to thy former feeling of my grace: returne, that both my felfe, & all the company of Angels, may fee, and reioyce in thee: and what fhall ye fee (O all ye hoaft of heauen) what fhall ye fee in my Church? euen fuch an awfull grace and maieftie, as is in a wel-marfhalled armie, ready to meet with the enemy.

that I may behold thee: what fhall you fee in the Shulamite, but as the company of an army?

CHAP. VII.

HOw beautiful are thy feet O daughter of the hyeft; being fhod with the prepara-tion of the Gofpell of peace,

1. How beautifull are thy goings with fhoues, O princes

and

daughter?
the compaſſe
of thy hyps
like iewels:
the worke of
the hand of a
cunning
workeman.

and readily addreſſed to run the way of the commaundements of thy God : thou art compaſſed about thy loynes with the girdle of verity;which is both precious for the matter of it, and cunningly framed by the skill of the ſpirit of truth.

2. *Thy*
nauell is as a
round cup,
that wanteth
not liquor:thy
bellie is as an
heap of wheat
compaſſed
about with
Lillies.

The nauell,whereby all thy ſpirituall conceptions receiue their nouriſhment, is full of all fruitfull ſupplie, and neuer wants meanes of ſuſtenance, to feed them in thy wombe: which alſo is ſo plentious in thy bleſſed increaſe, that it is as an heape of wheat, conſiſiſting of infinite pure grayns which conſort together with

much

much fweetneffe, and pleafure.

Thy two teftaments (which are thy two full and comely breafts; by whofe wholefome miike thou nourifheft all thy faithfull children, once borne into the light)are for their ex-cellēt & perfect agreement, & their amiable proportion, like two twins of Kids.

Thofe, who by their holy authority fupport thy gouern-mēt(which are as fom ftraight and ftrong necke to beare vp thy head) are for their height and defence like a tower; for their order, purenefle, and dignitie, like a tower of Iuo-ry: thy teachers and minifters

3. Thy two breafts are as two yong Kids that are twins.

4. Thy necke is like a tower of Iuo-ry: thine eies are like arti-ficiall pooles in a frequen-ted gate: thy nofe is as the tower of Le-banon, that looketh to-

(which

ward *Da-mafcus*.

(which are thine eyes) are like vnto fome cleare and artificiall ponds of water, in a place of greateſt refort : wherein all commers may fee the faces of their confciences ; & whence they may plentifully draw the waters of life. Thy nofe, by which all fpirituall fents are conuaied to thee, is perfectly compofed, and featured like fome curious turret of that goodly houfe in Lebanon ; fo as thy iudgement, and power of difcerning the fpirits, is admirable for the order and excellency thereof.

The whole tyre of thine head (which are the ceremonies vfed by thee) are very

5. *Thine head vpõ thee is as fcarlet, and the*

grace-

gracefull, and of hie eſtimation and price to all the behol-
ders : and as for me, I am ſo
enamoured of thee, that I am
euen tyed by my owne deſire,
to a perpetuall preſence in
thine holy aſſemblies.

*buſh of thine
head like pur-
ple: the king
is tied in thy
beames.*

Oh how beautifull & loue-
ly art thou therefore (O my
Church) in all thy parts and
ornaments ? how ſweete and
pleaſant art thou(O my loue)
in whatſoeuer might giue me
true contentment?

*6. How
faire art thou
& how plea-
ſant art thou,
O my loue,
in pleaſures?*

Thy whole frame is, for
goodlineſs & ſtreight growth,
like vnto ſome tall palme-
tree; which the more it is de-
preſſed by the violence of per-
ſecutions, riſeth the more; and

*7. This
thy ſtature is
like a palme-
tree, and thy
breaſts like
cluſters.*

the

the two breasts of thy Testaments are like two full iuicie clusters, which yeeld cōfortable and abundant refreshing.

8. *I said,
I will goe vp
into the
Palme-tree.
I will take
hold of her
boughes: thy
breasts shall
now be like
the clusters of
the vines, and
the fauour of
thy nose like
apples.*

Seeing then thou art my Palme-tree, I haue resolued in my selfe to adioyne my selfe to thee; to inioy thee, to gather those sweet fruits of thy graces, which thou yeeldest; and by my presence also will cause thee to bee more plentifull in all good works, and doctrine; so as thou shalt afford abundance of heauenly liquor vnto all the thirstie soules of thy children; and an acceptable verdure of holinesse and obedience vnto me.

4. *And the
roofe of thy*

And the deliuerie of my

word

word, by the mouthes of thy miniſters, ſhall bee as ſome excellent wine, which ſparkleth right vpward: being wel accepted of that God, in whoſe name it is taught, and looketh moſt pleaſantly in the glaſſe, being no leſs highly eſteemed of the receiuers: which is of ſuch wõderfull power, that it is able to put words both of repentance, and praiſe into the lips of him, that lies aſleepe in his ſinnes.

mouth like goodwine, which goeth ſtraight vp to my welbeloued; & cauſeth the lips of him that is aſleepe, to ſpeake.

The Church.

BEhold, ſuch as I am, I am not my owne ; much leſſe am I any others : I am wholely my Sauiours; and now I ſee, and feele, whatſoeuer I had

11. *I am my welbeloueds, and his deſire is toward mee.*

de-

deſerued, that he is mine alſo, in all intire affection ; who hath both choſen me, and giuen himſelfe for me.

Come therefore, O my deare Sauiour, let vs ioyne together in our naturall care : let thy ſpirit and my ſeruice be intent vpon thy congregations here below on earth ; and let vs ſtay in the place where our ſpirituall husbandry lieth.

Let vs with all haſt & cheerfulneſſe viſit the fruitfull vines of our beleeuing children ; & to our mutuall comfort, bee witneſſes and partakers of all the ſignes and fruits of grace, of all thoſe good workes, and thankeſgiuings, of thoſe holy

in-

indeauours and worthy pra-
ctifes, which they yeeld forth *the pomegra-*
nats bloſſom:
vnto vs: let vs iudge of their *there will I*
giue thee my
forwardneſſe, and commend *loue.*
it: whereupon it will eaſily ap-
peare, that the conſummati-
on of our happie marriage
draweth neere, in which there
ſhall bee a perfect vnion betwixt vs.

Behold: thy godly ſeruants, *13. The*
which not onely beare fruit *mandrakes*
haue giuen a
themſelues, but are power- *ſmell, and in*
full in the prouocation of o- *our gates are*
all ſweete
thers; preſent their beſt ſer- *things, new*
uices vnto thee ; and euen at *and old; my*
welbeloued, I
our doores(not farre to ſeeke, *haue kept thẽ*
not hard to procure) is of- *for thee.*
fer made vnto thee, of all
varietie of fruite ; whether

from thy yong conuerts, or thy more ſettled profeſſors:& all theſe I ſpend not lauiſhlie; but, in my louing care, duely reſerue them for thee, and for the ſolemne day of our full marriage.

CHAP. VIII.

The Iewiſh Church.

OH that I might ſee thee (my Sauiour) clothed in fleſh : Oh that thou which art my euerlaſting husband, mighteſt alſo be my brother, in partaking the ſame humane nature with me ; that ſo I finding thee below vpon earth,

1.Oh that thou wereſt as my brother that ſucked the breaſt of my mother. I would finde thee without, I would kiſſe thee, then

might

might familiarly intertaine thee, and conuerfe with thee, without the reproach of the world; yea, might be exalted in thy glory.

they fhould not defpife mee.

Then would I (tho I be now pent vp in the limits of Iudea) bring thee forth into the light, and knowledge of the vniuer-fall Church, whofe daughter I am: and then and there, thou fhouldeft teach me how per-fectly to ferue & worfhip thee, & I fhall gladly intertaine thee with a royall feaft of the beft graces that are in my holieft feruants; which I knowe thou wilt account better cheere, thē all the fpiced cups, and pom-granate wines in the world.

2. I will lead thee, and bring thee in-to my mo-thers houfe; there thou fhalt teach me: I will caufe thee to drinke fpiced wine, & new wine of the pomgranats.

3. *His left hand shall bee vnder my head, and his right hand shall imbrace mee.*

Then shall I attaine to a neerer communion with him; and both his hands shall bee imployed to susteine, and relieue me: yea, he shall comfort my head and my heart (my iudgement, and affections) with the liuely heat of his gracious imbracements.

4. *I charge you O daughters of Ierusalem, that you stirre not vp, nor waken my loue, vntill hee please.*

I charge you (O all ye that professe any friendship to me) I charge yee deepely, as yee will auoyd my vttermost censures; take heed how ye vexe and disquiet my mercifull Sauiour, and grieue his spirit: and doe not dare, by the least prouocation of him, to interrupt his peace.

Chrift.

CHRIST.

WHo is this, that from the comfortlefs defertes of ignorance, of infidelity, of tribulatiõs, afcendeth thus vp into the glorious light & libertie of my chofen? relying her felfe wholly vpon her Sauiour, and folacing her felfe in him? Is it not my Church? it is fhe, whom I haue loued, & acknowledged of olde : for, euen vnder the tree of offence , the forbidden fruit which thou taftedft to thy deftruction, I rayfed thee vp againe from death; Euen there , thy firft mother conceiued thee ; while by faith fhee layd hold on

5. VVho is this that cõmeth out of the wilderneſſe; leaning vpon her welbeloued? I raifed thee vp vnder an apple-tree: there thy mother conceiued thee : there fhe conceiued that bare thee.

S 3   that

that bleſſed promiſe of the Goſpel, whereby ſhe, and her beleeuing ſeed were reſtored.

Iewiſh Church.

6. *Set mee is a ſeale on thy hart, and as a ſignet on thine arme: for loue is ſtrong as death; Ielouſie is cruell as the Graue: the coales thereof are fiery coales, and a vehement flame.*

A Nd ſo haue thou me ſtill (O my Sauiour) in a perpetual and deare remébrance: keepe me ſure in thine heart, yea in thine armes, as that which thou holdeſt moſt precious; and let me neuer be remoued from thy loue; the leaſt ſhew and danger whereof I cannot indure: for, this my ſpirituall loue is exceeding powerfull, and can no more be reſiſted then death it ſelfe: & the ielous zeale which I haue for thee, and thy glory, conſumes

me,

me, euen like the Graue, and burnes mee vp like vnto the coales of fome moſt vehemẽt and extreame fire.

Yea, more then any fire; for any flame yet may be quenched with water: but al the water of afflictions & terrors (yea whole ſtreams of perſecutiõs) cãnot quench this loue: & for all tempting offers of wealth, of pleaſures & honor, how eaſily are they all contemned for the loue of my Sauiour ?

We haue yet a ſiſter (as thou knoweſt O Sauiour) ordained through thy mercy to the fame grace with me : the vncalled Church of the Gentiles ; ſmall (as yet) of groth, through

7. Much water cannot quench loue, neither can the floudes drowne it: if a man ſhould giue all the ſubſtance of his houſe for loue, they would greatly contemne it.

8. VVe haue a little ſiſter, and ſhe hath no breaſts: what ſhall we doe for our ſiſter,

S 4   the

when she shall
he spoken for?

the rarenefs of her conuerts, &
deftitute of the helpe of any
outward miniftery ; whereby
fhe might either bear, or nou-
rifh children vnto thee : when
fhe growes vnto her maturitie;
and the myftery of calling her
vniuerfally to thee, fhall be reuealed to the world, and her
felfe; what courfe will it pleafe
thee to take with her ?

CHRIST.

9. If she be
a wall, we will
build vpon
her a filuer
palace: and if
she be a doore,
we will keepe
her in with
boards of
cedar.

IF fhee fhall continue firme
and conftant, in the expectation of her promifes, and the
profeffion of that truth which
fhall bee reuealed ; wee will
beautifie and ftrengthen her,
with further grace, and make

      her

her a pure and coſtly palace,
fit to entertaine my ſpirit: and
if ſhe will giue free paſſage &
good entrance, to my word
and grace ; wee will make hir
ſure and ſafe from corruption, and reſerue hir to immortalitie.

Iewiſh Church.

BEhoulde : that condition
vvhich thou requireſt in
the Church of the Gentiles,
thou findeſt in me ; I am thus
firme and conſtant in my expectation , in my profeſſion: and that vvant thou findeſt in her of abilitie to nou-
riſh her Children , by the
breaſt of thy WORDE, is

10. *I am a wall, and my breaſts are as towers : then was I in his eyes as one that findeth peace.*

not

not in mee; who haue abundance both of nourifhment &
defence: vpon which my cō-
feffion and plea, I found grace
and peace in the eyes of my
Sauiour; and receiued from
him affurance of his euerla-
fting loue to me.

CHRIST.

11. Salomon
had a vine in
Baalhamon :
hee gaue the
vineyard vn-
to keepers:
euery one
bringeth for
the fruite
thereof a
thoufand pee-
ces of filuer.

MY Church is my Vine, &
I am the owner, and huf-
bandman: our thrift and profit therof farre exceedeth the
good husbandry of *Salomon*:
he hath a rich vineyard indeed
in a moft fruitfull foyle; but he
lets it forth to the hands of o-
thers, as not beeing able to
keepe and dreffe it himfelfe:

and

and therefore he is faine to be content with the greateſt part of the increaſe, not expecting the whole.

But my vine is euer before me, I am with it to the end of the world, I reſerue it in mine owne hands, and dreſſe it with mine owne labour: and therefore if thou (O *Salomon*) canſt receiue from thine, to the proportion of a thouſand, thy workemen and farmers vvill looke for the fift part to come vnto their ſhare; wheras the gaine of my vineyard ariſeth wholly, and onely, vnto my ſelfe.

Sith therefore ſuch is my care of thee, and ioy in thee

12. But my vineyard which is mine is before mee: to thee ô Salomon apper taineth a thouſand peeces of ſiluer, and two hundreth to them that kept the fruit thereof.

13. O thou that dwelleſt in the gardẽs,

(O

*the compani-
ons hearken
vnto thy
voice, cause
me to heare it.*

(O my Church;which cõsisteſt of the particular assemblies of men professing my name) see thou be diligent in declaring my will, & giuing holy coun-selles to all thy fellow-mem-bers: speake forth my prayse in the great congregations, (which al attend willingly vp-on thee) and let me heare the voice of thy conſtant & faith-full confession of mee before the world.

The Church.

*14. Oh
my welbelo-
ued, flee away
and be like
vnto the Roe*

I Will moſt gladly doe what thou commaundeſt, O my Sauiour but, that I may per-forme it accordingly; be thou

(which

(which art, according to thy bodily presence, in the hyest heauens) euer present with me by thy spirir, & hasten thy glorious comming, to my full redemption.

or to the yong Hart vpon the mountaines of spices.

FINIS.

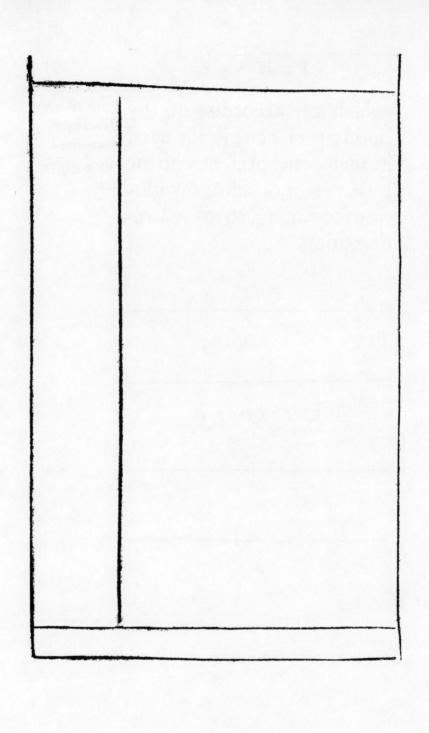

DATE DUE

NOV 28 1993			
DEC 08 1993			
DEC 27 1993			
NOV 15 1998			